Climbing New Hampshire's 48 4,000 Footers

From the summit of Mount Adams, you get a good view to Mount Madison to the northeast, with tiny Star Lake situated on the col separating the two peaks.

Climbing New Hampshire's 48 4,000 Footers

From Casual Hikes to Challenging Ascents

Eli Burakian

FALCONGUIDES

GUILFORD, CONNECTICUT

An imprint of The Rowman & Littlefield Publishing Group, Inc.
4501 Forbes Blvd., Ste. 200
Lanham, MD 20706
www.rowman.com

Falcon and FalconGuides are registered trademarks and Make Adventure Your Story is a trademark of The Rowman & Littlefield Publishing Group, Inc.

Distributed by NATIONAL BOOK NETWORK

All photos by Eli Burakian

Maps by The Rowman & Littlefield Publishing Group, Inc.

British Library Cataloguing in Publication Information available

Library of Congress Cataloging-in-Publication Data available

ISBN 978-1-4930-3111-5 (paperback)
ISBN 978-1-4930-3112-2 (e-book)

The paper used in this publication meets the minimum requirements of American National Standard for Information Sciences—Permanence of Paper for Printed Library Materials, ANSI/NISO Z39.48-1992.

Printed in the United States of America

Warning: Climbing is a dangerous sport. You can be seriously injured or die. Read the following before you use this book.

This is a guide about hiking that may involve some climbing, a sport that is inherently dangerous. Do not depend solely on information from this book for your personal safety. Your climbing safety depends on your own judgment based on competent instruction, experience, and a realistic assessment of your climbing ability.

There is no substitute for personal instruction in rock climbing, and climbing instruction is widely available. You should engage an instructor or guide to learn climbing safety techniques. If you misinterpret a concept expressed in this book, you may be killed or seriously injured as a result of the misunderstanding. Therefore, the information provided in this book should be used only to supplement competent personal instruction from a climbing instructor or guide. Even after you are proficient in climbing safely, occasional use of a climbing guide is a safe way to raise your climbing standard and learn advanced techniques.

There are no warranties, either expressed or implied, that this instruction book contains accurate and reliable information. There are no warranties as to fitness for a particular purpose or that this book is merchantable. Your use of this book indicates your assumption of the risk of death or serious injury as a result of climbing's risks and is an acknowledgment of your own sole responsibility for your safety in climbing or in training for climbing.

The author and The Rowman & Littlefield Publishing Group, Inc. assume no liability for accidents happening to, or injuries sustained by, readers who engage in the activities described in this book.

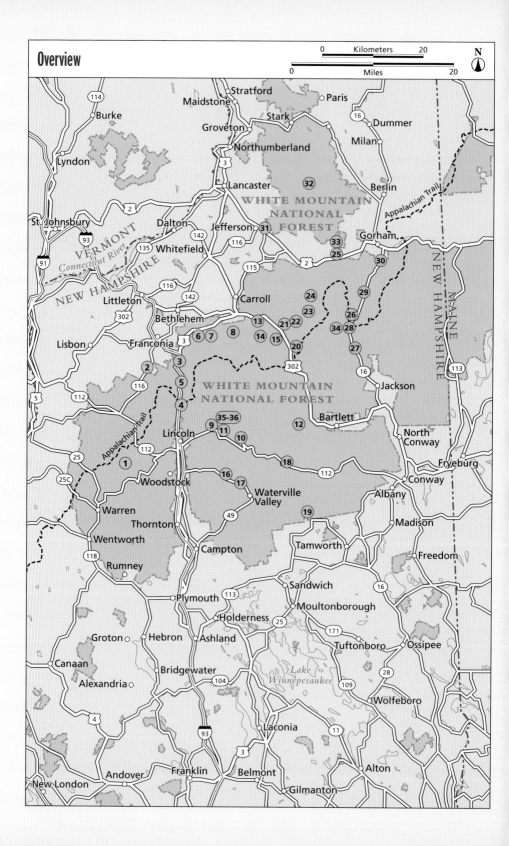

Contents

Acknowledgments

I'd like to thank my wife, Julia, and my children, Levon and Ani, for supporting me through the time-consuming process of planning, hiking, mapping, photographing, and writing. Without their support, there is no way I could have completed this project.

I would also like to extend my gratitude to all the authors and website creators whose helpful resources have been invaluable in the process of writing this book. Although I've hiked all of these mountains many times, there are many who have much more knowledge and experience than me.

Thank you to the friends and family who have joined me for these adventures and to everyone who supports the preservation of wild places. I have endless gratitude to those thousands of souls who have put in the hard work in making and maintaining the trails throughout the region.

Without a doubt, this book would not have been possible without the aid and support of Mike Dickerman and Steven Smith, who, in addition to writing the ultimate resource on the New Hampshire 4,000-footers, *The 4000-Footers of the White Mountains—A Guide and History,* have always been open and willing to answer my questions. I highly encourage anybody visiting the region to stop by Mike's Bondcliff Books retail location in Littleton, New Hampshire, and my favorite store in the whole world, Steve's Mountain Wanderer Books and Maps in Lincoln, New Hampshire.

Hikers enjoy the fine weather on an overnight hike in the Presidential Range.

Definitions of "4,000-Footer" and "Peak-Bagging"

"Peak-bagging" is the act of hiking all the peaks on a given list. In this case the list is the Appalachian Mountain Club (AMC) White Mountain 4,000-Footers List.

To make New Hampshire's 4,000-footers list, a peak must rise 200 feet above any ridge connecting it to a neighbor. This is why certain peaks, such as Mount Clay, Mount Guyot, and the South Peak of Mount Moosilauke do not qualify. Additionally, as the quality of measurements has improved over the years, the list has changed as the elevations of certain mountains have been adjusted.

When you have finished hiking the New Hampshire 4,000-footers, you can apply to the AMC Four Thousand Footer Club for membership to receive a certificate and a patch. There is no time limit, but you must ascend and descend all the peaks, although you can hike multiple peaks at one time. And if you bring your furry friend with you on every hike, he or she can also be recognized for completing the list!

Although catching sunset atop a peak means you have to walk down in the dark, sometimes it's worth it.

Introduction

No other location east of the Mississippi River has as many rugged and scenic peaks as the White Mountains of New Hampshire. For those not in the know, the relatively diminutive size (compared to mountains out West) and proximity to major metropolitan areas may at first glance suggest that these mountains are nothing special. Their geographic location, however, means they receive every type of weather. With incredibly harsh winters, and with the tree line around 4,500 feet in elevation, many of these mountains receive the full brunt of what Mother Nature can throw at them.

This also means the White Mountains have significant acreage in the alpine zone, with flora and landscape that are more closely related to climes significantly more northerly than the relatively low latitude would suggest.

As part of the incredibly old Appalachian Mountain chain, these mountains showcase the incredible power of uplift and erosion and are marked heavily by both recent (in geologic terms) and ancient ice ages, which have sculpted dramatic cirques such as Tuckerman Ravine.

But why climb mountains that rise over the seemingly random elevation of 4,000 feet? It is because above this level, you enter the rarified environment that separates these mountains from rolling hills and lush landscapes dominated by other mountain ranges in New England.

Over the course of your journey climbing the New Hampshire 4,000-footers, you will get to know the region well. You will stand atop a mountain and be able to name all the other 4,000-footers you can see. The steep climbs and rocky trails will force you to get in shape, and as you gain fitness, your appreciation for the mountains will rise.

Traversing the miles of ridgeline in the Presidential Range or along the dramatic spine of Franconia Ridge will remind you that you don't need to travel to exotic locations to experience jaw-dropping beauty. Admittedly, not all these peaks are as dramatic as Mount Lafayette or Mount Adams, but having a goal of climbing all the 4,000-footers, over months or even years, will get you to places you would not otherwise go.

Whether it's the journey to climb Owl's Head, which rises just a few dozen feet over 4,000 yet requires an 18-mile out-and-back hike through a rugged wilderness and up a rock slide, or to Mount Isolation, deep within a wilderness area that provides unique views of the popular Presidential Range, these hikes will challenge and reward in myriad ways. You truly will learn to enjoy the journey and may, like the author, find yourself looking forward to the solitude and wildness of these less-popular peaks more than the better known, and much more popular, high peaks that often come with high crowd levels.

If you are like many of us who need a little motivation to take that first step out the door, having a list of peaks to climb creates a goal. There's no reward at the end,

Two hikers traverse the Gulfside Trail above King Ravine.

just a sense of accomplishment, but having that goal might be the spark that ignites your fire.

You may also choose to share these hiking adventures with family or friends. These shared experiences live on in our memory, and each hike will be relived over and over again through stories and photos. There will definitely be times when you are not having fun, but the most challenging adventures often provide the biggest rewards and the best stories.

One thing is for sure. If you end up hiking all of the New Hampshire 4,000-footers, it won't be the end of your journey. The more you accomplish, the more you will be able to see what other opportunities await. I guarantee; once you have experienced the joy of summiting and exploring these peaks, you are bound to want more.

There's a lot of fun in store for you. I hope the pages of this book inspire you to get out of your comfort zone and see the world from new perspectives.

Be safe, and enjoy the journey!

How to Use This Guide

This guidebook is by no means a comprehensive resource of every route up every 4,000 footer in New Hampshire. This book contains thirty-six main hikes, with at least one route up each of the forty-eight peaks. The last four hikes are longer traverses, with a few possibly requiring multiple days.

Although a few of these peaks only have one true route, most of these mountains have many ways to ascend and descend; some mountains, such as those in the Northern Presidential Range, have innumerable possible route options. Some of these options are listed in the "Other Routes" section at the end of the route descriptions. Eight "Bonus Hikes," listed at the end of the book, describe in less detail traverses or optional routes recommended by the author.

Included with each route description are helpful pieces of information, such as average hiking time, distance and elevation gain, trails used, and special considerations. Driving directions and GPS coordinates are provided for the trailheads to each hike as well. Following the detailed route description is a more succinct list of turn by turn directions. Finally, a basic map is provided showing trails, distances, and key points along the route.

Please also check out the "Maps, GPS, Guides, Apps, and Resources" section for helpful information and resources that will aid you in acquiring all the information you need before and during your journey to have a safe and fun adventure.

The moon rises above the Presidential Range.

List of 4,000-Foot Mountains by Elevation

Rank	Name	Elevation	Rank	Name	Elevation
1	Washington	6,288	25	Flume	4,328
2	Adams	5,799	26	South Hancock	4,319
3	Jefferson	5,716	27	Pierce	4,312
4	Monroe	5,372	28	North Kinsman	4,293
5	Madison	5,366	29	Willey	4,285
6	Lafayette	5,260	30	Bondcliff	4,265
7	Lincoln	5,089	31	Zealand	4,260
8	South Twin	4,902	32	North Tripyramid	4,180
9	Carter Dome	4,832	33	Cabot	4,170
10	Moosilauke	4,802	34	East Osceola	4,156
11	North Twin	4,761	35	Middle Tripyramid	4,140
12	Eisenhower	4,760	36	Cannon	4,100
13	Carrigain	4,700	37	Wildcat D	4,062
14	Bond	4,698	38	Hale	4,054
15	Middle Carter	4,610	39	Jackson	4,052
16	West Bond	4,540	40	Tom	4,051
17	Garfield	4,500	41	Moriah	4,049
18	Liberty	4,459	42	Passaconaway	4,043
19	South Carter	4,430	43	Owl's Head	4,025
20	Wildcat A	4,422	44	Galehead	4,024
21	Hancock	4,420	45	Whiteface	4,020
22	South Kinsman	4,358	46	Waumbek	4,006
23	Field	4,340	47	Isolation	4,003
23	Osceola	4,340	47	Tecumseh	4,003

Before You Hit the Trail

Weather and Seasons

To those from outside the region, the relatively diminutive heights of the peaks in the White Mountains compared to those out West or in other locales may suggest a corresponding lack of severe weather. That could not be further from the truth, with the Mount Washington Observatory proclaiming the peak to be the "Home of the World's Worst Weather." Until very recently in fact, Mount Washington held the record for the highest recorded wind speed in the world—231 miles per hour, observed in 1934.

In addition to the variable weather associated with northern New England, the mountains create their own weather. Orographic uplift can create clouds and precipitation at higher elevations, while down in the valleys, the weather can be dry and calm. Generally, the higher you climb, the more likely there will be wind and the stronger that wind will blow.

The highest temperature ever recorded at the summit of Mount Washington was 72°F. Snow has fallen during every month of the year on the summit, and precipitation is recorded more than 210 days per year on average. The lowest temperature ever recorded on Mount Washington was -47°F, and windchill values have been recorded below -100°F.

Even on lesser peaks than Mount Washington, temperatures at the trailhead can be in the 60s, with temperatures higher up in the 40s and 30s. Additionally, the

Hoar frost collects on a stick high up on a mountain during a crisp winter day.

summits are often in the clouds. When hiking in the alpine zone, whiteouts can be very disorienting, and it is easy to get lost. It is important to be prepared by checking the weather, having the proper equipment, and, most importantly, being flexible with your hiking plans if the weather is not cooperating.

Winter is long and summer short in the White Mountains. The best hiking months are June through September. October is a great time to hike too, with incredible foliage in the valleys, but be prepared for snow and ice as well.

One of the most dangerous periods to hike in the White Mountains is during spring, which can last from late March all the way through mid-June. During the spring melt, rivers can be raging, making many of the hikes with river crossings completely impassable. Snow bridges, which form in winter over streams and rivers, can collapse in spring, creating a significant hazard for unsuspecting hikers who aren't aware that they are crossing over what could be a raging torrent.

Additionally, trails are very susceptible to erosion during the spring months. During this season, some trails can become streams themselves. In addition to the dangers of hiking steep slopes on wet mud and rocks, hikers who go off-trail to avoid walking in the mud exacerbate erosion issues. Many hiking trails are closed to traffic for weeks or months in spring, and it is imperative that hikers respect these closures. Use common sense; even if the trail isn't closed, if it is very wet, it is best to stay away.

Another important issue to consider regarding the weather in the White Mountains is lightning. Lightning is a frequent occurrence among the high peaks, and many people have been hit, even killed, by lightning strikes. If you hear thunder, drop down in elevation and get under cover as soon as possible.

Safety, Preparation, and Gear

A safe hike is an enjoyable hike. The most important thing to remember is that if you use common sense to prepare for a hike, you most likely will be just fine. Be sure to look at the weather ahead of time. If it's going to be raining, bring not only a rain jacket but also rain paints and a pack cover of some sort, as well as a change of clothes in case you get wet. Remember: If your pack gets wet, everything inside will get wet too.

If there's a chance of snow, or if you are hiking in any season but summer, bring enough warm clothing to make sure you won't have to worry about hypothermia or frostbite. Hiking in winter is very challenging, and the most important thing to remember is that you want to be warm but not too hot. Stop and remove layers if you get hot, as sweating leads to wet clothes. Once your clothes are wet, they will suck the heat right out of you, and if you stop for any significant time on a cold hike with wet clothes, you are much more likely to suffer from hypothermia and frostbite. You may want to pack chemical hand/foot warmers as a backup in case your extremities get cold. As your core drops in temperature, your body pulls circulation from the extremities to keep your vital organs operational, leaving your fingers and toes much more susceptible to frostbite.

From an opening above rock steps along the Gorge Brook Trail on Mount Moosilauke, you can see the Franconia Ridge in the distance (hike 1).

Make sure that everyone in your party is prepared; one unprepared hiker can ruin a trip for everyone else. Obviously, make sure you have the proper footwear—nothing ruins a hike more easily than blisters. Be sure you have enough water, either by bringing multiple containers on a long hike or by using purification tablets or a water filter if you plan on refilling during your hike from anywhere but a guaranteed potable water source, such as the AMC huts. No natural water sources are guaranteed to be safe to drink

Here is a list of items to consider bringing on any hike:

- ❑ Backpack
- ❑ Hiking boots or sneakers
- ❑ Poles
- ❑ Rain and/or wind gear
- ❑ Extra layers for warmth or to replace wet clothing
- ❑ Extra socks
- ❑ Sunglasses
- ❑ Hat
- ❑ Gloves
- ❑ Water bottles
- ❑ Snacks and/or meals
- ❑ Water filter or chemical tablets
- ❑ Lighter
- ❑ Map (and possibly a compass and/or GPS device)
- ❑ Insect repellent
- ❑ Sunscreen
- ❑ Toilet paper and wet wipes
- ❑ Ziplock bag for trash
- ❑ Headlamp with extra batteries
- ❑ Mobile phone
- ❑ Camera
- ❑ Knife
- ❑ Duct tape
- ❑ Identification and medical information
- ❑ Emergency kit containing fire starter, knife, bandages, antibacterial ointment, personal medications, and water purification tablets
- ❑ Extra prescription glasses or contact lenses if necessary
- ❑ NH Hike Safe Card (available for purchase at NH Fish and Game Department's website)
- ❑ Tracking or emergency communication device such as a SPOT or InReach

Additionally, if you plan on going out for at least one night, you may need:

- ❏ Shelter (tent or bivy sack)
- ❏ Ground sheet
- ❏ Sleeping bag
- ❏ Cook stove
- ❏ Money (for staying at AMC campsites and for emergency purposes)

Most importantly, especially if you are alone, make sure to let somebody know where you will be hiking, the route you plan on taking, and when you plan on returning. Cell reception is pretty good on the ridges and peaks but can be spotty or nonexistent in the wooded valleys. A personal locator device that uses satellites, such as a SPOT or InReach, is increasingly becoming a standard addition to a hiking kit. In addition to tracking your adventure and sharing your route, these devices provide an extra level of security so that if you get in a bind, you can contact someone for help. A smartphone can be used in multiple ways, including functioning as a GPS device and map even if you don't have cell reception.

Crossing rivers and streams can be very dangerous, so it is important that you know what you are doing. Using hiking poles can help you cross safely. The higher the water, the more force it exerts, and even knee-high water can be enough to push you off balance. Make sure your feet (and poles, if you have them) are set and stable before taking the next step, and understand that water depths can be deceiving. On big river crossings, you may want to unstrap the buckles of your backpack so that the wet bag will not drag you under in case of a dunking. It is better to lose your belongings than to lose your life. Also be aware that even during the peak of summer, mountain rivers and streams can be extremely cold; in spring, water from snowmelt is barely above freezing.

Be especially careful during hunting season. Make sure everyone in your party is wearing bright-colored clothing, and put hunter's orange on any dogs. Check with state fish and wildlife divisions for specific dates, and be sure to stay on the trail when hiking during hunting season.

If you see wildlife, be respectful and give the animal space. You never know how a wild animal will respond to any type of movement. It is always exciting to see a moose in the woods, but these large creatures can be unpredictable; if you happen to get between a mother and her calf, she may become aggressively protective.

Black bears roam the region but are rarely seen on the trail. If you do encounter a bear, stay calm, give it space, and don't continue until the bear has left the area.

Mosquitoes are common, and during late spring and early summer, blackflies can be vicious. They seem to hover closer to the ground in swarms. Beyond using insect repellent and wearing long pants and a long-sleeved shirt, the only real option is to continue moving. Although blackflies are more annoying than dangerous, they can turn your hike into a nightmare. You can also spray or wash your clothing with

The moon rises high above Mount Liberty and Mount Flume (hike 4).

permethrin, which usually does a good job of keeping the insects away and is less toxic than putting DEET directly on your skin. Lemon eucalyptus is a good alternative to DEET but does require more frequent application.

Giardia lamblia is a parasite found in untreated water sources and can cause severe gastrointestinal issues that don't surface until days, or even weeks, after ingestion. Most springs are usually clean, assuming you can see where the water is coming out of the ground, but no water source is guaranteed safe to consume. It is always best to filter your water or use chemical treatment such as iodine or chlorine to kill/filter out any viruses, bacteria, or parasites. Many companies now make lightweight bottles with in-line filters that allow you to drink straight from the source without having to pump water through a filter or wait until the chemical treatment has worked.

Ticks, of which there are multiple varieties, carry many diseases, including the well-known Lyme disease. Due to the changing climate and other reasons, ticks are increasingly found in this region, especially at lower elevations. When possible, wear long pants while hiking. When you are done with your hike, check your entire body, including your head, for any ticks. If you find one that is attached, use tweezers or a tick scoop to remove the buried head. Generally, if you find a tick within 24 hours and remove it right away, transmission of disease is unlikely. Do not squeeze the body of the tick while removing it.

Ticks vary in size by species as well as life stage. Unfortunately, some ticks, such as deer ticks during the nymph stage, can be as small as poppy seeds and may be missed even with a careful search. If you do find an engorged tick and are worried as to whether it carries disease, try to save it once you remove it. Take it to your doctor or a professional for identification if you are concerned that it may have been embedded long enough to transmit a disease. Although a bullseye rash can be a telltale sign of Lyme infection, not all people get this rash and ticks carry many more diseases than Lyme.

The only poisonous plant to be aware of in the area is poison ivy. This three-leafed plant is often found at lower elevations, generally near water. If you think you have come into contact with poison ivy, wash the area with soap and water as soon as possible; try not to touch anything else until you do so that you don't spread the toxic oil.

Finally, it is highly recommended that you purchase a "New Hampshire Hike Safe Card" from the New Hampshire Fish and Game Department's website. At $25 per person or $35 per family, having the card means that if you need to be rescued, even due to negligence, you will not be responsible for rescue costs.

Leave No Trace

Leaving no trace of your passing can be extremely difficult. Most people would agree that a primary reason for going on a hike is to enjoy nature. Unfortunately, we humans adversely affect nature more than any other species, and true natural places are becoming increasingly rare. To continue to enjoy what nature provides and to allow future hikers to enjoy it as well, along with just doing what is decent, all hikers should strive to make as little impact as possible while traveling through these natural places.

By following the basic principles listed below and using common sense, you can ensure that the places you visit will remain as natural as possible.

- **Pack out all your trash,** including such biodegradable items as apple cores, which have as great an impact as other trash. When possible, pick up and remove any trash others have left behind.
- **Avoid going off-trail whenever possible.** This is especially true in the alpine zones above tree line. The unique landscapes of these high-elevation ecosystems are very sensitive and include endangered and threatened species. Although some of these zones may feel large, such as the extensive alpine landscape in the Presidential Range, they actually compose a very small percentage of the overall regional landscape; heavy use by hikers is creating an existential threat to the long-term survival of these areas.

  By staying on the trails, you keep soil damage and erosion from spreading beyond the narrow route. It takes just a few hikers to create a new route, such as a short bushwhack around a wet section of trail, and when this new path becomes obvious, it turns into a trail. You'll also decrease your chances of getting poison ivy or picking up ticks by remaining on the trail.
- **Use outhouses and restrooms whenever possible.** When it is not possible, make sure you go well away from the trail and water sources (at least 200 feet) and bury waste 6 to 8 inches deep in the soil. Pack out all hygiene products.
- **Don't pick flowers or destroy wildlife, and don't remove natural objects.**
- **Don't feed or approach wild animals.**
- **Be courteous on the trail,** allowing people moving in the opposite direction or at quicker speeds to pass. If you need to get off the trail to do this, try to stand on rocks or wood so as not to disturb the trailside plant life.

For more information visit LNT.org.

Hiking Tips and Suggestions

As the adage goes, "Hike your own hike." Whether you are a trail runner who likes to race across the mountains or a landscape photographer who likes to take time to capture vivid photographs of your adventure, the most important thing is that you are prepared and adaptable. If you have your mind set on a hike and the weather does not cooperate, that's okay. Be willing to change your plans. There is so much to do in the White Mountains that you will certainly be able to find something fun, and safe, to do.

Some hikers prefer boots with ankle protection and stiff toes and soles to prevent bruising your feet on sharp rocks. Others prefer lighter footwear with the maneuverability and ground feel you don't get with boots. As long as you know your abilities and limitations, and have tested your gear before doing a big hike, you should feel confident that you are making the proper choice. Never start a hike with brand new untested boots, as that is a recipe for blisters which can bring a hike to a painful, screeching halt.

It is always best to overestimate how long the hike will take. You never want to be rushed—that can lead to small mistakes that can quickly become big mistakes in the mountains.

Whether to carry hiking poles is a personal choice, although this author believes they should be part of every hiker's gear. Poles transfer some of the energy expenditure to your upper body, making a hike a full-body effort. They can help save your knees on the downhills and provide stability and aid in crossing rivers and streams. If your hands often swell during hikes, using poles can relieve that. Modern poles are very lightweight and can fold up or collapse to a small enough size to fit in your pack.

Most modern smartphones have integrated GPS chips, and even without reception they can provide navigation aid. We'll discuss more about this later, but it's a good idea to download maps onto your device so that you can track your hike even if the phone is in airplane mode. In addition to providing a record of your trip, and locations of your photos, having your track visible can be very helpful, even lifesaving, if you get lost or end up out on the trail after dark. If you have mapped your hike with a GPS, and don't know where you are or need to turn around, you can always follow your track back to the starting point. (In cold weather, keep your phone near your body to preserve the battery and keep a charge.)

Photography Tips and Suggestions

Whether you bring a fancy camera with multiple lenses or just use your smartphone, there is a good chance you will take photos on your journey. The most important advice for taking good photos is to keep your camera readily accessible. If your nice digital SLR is tucked away in your backpack, you'll be much less likely to use it when the opportunity for a good photo arises.

If you are using a smartphone, keep it in your pocket or an accessible pocket in your backpack. If you are using a larger camera, devise a method to have the camera nearby. One method is to use a small camera case and slip the sternum strap of your pack through the belt loop of the case. Your camera will always be within hand's reach.

Make sure to bring any accessories you might need, including extra batteries and memory cards as well as lens cleaning solution and a lens cloth. For longer exposures, you may want to bring a tripod.

Shooting in RAW format gives you much more information in your image files and the ability to process the image with much more flexibility than with JPEGs. Even smartphones now provide the ability to shoot in RAW or DNG (Digital Negative) format using third-party apps. Be aware of the light, and try not to overexpose the image. Take multiple shots each time. It is always upsetting to think you have a good photo because it appears sharp on the camera or phone screen, only to get home and discover that the image is blurry. By taking multiple shots of the same scene, you are more likely to come away with a keeper.

Make sure that you focus on the most important part of your image. Use simple rules such as the "rule of thirds" to help aid your composition.

If capturing good photos is a priority, you may want to adjust your hiking schedule so that you are in the right place during the golden hours—just after sunrise and just before sunset. This may mean leaving early in the morning while it is still dark or being willing to finish the hike after the sun has set.

Websites and Resources for Weather and Trail Conditions

Weather changes quickly in the White Mountains, and the mountainous terrain creates microclimates. Whatever source of weather information you use, be sure to check it as close to your hike as possible and use a location near where you will be hiking. The Mount Washington Observatory posts weather forecasts for the higher summits every day and is a great resource:

www.mountwashington.org/experience-the-weather/higher-summit-forecast
.aspx

If you want to know more about the trail conditions on your specific route, there are multiple sources online. Two of the best resources are:

www.newenglandtrailconditions.com
https://trailsnh.com/lists/New-Hampshire-4000-Footers.php

The Appalachian Mountain Club also posts weather reports from their huts and important locations like Tuckerman Ravine and the summit of Mount Washington here:

www.outdoors.org/outdoor-activities/backcountry-weather

Maps, GPS, Guides, Apps, and Resources

Although this book provides a good starting place for planning your hike, you are definitely going to need some good topographic maps with hiking trails and distances listed. You will most likely want to get a few other books as well.

There are basically three sets of maps that provide the information you need to plan and navigate your hike:

- **Appalachian Mountain Club's White Mountain Trail Maps.** These are the standard maps that provide all the information you need to hike safely in the White Mountains. Each of the three (or four) separate paper maps covers two regions, one on each side. (One version of the maps separates the Presidential Range and Franconia/Pemigewasset regions onto separate maps, making a set of four maps.) These maps come with the *AMC White Mountain Guide* in plain paper and can also be purchased separately on waterproof tear-resistant material.

- **Map Adventures White Mountains Map.** This two-sided map is a little larger than the AMC set, but it covers the entire White Mountain region and lists all trail distances. If you want to buy just one map, this is the one to get. It is printed on waterproof material as well.
- **National Geographic White Mountain National Forest Maps.** These two-sided waterproof maps cover the entire region, with the maps divided into WMNF East (#741) and WMNF West (#740). These maps also list the mileage for all trail segments.

The following books will be helpful for planning:

- *Appalachian Mountain Club White Mountain Guide*. This guidebook, now in its thirtieth edition, is the standard resource that all White Mountain hikers should have. The book, compact but thick, describes every maintained trail and is updated every few years as trails change. This book also comes packaged with the full set of AMC White Mountain Trail Maps. It is compiled and edited by Steven D. Smith, who owns and operates The Mountain Wanderer, a bookstore (and website) in Lincoln, New Hampshire, that is completely devoted to hiking in New Hampshire and New England. (If you stop by the store, Steve can probably answer any hiking question you may have, as he knows the region and its trails inside and out.)
- *The 4000-Footers of the White Mountains: A Guide and History* by Steven D. Smith and Mike Dickerman. At first blush, this guide might seem unnecessary because you already have a guidebook on the 4,000-footers. Whereas this book chooses a selection of hikes, Smith and Dickerman's guide contains the history, nomenclature, and geology of every 4,000-foot peak along with descriptions of every major route up each mountain. It is a big book, with just a few black-and-white photos and no maps, but makes an invaluable resource for a peak-bagger and supplements the information in this book well.

Smartphones have for the most part replaced separate GPS devices. Smartphones such as the iPhone, via third-party apps, allow you to download detailed topographic maps that can then be viewed offline. By using a mapping/tracking app with a downloaded map, you can keep your phone in airplane mode to preserve the battery life. Two of the most highly regarded mapping apps are Gaia GPS and GPS Kit, but there are many others available as well.

Some people still prefer separate GPS devices because of their rugged build and longer battery life. Additionally, personal locator devices such as SPOT and the Garmin InReach allow for tracking and have a button for emergency rescue if you're in distress. The InReach also has a screen where maps can be preloaded and allows for texting via satellite. These do require a subscription to the service, so you need to

If you have some extra time in the area, make sure to visit some of the region's incredible water-falls, including the largest, Arethusa Falls.

decide if this is right for you. If you are going on a big adventure, it is great to know that your friends and family can track and follow your progress.

Here are some very helpful websites:

- **Peakfinder.org.** This website provides line drawings showing all the visible peaks from the summits of every New Hampshire 4,000-footer, as well as many more.
- **4000footers.com** contains basic information about all the New England 4,000-footers.
- **amc4000footer.org.** This is the official site of the Four Thousand Footers Club.
- **Viewsfromthetop.com** provides a general resource for hiking information in the Northeast.
- **www.fs.usda.gov/main/whitemountain/.** This is the official USDA National Forest Service website for the region, with trail information, road closures, and so forth.
- **Outdoors.org.** This is the official Appalachian Mountain Club (AMC) website. The AMC is responsible for running many of the huts in the White Mountains, as well as much of the trail work and educational programs.

There are multiple Facebook groups with thousands of members that are invaluable resources if you have any questions about hiking in the White Mountains or would just like a little support.

If you are interested in the history of the White Mountains, be sure to check out whitemountainhistory.org.

Driving and Parking

Most of the trailheads and trails in this book are within the White Mountain National Forest (WMNF). Many of the parking areas require a fee. The daily use fee can be paid through self-service stations at the trailheads. (Remember to bring cash or a check!) These passes are then displayed on the dashboard of the vehicle.

If you plan on hiking multiple times throughout the year, you should get the WMNF annual pass or annual family pass. These are stickers that go on your windshield and are valid for a year from the date of purchase. The annual pass provides one sticker for one car; the family pass provides two stickers. They can be purchased at various local vendors, online, or at the WMNF offices. For more information visit www.fs.usda.gov/detail/whitemountain/passes-permits/recreation/.

As you explore the White Mountains, you will notice that some trailheads are located at big parking lots while others require you to park along the edge of a road. If parking along a road, do so in a safe, visible spot that is wide enough for your vehicle to be completely off the road.

Busy parking areas, such as Pinkham Notch, Appalachia Trailhead, and the parking for the Falling Waters Trail in Franconia Notch, fill up very quickly on busy weekend days, so arrive early to guarantee a spot.

As you drive around the region, be aware that hikers may be crossing or walking along the road. Deer, moose, and birds are frequently on the roadways and can be difficult to see at night. Drive slowly; always be aware and ready to stop at any moment.

Some dirt roads that access trailheads are closed in winter. For these hikes you will need to park near the gate and walk the extra distance, wait until the roads open to do the hike, or find an alternative hike. Big rains occasionally wash out these roads and may require that you adjust your plans.

Flora and Fauna

Throughout your exploration of the White Mountains, you will traverse numerous ecosystems, from low elevation mixed-hardwood forests to higher elevation boreal forests and, above tree line, the unique alpine ecosystems that provide a rare opportunity to experience an environment closely resembling that found far to the north.

Mammals you may run across include red squirrel, snowshoe hare, and North American porcupine, which are hilarious as they try to run away by slowly climbing trees! In ponds and marshy areas, you may see American beavers, which leave pointed gnawed stumps around the area.

At lower elevations you may encounter white-tailed deer. Moose live throughout the region and are usually found in the mid-lower elevation forests; they are occasionally spotted higher up on the mountains. The changing climate has allowed the moose tick/winter tick to thrive, which has begun decimating the moose population. Thousands of ticks have been found on individual moose. Unlike deer, which become aware of the ticks in their larval stage and rub or bite them off, moose are unaware of the ticks until they become fully mature and engorged. Blood loss from the ticks themselves, as well as the associated blood loss and infections that can result from the moose scraping themselves raw in an attempt to rid themselves of the engorged ticks, have led to the massive decline.

Black bears also roam the White Mountains but are more rarely seen. Generally, neither bears nor moose are likely to cause harm, but if you see either animal, stay calm and keep your distance. These larger animals can become aggressive when you get close to or between them and their young. Black bears have a keen sense of smell, so if you are camping, make sure to prepare food away from your campsite and hang your food or put it in bear boxes. If a single moose is blocking your path, shouting might be enough to make it move, but during spring calving season or fall rutting season, they may be more aggressive; you may need to find an alternative route around them.

Although the large animals are exciting, keep your eye out for smaller creatures such as frogs and the bright red-and-orange red efts, the juvenile stage of eastern newts. You also may see many kinds of insects, including brightly colored butterflies.

An American toad waits by the side of the trail.

Mosquitoes and blackflies are the region's annoying stinging insects. If unlucky, you may run across a yellow jacket nest—holes in the ground near the base of trees. If you or someone in your hiking party steps on a nest, run until the yellow jackets are no longer chasing you. Warn others as soon as you can, although your involuntary shouts will probably be sufficient warning!

Wild turkeys roam the forest, and you will be forgiven for jumping if you startle a grouse, which can seemingly burst out of nowhere. Other birds you may encounter include thrushes, nuthatches, and even birds of prey, including owls and hawks.

Lichens cover rocks and break them down into minerals that eventually end up in the soil. There are many varieties, including the yellow map lichen, the orange sunburst lichen, and the target lichen, which grows in concentric rings. Old man's beard is a wiry branching lichen that hangs off tree branches. You'll see mosses everywhere too, including the bright green peat moss that grows along trails at mid and higher elevations.

Mushrooms and various other fungi are found throughout the forests. There are hundreds of flower species in the region; in alpine zones at certain times of year, they can create a dazzling variety of colors. In the forest, spring brings out varieties of trillium, identifiable by their three big leaves and three brightly colored petals. If you are lucky, you may even come across the rarer and beautiful jack-in-the-pulpit with its hooded sheath and the pink lady's slipper, a species of orchid.

Leaves catch the rain on a moist autumn day.

Hobblebush is everywhere and is easily identifiable by its broad leaves on long branches that grow up to several feet in height. They produce beautiful white flowers and red berries, and during fall the leaves turn varieties of bright colors, often in distinct segments.

In the alpine zones, you need to look closely to see an amazing variety of flowers, the most common being the diapensia, or pincushion plant (*Diapensia lapponica*), which grows in rugged exposed areas in green mats. The small flowers have five white petals and bloom in late spring and early summer.

Forests are the defining landscape of northern New England, and although forest covers most of the region today, it wasn't always this way. A long history of logging, especially in the White Mountains, means there are very few true old-growth forests here. (Small pockets of old-growth forest do exist, including "The Bowl," which lies between Mount Whiteface and Mount Passaconaway and the Gibbs Brook Scenic Area, which you pass through on your way up Mount Jackson.)

Lower and middle elevations are dominated by deciduous broadleaf trees. These include white and American mountain ash, red and sugar maple, pin and black cherry, American beech, and red oak. Paper and yellow birch trees are also very prevalent and often are found in the transition zone between lower and higher elevations. Conifers found at lower elevations include eastern white pine and eastern hemlock.

Red spruce and balsam fir dominate the higher elevations, with an increasing prevalence toward fir near the extremes just below tree line. Interestingly, although black spruce is not found as readily in these boreal zones, the krummholz, the gnarled and matted miniature trees in the alpine zone, is actually composed mostly of black spruce and balsam fir, not red spruce. Higher elevations can also contain mountain maple and mountain ash.

If you are interested in the flora and fauna of the White Mountains and want to learn while you hike, the *Nature Guide to the Northern Forest* by Peter Marchand and *Field Guide to the New England Alpine Summits* by Nancy Slack and Allison Bell, both published by the Appalachian Mountain Club, are highly recommended and are the perfect size for throwing in a backpack. Another more comprehensive book about all of New Hampshire, not just the White Mountains, is *The Nature of New Hampshire—Natural Communities of the Granite State* by Dan Sperduto and Ben Kimball.

Geology

In addition to forests, the other defining feature of the White Mountain landscape is its rocks, and you will get your fill of them as you hike up almost any trail in the region. New Hampshire is known as the Granite State for good reason—granite, or variations such as quartz monzonite, is the predominant rock type in the region. Mica schist, pink quartz, black tourmaline, and white feldspar are also common.

The mountains of this region were originally formed by magma intrusions created by the New England hotspot as the North American Plate moved over it between 124 and 100 million years ago. In colonial times the White Mountains were named not only for the snowcapped peaks in winter but also for the white appearance created by sunlight reflecting off mica flecks in the snowless months.

Many defining characteristics of the White Mountains were created by two major ice ages, one around 2 million years ago and another more recent, just 12,000 years ago. Much of this region was covered by thick ice that, with enough mass and pressure, had the power to transform the landscape. Ice would get in cracks of the rock, breaking off large pieces as it expanded. The movement of the ice scoured the landscape, creating both smooth polished rock faces and glacial striations, lines in the rocks caused by the dragging of ice and other rocky debris.

Tuckerman Ravine is an example of a glacial cirque. Unlike the more V-shaped valleys created by the eroding power of streams and rivers, glacial cirques were created by ice and have a U-shaped appearance. As you peer up Tuckerman Ravine from the Hermit Lake area, notice the smooth appearance and obvious bowl shape, which differs dramatically from other valleys in the area.

You will also come across glacial erratics—large rocks, often of a different type than the local bedrock, that you can find scattered throughout the region. These rocks were dragged by the movement of the glaciers and then randomly dropped. Tarns are lakes and ponds created by glaciers and are found in glacial cirques. Hermit Lake, at the base of Tuckerman Ravine on Mount Washington, is an example of a tarn.

Even now, the slow but steady erosion of the landscape is occurring. Rockslides happen throughout the White Mountains, with some occurring even in recent years. The Old Man of the Mountain, an outcrop on the Cannon Cliffs that when viewed from a certain angle resembled the profile of a man's face, and that adorns the road signs and license plates of New Hampshire, no longer exists. Despite humans using

Gray jays like to hang around summits. They know hikers are constantly dropping sunflower seeds from their trail mix.

bolts and wires to maintain the landmark, Mother Nature eventually had her way; the Old Man fell into oblivion in 2003.

If you would like to learn more about the geology of the White Mountains, *The Geology of the White Mountains* by Eusden, Thompson, Fowler, Davis, Bothner, Boisvert, and Creasy is an invaluable resource.

History

Although the White Mountains region was settled by people of European descent over the past few hundred years, Native Americans have inhabited the region for 12,000 years. By the time white settlers came to New Hampshire, the Abenaki people and related tribes such as the Penacook were living throughout the region. As with much of the sordid history of the United States, disease and war rapidly decimated the native populations.

Many of the names of rivers, lakes, and mountains in the region hark back to these earliest settlers. Names such as Winnipesaukee, Passaconaway, and Chocorua come from the stories and famous leaders of these tribes.

The earliest settlers of European descent came to the area in the 1600s, and by the 1800s the White Mountains were dominated both by tourism and by logging. One notable family, the Crawfords, settled in and around Crawford Notch. They built hotels, roads, and trails throughout the region. In 1819 Abel Crawford and his son Ethan Allen Crawford opened up the Crawford Path, a hiking and, later, horse path along the spine of the southern Presidential Range.

Throughout the nineteenth and early twentieth centuries, hotels, inns, and guest houses spread throughout the White Mountains, including atop some of the high peaks. At the same time, the area was logged heavily, both for timber and for farming. Railroads spidered through the region, and most of the virgin timber was harvested.

In 1911 Congress passed the Weeks Act, which opened the door for the federal government to begin purchasing land. Over time, the White Mountain National Forest has grown to encompass most of the region and its 4,000-foot peaks. The current national forest comprises 750,000 acres and includes six federal wilderness areas, specific defined areas where very little development can occur, in an effort to keep them in a natural state. These include the Presidential Range–Dry River Wilderness, the Great Gulf Wilderness, the Pemigewasset Wilderness, the Sandwich Range Wilderness, the Caribou–Speckled Mountain Wilderness, and the Wild River Wilderness, totaling more than 150,000 acres in all.

The State of New Hampshire also oversees several state parks in the region, including Franconia Notch, Crawford Notch, and Mount Washington State Parks.

Map Legend

Municipal

═〔93〕═	Interstate Highway
═〔302〕═	US Highway
═〔16〕═	State Road
═〔000〕═	Local/County Road
├──┼──┤	Railroad
─ ─ ·· ─ ··	State Boundary
─────	Leader Line

Trails

─ ─ ─ ─	Featured Trail
- - - - -	Trail or Fire Road
··········	Ski Lift

Water Features

⬭	Body of Water
≈	Marsh
∿	River/Creek
⌒⌒	Intermittent Stream
♂	Spring
∥	Rapids
≋	Waterfall

Symbols

⊻	Bridge
■	Building/Point of Interest
⛺	Campground
▲	Campsite (backcountry)
⬛	Inn/Lodging
🅿	Parking
▲	Peak/Elevation
🏢	Ranger Station/Park Office
◈	Scenic View
○	Town
⑳	Trailhead
❷	Visitor/Information Center
▬	Water

Land Management

▭	National Park/Forest
▭	National Monument/Wilderness Area
▭	State/County Park

Mount Moosilauke and the Kinsman Range

Mount Moosilauke can be seen from Bald Peak, along the Mount Kinsman Trail.

1 Mount Moosilauke

Often called the Entrance to the White Mountains, Mount Moosilauke is the south-westernmost of the 4,000-footers; the broad alpine summit provides amazing views out to the Whites as well as across Vermont and down the Connecticut River Valley. Unlike most of the mountains in the region, which lie within the White Mountain National Forest, most of the land and trails on the mountain are owned and maintained by Dartmouth College, which also runs the Moosilauke Ravine Lodge, rebuilt in 2017.

Distance: 8.1-mile lollipop loop
Summit elevation: 4,802 feet
4,000-footers rank: 10
Elevation gain: 2,500 feet
Difficulty: Moderate
Hiking time: About 4 hours
Trails used: Gorge Brook Trail, Carriage Road, South Peak Spur, Snapper Trail

Views: Excellent
Canine compatibility: Great
Special considerations: Parking is along the side of the road, so the earlier you get there, the less walking you will have to do to reach the trailhead. Reservations are required to eat or stay at the Moosilauke Ravine Lodge.

Finding the trailhead: *From I-93,* take exit 32 and head west on NH 112 (Kancamagus Highway). In approximately 3 miles, turn left onto NH 118. Go 7.1 miles and turn right onto Ravine Road. Follow this for 1.5 miles to the end of the road, where you can turn around and park along the west side of the road before the service road entrance. *From I-91 (south of junction with I-93),* take exit 16 and head east on VT 25 South toward Bradford. Go through the lights, and stay on the road as it crosses the bridge into New Hampshire and becomes NH 25. Continue heading east, and at the next light go straight, continuing onto NH 25C. In 13 miles, head left onto Water Street in Warren, near the Warren Rocket. Go just 0.1 mile; turn left at the stop sign onto NH 118 North/NH 25 West, and in 0.6 mile turn right onto NH 118. In 5.9 miles take a left onto Ravine Road. Follow this for 1.5 miles to the end of the road, where you can turn around and park along the west side of the road below the service road (unless you are a guest at the Ravine Lodge). Either follow signs from the turnaround to the trailhead at the river or head down to the Ravine Lodge before walking down to the river to begin the hike. **GPS:** N43 59.63' / W71 48.89'

The Hike

As the most southwestern of the New Hampshire 4,000-footers, Mount Moosilauke's location and broad summit provide a unique view. You can see far down the Connecticut River Valley and over to the high peaks of Vermont along the central spine of the Green Mountains. The name Moosilauke, which means "bald summit," is an Abenaki word that describes the peak aptly.

The traditional route following the Gorge Brook Trail to the summit, then the old Carriage Road to Snapper Trail back down makes for one of the easier hikes in this

There is no better view on Mount Moosilauke than that from South Peak out toward the main summit.

book. With a short spur to South Peak, you'll be rewarded with a second impressive view where you will be unlikely to run into other hikers.

Dartmouth College owns thousands of acres that encompass the east side of Mount Moosilauke. The Ravine Lodge is owned by the college and is staffed by current and former students. Over a thousand incoming first-year students are introduced to Mount Moosilauke and the Ravine Lodge every year before they begin classes as part of the Dartmouth Outing Club's First Year Trips Program, and many will work and live on the mountain at some point before or after they graduate.

From the parking turnaround at the end of the access road, head straight along a gravel path; in a few hundred feet, make two left turns, following signs down toward the river. (**Note:** Parking is along the road below the service entrance, and you may have to walk a distance back up the road on busy weekends, when cars can be parked up to 0.5 mile from the turnaround.) You can also take the path down to the Moosilauke Ravine Lodge and follow the road below it to the trail down to the river. Either way, a 0.2-mile hike takes you down to the bridge over the river.

After crossing the bridge over the Baker (or Asquamchumaukee) River, turn left, following signs for the Gorge Brook Trail. In 0.1 mile (0.3 mile from the parking turnaround), turn right (north), following signs for the Gorge Brook Trail. The rocky

Two hikers make their way up the Gorge Brook Trail.

trail climbs through mixed forest along a wide, eroded route and makes a slight dip before crossing over Gorge Brook at 0.6 mile.

The Gorge Brook Trail, which used to follow the river here until a major washout in 2011 during Tropical Storm Irene, joins the Snapper trail and heads slightly away from the main brook, reaching the new junction at 0.8 mile. Turn right (north) onto the Gorge Brook relocation (called the Wales Carter Connection) as the Snapper Trail continues straight. A winding, fairly easy path heads back up toward the river, rejoining the old route and crossing a bridge at 1.3 miles. The Gorge Brook Trail continues along a sometimes-muddy section by the east bank of the brook, reaching the Ross McKenny Forest plaque at 1.6 miles.

The plaque location is also informally known as "last water," because it's the last place to get water for most of the remainder of the loop. At this point, the trail makes a sharp turn to the east and begins contouring up the side of the mountain as the trail becomes a little steeper. The Gorge Brook Trail joins an old logging road, becoming less steep before reaching the first overlook at 2.4 miles.

As you continue, the trail turns to the left (north) and soon begins a series of switchbacks. Another opening provides a view at 2.9 miles, and just above this a view at 3.0 miles reveals Mount Jim just across Jobildunc Ravine, with the Kinsman and Franconia Ranges rising behind it. As the trail heads in a westerly direction, you climb over boulders while views become more prevalent.

At 3.3 miles the trail turns north, and as you climb over a shoulder (known as the East Peak, the highest point visible from the Ravine Lodge), you get a view of the summit. Pass through a scrubby tree-lined section before popping out below the summit to make the final 0.25-mile push in open alpine terrain to reach the summit at 3.8 miles.

The broad Connecticut River Valley separates New Hampshire and Vermont, with the high peaks of Vermont's Green Mountains rising to the west. All five of Vermont's 4,000-foot peaks are visible (from south to north): Killington Peak, Mount Abraham, Mount Ellen, Camel's Hump, and Mount Mansfield. On particularly clear days the high peaks of the Adirondacks can be seen in the distance. Due south and due north, the mountains are small and rolling, but all the big peaks of the White Mountains are visible to the east.

The Kinsman and Franconia Ranges are visible to the northeast, with the high Presidentials rising in the distance. Due east, the Tripyramids can be seen, flanked by Mount Osceola closer to the north and Mount Tecumseh nearer to the south. Thirty-four 4,000-footers are visible from the summit.

A series of summit houses once entertained and accommodated guests atop the mountain. Short rock walls (good wind shelters) provide evidence of this past. Guests took carriages all the way up from Breezy Point on the Baker River, a spot much lower than the Ravine Lodge. (The Carriage Road from Breezy Point makes for a nice ski trip up the mountain in winter.)

From the summit, follow the Carriage Road southwest along the ridge separating the main peak from South Peak. Wide-open views in both directions eventually become obscured as the trail is lined with stunted fir and spruce. This section of ridge is white-blazed, as it is part of the Appalachian Trail. At 4.7 miles (0.9 mile from the summit), Glencliff Trail heads off to the right while the Carriage Road heads left (southeast). Before descending the Carriage Road, however, follow Glencliff Trail for 30 feet then take the signed spur on the left to South Peak. Although there isn't the requisite 200 feet of prominence needed to make South Peak an official 4,000-footer, a short rocky 0.2-mile climb to the open summit provides outstanding views of Mount Moosilauke's main peak, and you are very likely to have the summit to yourself.

From the junction, follow the Carriage Road southeast down along an arm of the mountain. Although wide, the road is rocky and at times drops fairly steeply. Take a few minutes to stop and enjoy the views to the south as you descend. Several switchbacks lead to the junction with the Snapper Trail at 6.3 miles, just below 3,400 feet in elevation.

Turn left onto the Snapper Trail as it first contours fairly gently toward the northeast before turning southeast and reaching the junction with the Gorge Brook Trail

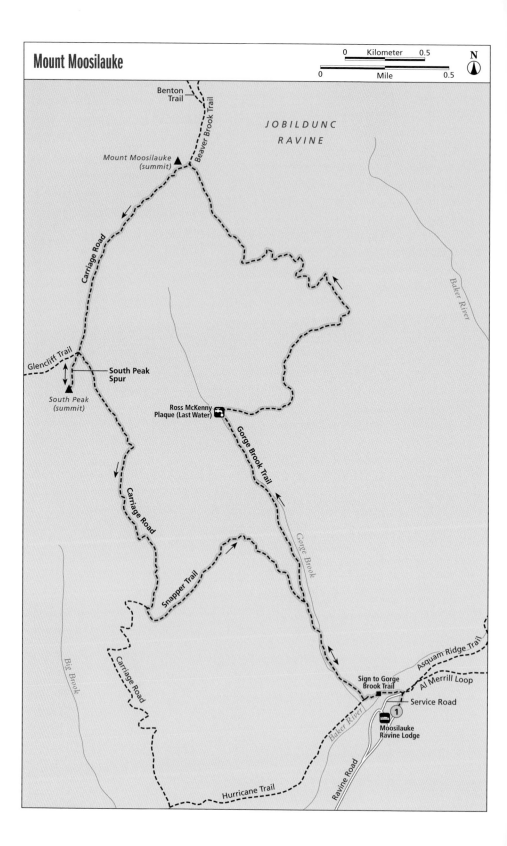

Mount Moosilauke

0   Kilometer   0.5

0   Mile   0.5

N

Benton Trail

Beaver Brook Trail

JOBILDUNC RAVINE

Mount Moosilauke (summit)

Carriage Road

Baker River

Glencliff Trail

South Peak Spur

South Peak (summit)

Ross McKenny Plaque (Last Water)

Gorge Brook Trail

Gorge Brook

Carriage Road

Snapper Trail

Big Brook

Carriage Road

Asquam Ridge Trail

Al Merrill Loop

Sign to Gorge Brook Trail

Service Road

Baker River

Moosilauke Ravine Lodge

1

Hurricane Trail

Ravine Road

in 1.0 mile, at 7.3 miles. From here follow the Gorge Brook Trail 0.8 mile back to the parking turnaround (go left after crossing over the Baker River), or stop by the Ravine Lodge by heading straight from the bridge.

Miles and Directions

0.0 Start at the end of the parking turnaround and follow the gravel path, making a left down to the river and the Gorge Brook Trail.

0.2 Cross the Baker River and turn left, following the sign for the Gorge Brook Trail.

0.3 Turn right (north) onto the Gorge Brook Trail as the Hurricane Trail continues straight.

0.6 Cross over Gorge Brook. Stay straight.

0.8 Turn right, following Gorge Brook Trail as Snapper Trail heads straight/left.

1.3 Cross over Gorge Brook.

1.6 The trail turns right (east) at Ross McKenny plaque and "last water" on the hike.

2.4 Reach the first overlook.

3.3 Reach East Peak.

3.8 Reach the summit of Mount Moosilauke. Head left (southwest) on the Carriage Road.

4.7 Reach the junction with Glencliff Trail and Carriage Road. Take the side trail to the summit of South Peak, which is left off the Glencliff Trail just a few yards from the junction.

4.9 Reach the summit of South Peak.

5.1 Return to the junction with Carriage Road. Head left (southeast) down Carriage Road.

6.3 Turn left onto Snapper Trail.

7.3 At the junction with the Gorge Brook Trail, continue straight on Gorge Brook Trail to the trailhead.

7.9 Reach the Baker River. Go left after crossing the river to get to the parking turnaround, or head straight and up to the right to visit the Ravine Lodge.

8.1 Arrive back at the parking turnaround.

Other Routes

1. Glencliff Trail to Carriage Road out-and-back—distance: 7.8 miles; elevation gain: 3,400 feet

2. Beaver Brook Trail out-and-back—distance: 7.6 miles; elevation gain: 3,300 feet

3. Ridge Trail to Beaver Brook Trail to Carriage Road to Snapper Trail to Gorge Brook Trail—distance: 9.6 miles; elevation gain: 2,800 feet

2 North and South Kinsman Mountains (with spur to Bald Peak)

The Kinsman Ridge rises out of Franconia Notch, forming its western wall. On this hike you get great views across to the high peaks of Franconia Ridge, unique views of Mount Moosilauke from the north, and into Vermont as well. Most people ascending these peaks embark from Franconia Notch, but the Mount Kinsman Trail from the west is a less-crowded alternative, with a bonus summit of Bald Peak halfway up—a good spot to enjoy a snack and catch your breath.

Distance: 10.4 miles out and back
Summit elevation: North Kinsman, 4,293 feet; South Kinsman, 4,358 feet
4,000-footers rank: North Kinsman, 28; South Kinsman, 22
Elevation gain: 4,000 feet
Difficulty: Moderate

Hiking time: About 6 hours
Trails used: Mount Kinsman Trail, Kinsman Ridge Trail
Views: Great; east view from North Kinsman ledges; best view from South Peak on South Kinsman
Canine compatibility: Good

Finding the trailhead: *From I-93,* take exit 34C from I-93 North. Turn left onto NH 18 North and in 2.1 miles turn left onto Kerr Road. In 0.25 mile the road becomes Wells Road, which you will follow for 1.7 miles. Turn left onto NH 116 South; the trailhead parking area will be on the left side of the road in 2 miles. (From I-93 South, take exit 38 and follow NH 116 south for 4.6 miles. *From I-91 (from the south),* take exit 16 and head east on VT 25 South toward Bradford. In 0.5 mile, turn left onto US 5 North. Turn right onto Newbury Crossing road in 7.7 miles; after 0.5 mile, cross the Connecticut River and turn left onto NH 10. In 2.3 miles turn right onto NH 116 East and follow this winding road for 10.2 miles until its junction with NH 112. Turn right and in 0.9 mile turn left onto NH 116 North. The parking for the Mount Kinsman Trail will be on the right in 6.5 miles. **GPS:** N44 09.90' / W71 45.95'

The Hike

Although the distance is the same and the vertical gain slightly more, by hiking the Mount Kinsman Trail instead of the more popular route(s) on the east side of the ridge from Franconia Notch, you get the opportunity to visit a cool minor summit on the way, check out a narrow flume, and, most importantly, avoid the crowds on the other trails and parking hassle on the weekends.

This is a quintessential White Mountain hike, with sections of both smooth and rocky trail and even some sections where you will need to use your hands. Since you start under 1,000 feet in elevation, you climb through multiple ecosystems and your hard work is rewarded with stunning views. **Option:** A nice day trip of 4.6 miles can be made by just going to Bald Peak and back.

Four hikers traverse the summit of South Kinsman Mountain.

The Mount Kinsman Trail begins very gradually, and you soon find yourself in a beautiful hemlock forest. This section of trail is fairly new, and in 0.5 mile you meet back up with the old Mount Kinsman Trail. After the hard right at the junction, you curve around to the left; when you pass near an old sugarhouse, the trail makes a turn to the right.

You begin to climb again, not very steeply at first. When you enter the White Mountain National Forest at 1.1 miles, you take a right then a quick left onto another older and steeper logging road. Cross a brook at 1.5 miles and at 1.8 miles pass a nice set of small falls tumbling through rocks coated in a thick blanket of verdant moss. Kendall Brook is crossed at 2.1 miles and provides the opportunity for a short side trip. A steep but short trail on the far bank leads down to the right; at the end of this 500-foot spur, you reach the top edge of a long eroded basaltic dike that has created a long flume. This stunning geologic feature, Kinsman Flume, stretches down for about 100 feet and provides a great example of how water erodes different types of rock.

Just past the brook is the spur trail on the right (west) to Bald Peak. This 0.2-mile spur takes you on a quick down and up to a nice open ledge where you get a great view of the western side of the Kinsman Range and North Kinsman. Almost due south is Mount Moosilauke, the westernmost of the White Mountains.

Back at the junction, the trail makes a sharp left (east) turn and soon begins to wind steadily up the mountain, climbing 1,500 vertical feet in 1.6 miles, mostly at a moderate grade with a few short steep sections. At 3.7 miles, reach the junction of

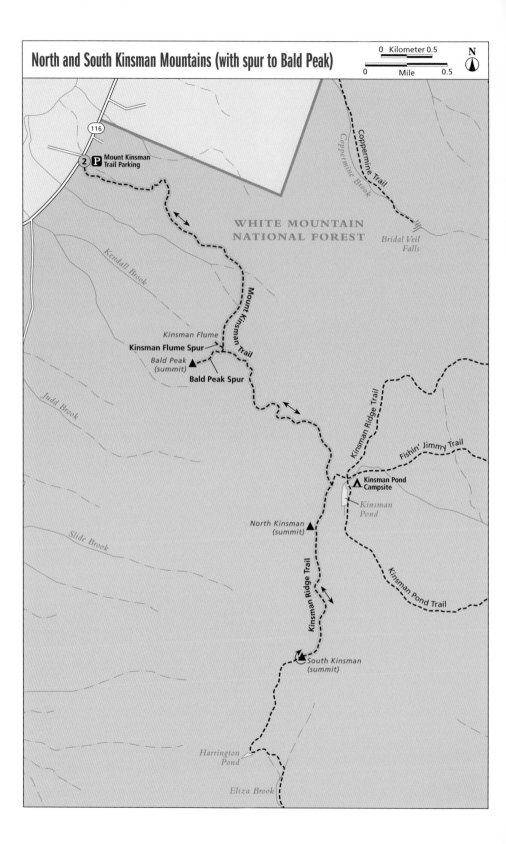

North and South Kinsman Mountains (with spur to Bald Peak)

0 Kilometer 0.5

0 Mile 0.5

N

116

P Mount Kinsman
Trail Parking

2

Coppermine Trail

Coppermine Brook

WHITE MOUNTAIN
NATIONAL FOREST

Bridal Veil
Falls

Kendall Brook

Kinsman Flume
Kinsman Flume Spur

Mount Kinsman Trail

Bald Peak
(summit)

Bald Peak Spur

Judd Brook

Kinsman Ridge Trail

Fishin' Jimmy Trail

Kinsman Pond
Campsite

Kinsman
Pond

Slide Brook

North Kinsman
(summit)

Kinsman Ridge Trail

Kinsman Pond Trail

South Kinsman
(summit)

Harrington
Pond

Eliza Brook

the Kinsman Ridge Trail. While the Mount Kinsman Trail is marked with blue blazes because it connects with the Appalachian Trail, the Kinsman Ridge Trail is marked with white blazes signifying that you are now on the Appalachian Trail.

Turn right (south) and make the short but sometimes very steep climb to the summit of North Kinsman. The summit is the large boulder on the left; just beyond, a short side trail leads down to ledges with great views across to the Franconia Ridge. A side path to the left from the ledge will take on you a short scramble down to a view directly over Kinsman Pond.

Continue following the Kinsman Ridge Trail south as it descends a few steep pitches to the flat low point at 4.5 miles. The trail climbs a tiny bit then levels out, giving you a chance to enjoy the beautiful high-elevation fir forest before making the final rocky ascent to the summit of South Kinsman. Pass the somewhat obscured north knob of South Kinsman at 4.9 miles (possibly near the true summit) and continue ahead to the accepted summit, with better views on the south knob (marked by a rock cairn), at 5.0 miles. The mostly flat summit provides great views in all directions.

You get a unique perspective of Mount Moosilauke to the south and Bog Pond to the southwest under Mount Wolf. The Franconia Range dominates the view to the east. See if you can spot the distinctive Camels Hump in Vermont, which is 60 miles to the west. Return the way you came, enjoying the nice views north to the Cannon Balls and Cannon Mountain as you descend from North Kinsman.

Miles and Directions

0.0 Start from the parking area on the Mount Kinsman Trail.

2.1 Reach Kendall Brook and a short side trail to the right down to Kinsman Flume; just beyond this first junction, reach the junction of the side trail to Bald Peak. Head right (west) to Bald Peak.

2.3 Reach Bald Peak.

2.5 Return to Mount Kinsman Trail, heading east at the junction.

4.1 Reach the junction with the Kinsman Ridge Trail (AT). Head right (south) up a short but steep climb to the summit of North Kinsman.

4.5 Reach the summit of North Kinsman. The side trail to a ledge with views is just beyond on the left.

5.4 Reach the summit of South Kinsman; continue to the second knob/highpoint to the rock cairn. Enjoy the views before returning the way you came.

10.4 Arrive back at the trailhead.

Other Routes

1. Lonesome Lake Trail to Cascade Brook Trail to Fishin' Jimmy Trail to Kinsman Ridge Trail out-and-back—distance: 8.1 miles; elevation gain: 3,000 feet

2. Kinsman Ridge Traverse (bonus hike 1)—distance: 16.9 miles; elevation gain: 3,000 feet

3 Cannon Mountain

Cannon Mountain is best known for the ski area on its slopes and the aerial tramway that runs most of the year. Although short, this hike is steep and the trail is eroded, but it rewards the hiker with a great clifftop view and an observation tower, both of which provide a dazzling perspective of Franconia Ridge.

Distance: 4.4 miles out and back with loop to observation tower
Summit elevation: 4,100 feet
4,000-footers rank: 36
Elevation gain: 2,300 feet
Difficulty: Moderate; the first mile is steep, but the hike is short.
Hiking time: About 3 hours

Trails used: Kinsman Ridge Trail, Rim Trail
Views: Excellent; best views from ledge on Cannon Cliffs and from observation tower
Canine compatibility: Good, but summit can be crowded with nonhikers.
Special considerations: Watch out for downhill skiers in winter. The summit can be crowded on summer weekends.

Finding the trailhead: *From I-93,* take exit 34B toward the Cannon Mountain Tramway. Turn left onto Tramway Drive; then take the first left into the main parking area. In a few hundred feet, you will see a dirt road on the left. You can park in the main lot; the dirt road leads to an open area and the trailhead is at the southeast corner of the open area. *From I-91 (from the south),* take exit 16 and head east on VT 25 South toward Bradford. In 0.5 mile turn left onto US 5 North. Turn right onto Newbury Crossing road in 7.7 miles. After 0.5 mile cross the Connecticut River and turn left onto NH 10. In 2.3 miles turn right onto NH 116 East; follow this winding road for 10.2 miles until the junction with NH 112. Turn right, and in 0.9 mile turn left onto NH 116 North. Take NH 116 North for 8.5 miles and then turn right onto Wells Road. In 2.0 miles turn right onto NH 18 South and after 2.1 miles get onto I-93 South. Take exit 34B and turn right onto Tramway Drive. In a few hundred feet, you will see a dirt road on the left. You can park in the main lot; the dirt road leads to an open area and the trailhead is at the southeast corner of the open area. **GPS:** N44 10.17' / W71 41.25'

The Hike

Although this ties for the shortest hike in the book, don't be fooled. The hike up is very steep—climbing 1,500 feet over the course of just 1.0 mile. Don't let that deter you, however; this is a premier hike with multiple viewpoints, including a magnificent ledge overlooking Franconia Notch and the Franconia Ridge. This is a great hike for a mixed party: Those who only want a short loop at the summit can take the Aerial Tram up, while the fit and adventurous can put in the hard work and climb to the top.

Interestingly, Cannon Mountain, also known as Profile Mountain, is not named for a person but for a small geologic feature. A long flat rock that sits on a smaller one

Mist floats through the high-elevation forest during a late-fall hike up Cannon Mountain. ▶

The sun sets over the Green Mountains in Vermont as Cannon Mountain rises above the hills to the west.

resembles a cannon. The lesser used Profile Mountain name refers to the Old Man of the Mountain, which, until 2003 when it collapsed, described a prominent outcrop on the dramatic Cannon Cliffs that when viewed from a certain angle, looked like the profile of a man and remains as the image on the New Hampshire state license plate.

From the trailhead at the southeast edge of the side parking area, the Kinsman Ridge Trail enters the woods and briefly heads east on a mellow grade before turning right to begin the steep ascent. Here you get an up-close-and-personal view of extreme erosion. Notice the gravelly unconsolidated consistency of the soil on the bottom section of the hike that has been eroding for years. At times the trail can look more like a bobsled run than a hiking trail.

Climb steeply up the trail as it heads south, then southwest on a contour, then due south, with some small switchbacks along the way. The trail gets rockier as you gain elevation, and at 0.8 mile you reach the edge of a ski trail. From here you will cross the ski trail four times over the next 0.25 mile, with occasional views down to Echo Lake and to the north. After the last crossing, the trail hugs the left side of the ski trail. The rocks are angled and often slippery here, so be careful. Also make sure to turn around for views of the cliffs near Eagle Cliff across the valley.

At 1.2 miles the trail heads left off the ski trail. Rocks are coated in moss as you continue to climb to the southeast. The trail continues to level further, while the surrounding vegetation becomes denser and shorter until you reach the junction with a short spur trail on the left at 1.5 miles to a magnificent view atop Cannon Cliffs. This large open slab is perfect for enjoying a bite or a drink while admiring the stunning profile of Franconia Ridge across the valley.

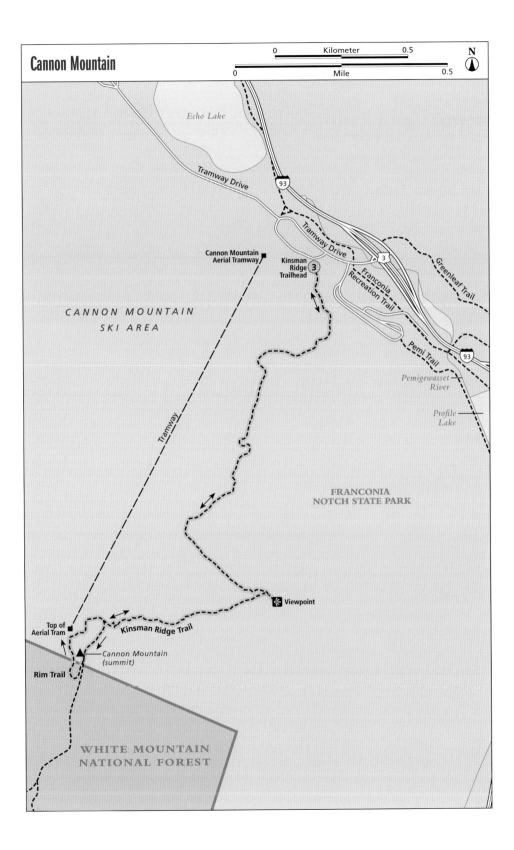

Cannon Mountain

Echo Lake

Tramway Drive

93

Tramway Drive

3

Greenleaf Trail

Cannon Mountain
Aerial Tramway

Kinsman
Ridge
Trailhead

3

CANNON MOUNTAIN
SKI AREA

Franconia
Recreation
Trail

Pemi Trail

93

Pemigewasset
River

Tramway

Profile
Lake

FRANCONIA
NOTCH STATE PARK

Viewpoint

Top of
Aerial Tram

Kinsman Ridge Trail

Cannon Mountain
(summit)

Rim Trail

WHITE MOUNTAIN
NATIONAL FOREST

Kilometer

0   0.5

0   Mile   0.5

N

From the junction with the short spur, the trail makes a sharp turn to the right (west), where you quickly climb over the hump of the east peak. Make a short descent and then climb up toward the peak, first through an often-wet section with scrub and boulders, until you pop out onto the talus field and make the final few switchbacks to the junction with the Rim Trail at 2.0 miles.

Head left (south) on the Rim Trail to make a 0.4-mile loop of the summit. The trail is level, with some benches at viewing areas along the way. At 2.2 miles take the trail on the right with a sign labeled "Short Path," which will quickly take you to the Summit Observation Tower. This big platform provides great views in every direction. There should be a nice panorama with peak names on the tower. You can see north into Canada, and there's a great westerly view of the high peaks of Vermont's Green Mountains, including Mount Mansfield, Vermont's tallest peak. To the east is one of the best views of Franconia Ridge. North and South Kinsman are visible along Kinsman Ridge to the southwest, with the humps known as the Cannon Balls the closest peaks on the ridge.

From the summit tower, follow the Rim Trail down to the top of the tramway station. Stay to the right and follow the Rim Trail back into the woods, where you return to the junction with the Kinsman Ridge Trail. Turn left (east) and follow the Kinsman Ridge Trail back down to the parking lot.

Miles and Directions

0.0 Start from the southeast edge of the side parking area on the Kinsman Ridge Trail.

1.5 The trail reaches a short spur on the left to an open rocky slab with great views. The main trail turns right (southwest).

2.0 Turn left onto the Rim Trail.

2.2 Leave the Kinsman Ridge Trail, which heads left, and follow "Short Path" up to the right to the observation tower. At the observation tower, continue along the gravel path to the top of the tramway.

2.3 At the tramway station, head right and back into woods, following the Rim Trail back to the junction with the Kinsman Ridge Trail.

2.4 Turn left (east) onto the Kinsman Ridge Trail.

4.4 Arrive back at trailhead.

Other Routes

1. Lonesome Lake Trail to Hi-Cannon Trail to Kinsman Ridge Trail to Rim Trail out-and-back—distance: 5.5 miles; elevation gain: 2,600 feet

2. Kinsman Ridge Traverse (bonus hike 1)—distance: 16.9 miles; elevation gain: 3,000 feet

The Franconia Range and the Pemigewasset Wilderness

The dramatic cliffs of Bondcliff are seen from Mount Bond.

4 Mount Liberty and Mount Flume

The journey up the Flume Slide Trail is steep and challenging, ascending straight up the west side of Mount Flume. The slide is old, meaning there are plenty of trees to grab onto as you climb, but only do this hike when conditions are dry. The challenging climb rewards you with dramatic clifftop views from the summit of Mount Flume and equally impressive views from Mount Liberty. *Note:* If conditions are wet, or you're looking for an easier option, go out and back on the Liberty Spring Trail.

Distance: 9.9 miles lollipop loop
Summit elevation: Mount Flume, 4,328 feet; Mount Liberty, 4,459 feet
4,000-footers rank: Mount Flume, 25; Mount Liberty, 18
Elevation gain: 3,900 feet
Difficulty: Very difficult. The Flume Slide Trail is extremely steep; an easier option is out and back on the Liberty Spring Trail and Franconia Ridge Trail.
Hiking time: About 6.5 hours
Trails used: Whitehouse Trail, Franconia Notch Recreation Path, Flume Slide Trail, Franconia Ridge Trail, Liberty Spring Trail

Views: Excellent
Canine compatibility: Not dog friendly; out and back on Liberty Spring and Franconia Ridge Trails is doable for fit dogs.
Special considerations: Parking can be crowded on the weekends. You can also park at the northern lot at the Flume Visitor Center and take the recreation path to the Liberty Spring Trail instead of using the Whitehouse Trail. Do not attempt to climb the Flume Slide Trail in wet weather.

Finding the trailhead: *From I-93 (from the south),* take exit 34A and merge onto US 3 North. The road to the parking lot for the Liberty Spring Trail will be on the right in 0.9 mile, past the main entrance to the Flume Gorge. *From I-93 (from the north),* take exit 33 and turn left onto US 3 North. The road to the parking lot for the Liberty Spring Trail will be on the right in 2.8 miles, past the main entrance to the Flume Gorge. The Whitehouse Trailhead is located at the south end of the parking area. **GPS:** N44 06.05' / W71 40.90'

The Hike

Mount Liberty and Mount Flume are the southernmost peaks along Franconia Ridge. Although not above tree line, both afford open clifftop views. The route up the Flume Slide Trail follows a long-overgrown rockslide and is very difficult, requiring use of your hands to navigate steep rocky terrain that is often wet. In just over 0.5 mile, you will climb more than 1,300 feet in elevation! In dry conditions with adequate time, it is a doable and memorable challenge for most fit hikers. *Note:* Consider Other Route 1 below for an out-and-back on the Liberty Spring Trail; it is 0.3 mile longer, with 500 more vertical feet of climbing, but is significantly easier.

A hiker stands atop the cliffs on Mount Flume, high above the Pemigewasset River valley, as Mount Moosilauke rises high in the distance.

From the parking area, follow the Whitehouse Trail into the woods as it climbs over a gentle rise and parallels the highway before coming out on the Franconia Notch Recreation Path at 0.6 mile. Turn left onto the bike path, cross the Pemigewasset River, and turn right onto the Liberty Spring Trail at 0.8 mile.

Climb gradually in a northeasterly direction as you contour up through a beautiful hardwood forest, making a turn to the southeast before reaching the junction with the Flume Slide Trail at 1.4 miles. Turn right (south) onto the Flume Slide Trail.

The Flume Slide Trail starts innocently enough, contouring south then southeast as it gently climbs up toward Flume Brook, gaining 500 feet in the first 1.7 miles from the junction. At 3.3 miles (from the trailhead) you cross over Flume Brook, crossing back over at 3.4 miles. At 3.8 miles the trail crosses an upper branch of Flume Brook and shortly after reaches the gravelly path that heads straight up and signals the beginning of the real climb.

Here, at 4.0 miles (around 2,900 feet elevation), you reach the first series of ledgy slabs. The pitch increases, and you need to use your hands. Although there often are areas of runoff, if it hasn't rained recently, you should be able to find some nice holds. Take your time and be sure to test your footing before making the next step. On the steepest sections, use the "three points of contact" rule and only move one hand or foot at a time. If you feel uncomfortable on the ledges, numerous bushwhacks along

A sign lists mileage at the junction of the Franconia Ridge and Liberty Spring Trails.

the edge allow you to pull yourself up using trees, roots, and branches. Some rocks may be loose, so if you are traveling in a group, make sure to provide adequate spacing and don't climb directly above or below another person.

The climb is relentless but straightforward, and near the top the trail turns left onto a steep path that no longer climbs directly up. Just before reaching the ridge crest, follow a short spur to the left for nice views of Mount Flume's cliffs. Reach the junction with the Franconia Ridge and Osseo Trails at 4.7 miles. Head left (north) onto the Franconia Ridge Trail to the summit of Mount Flume at 4.8 miles.

Cliffs jut out along the last climb to the peak, soaring over the valley and the rockslides that pour off the mountain. With views to the south, west, and north, it's hard to know where to look. To the west, the Kinsmans rise from Franconia Notch. Mount Liberty stands slightly taller to the immediate northwest, while from this vantage point you can see the eastern sides of the Mount Lincoln and Mount Lafayette summit cones. The ski trails on Loon Mountain are visible to the south, with Mount Osceola farther to the east.

From the summit, the Franconia Ridge Trail heads north then northwest, dropping 450 feet to the col between Mounts Flume and Liberty. The climb up to Mount Liberty starts off easily enough but ends in a steep section of large rocks as you gain 550 feet to reach the summit at 6.0 miles.

The summit of Mount Liberty provides views in all directions, with all the peaks in the Pemigewasset Wilderness spreading out from the northeast to the southeast. Beyond Owl's Head, which is the lower broad north–south ridge directly to the northeast, you can see a higher ridge extending from the Twins in the north to the Bonds and Bondcliff to the south. To the northeast over Mount Guyot, the highest peaks of the Presidential Range rise beyond. To the north, Mount Lincoln juts high above, obscuring the taller peak of Mount Lafayette beyond. Just to the west of the

Mount Liberty and Mount Flume

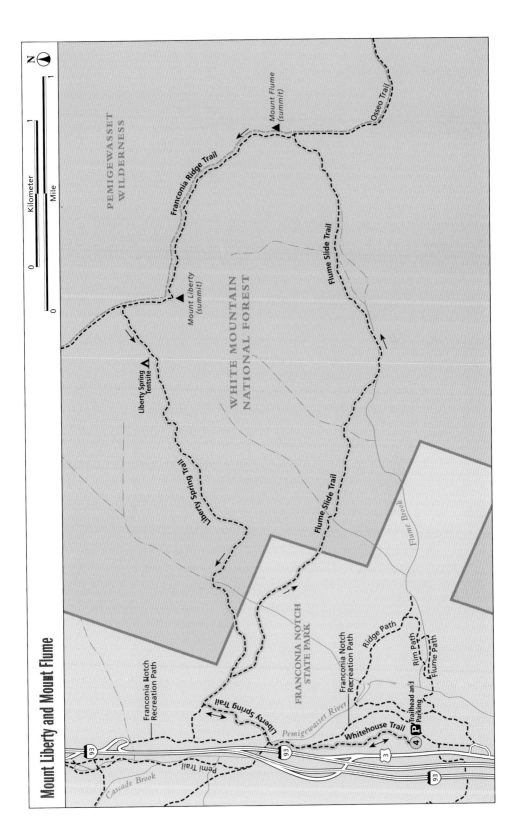

PEMIGEWASSET WILDERNESS

Mount Flume (summit)

Osseo Trail

Franconia Ridge Trail

Mount Liberty (summit)

Liberty Spring Tentsite

Flume Slide Trail

WHITE MOUNTAIN NATIONAL FOREST

Liberty Spring Trail

Flume Slide Trail

Franconia Notch Recreation Path

Franconia Notch Recreation Path

Ridge Path

Rim Path

Flume Path

Flume Brook

FRANCONIA NOTCH STATE PARK

Pemigewasset River

Liberty Spring Trail

Pemi Trail

Cascade Brook

Whitehouse Trail

Trailhead and Parking

N

Kilometer

Mile

0   1

0   1

ridge, the dramatic cliffs of Cannon Mountain create the gateway to the northern entrance of Franconia Notch.

Continue north along the Franconia Ridge Trail, dropping off the summit plateau to the right, down along some steep rock, then curving back out to the left just below a gigantic rock outcrop. The trail continues into the woods, descending steeply at first before mellowing as it travels through a high-elevation fir forest. At 6.3 miles you reach the junction with the Liberty Spring Trail.

Turn left (west) onto the Liberty Spring Trail and begin descending. At 6.6 miles reach the Liberty Spring Campsite with tent platforms. During summer there is a caretaker; camping requires a fee. There's a small spring to the left if you need some water. Continue descending fairly steeply through a mix of fir, spruce, and birch. Over the next 1.2 miles you descend 1,500 feet, with some big rock steps and occasional switchbacks. A sharp turn to the right around 2,400 feet signals an easing of the grade, and you reach the junction with the Flume Slide Trail at 8.6 miles and the recreation path in the valley at 9.1 miles. Head left to the Whitehouse Trail and reach the parking area at 9.9 miles.

Miles and Directions

0.0 Start from the parking area and follow the Whitehouse Trail north.

0.6 Turn left onto the (paved) Franconia Notch Recreation Path.

0.8 After crossing the Pemigewasset River on a bridge, turn right (east) onto the Liberty Spring Trail.

1.4 Turn right (south) onto the Flume Slide Trail.

4.0 Reach the bottom of the slide.

4.7 Reach the junction of Osseo and Franconia Ridge Trails. (Just before the junction, a short spur to left leads to nice view.) Turn left (north) onto the Franconia Ridge Trail.

4.8 Reach the summit of Mount Flume. Continue north on the Franconia Ridge Trail.

6.0 Reach the summit of Mount Liberty. Continue north on the Franconia Ridge Trail.

6.3 Turn left (west) onto the Liberty Spring Trail.

6.6 Pass the Liberty Spring tentsite.

9.1 Turn left onto the Franconia Notch Recreation Path.

9.3 Turn right onto the Whitehouse Trail.

9.9 Arrive back at the parking lot.

Other Routes

1. Whitehouse Trail to Liberty Spring Trail to Franconia Ridge Trail out-and-back—distance: 10.1 miles; elevation gain: 4,300 feet

2. Pemigewasset Loop (hike 36)—distance: 38.5 miles (extended), 31.5 miles (basic); elevation gain: 12,500 feet (extended), 10,000 feet (basic)

3. Franconia Ridge Traverse (bonus hike 2)—distance: 13.9 miles point to point, 17.4-mile loop; elevation gain: 5,800 feet

5 Mount Lincoln and Mount Lafayette

Although Mount Washington is the most famous peak in the White Mountains, most knowledgeable hikers agree that the alpine traverse along the dramatic Franconia Ridge is second to none, with steep drops on both sides along a remarkably straightforward walk to the highest peak outside the Presidential Range. Along the loop you will pass several gorgeous waterfalls, and the descent off Mount Lafayette takes you by Greenleaf Hut with continuing views along the Old Bridle Path. This is an extremely popular classic hike that showcases the best of what makes hiking in the White Mountains so special.

Distance: 8.9-mile loop
Summit elevation: Mount Lincoln, 5,089 feet; Mount Lafayette, 5,260 feet
4,000-footers rank: Mount Lincoln, 7; Mount Lafayette, 6
Elevation gain: 4,100 feet
Difficulty: Difficult
Hiking time: About 6 hours

Trails used: Falling Waters Trail, Franconia Ridge Trail, Greenleaf Trail, Old Bridle Path
Views: Excellent
Canine compatibility: Difficult; a few water crossings, lots of people on weekends, some steep rocky sections
Special considerations: Parking can fill up quickly, so get there early.

Finding the trailhead: *From I-93 (from the south),* take the "Trailhead Parking" exit in Franconia Notch. This exit is two exits past exit 34A and one exit past the exit signed for "The Basin." *From I-93 (from the north),* take exit 34A and get back on I-93 North/US 3 North. In 3.1 miles take the "Trailhead Parking" exit. This is one exit past the exit for "The Basin." **GPS:** N44 08.52' / W71 40.88'

The Hike

This hike has it all: big waterfalls, ruggedly steep trails, dramatic ridge-line walking, and endless views. This iconic Franconia Ridge hike, with its narrow path along steep drop-offs high above tree line, is unlike any other hike in the White Mountains and is guaranteed to instill a sense of wonder and awe even for those who have hiked this route many times.

This is one of the most popular hikes in the White Mountains, so you'll want to get to the parking lot very early if you plan on doing this on a weekend. The parking situation can be a nightmare, and on busy days cars are parked all along the edge of I-93/US 3. Also, since the ridge is very exposed to wind, precipitation, and lightning, do not attempt this route if there's a chance of bad weather or if the higher summits' forecast calls for high wind.

From the east side of the parking lot, take the combined Old Bridle Path / Falling Waters Trail into the woods. In 0.2 mile, head right onto the Falling Waters Trail as the Old Bridle Path turns left (north). Immediately cross over Walker Brook; continue to

A hiker traverses Franconia Ridge below Mount Lafayette.

climb to the east and then make a short descent to cross over Dry Brook at 0.7 mile. The trail makes a sharp left turn (east) and climbs along the brook, passing Stairs Falls at 0.8 mile and crossing back over the brook at 0.9 mile, just below Swiftwater Falls.

Carefully traverse the slippery rocks on the other side of the brook; make a short ascent of steep stone steps then gradually ascend, following the route of an old logging road. Reach the base of Cloudland Falls at 1.3 miles. The beautiful series of cascades drops more than 80 feet, and the short but steep, technical rocky climb up the north side of the falls takes you to the top edge, where you can peer over and see people at the bottom.

From here the trail climbs steeply as it follows the Lincoln Branch of Dry Brook, which you cross numerous times, finally turning to the south at 1.6 miles. Continuing to climb, the trail follows an old logging road to the South Branch of Dry Brook then turns away to the north and climbs toward the ridge along a series of switchbacks. At 2.8 miles, just over 4,000 feet in elevation, a short side trail leads to Shining Rock, a huge cliff with impressive views. This junction is at the last switchback. After a short climb to the north, the trail makes a final turn to the east. At 3.2 miles you reach the Franconia Ridge Trail on the summit of Little Haystack Mountain, just above tree line.

Head left (north) along the Franconia Ridge Trail, following the broad spine. As you near Mount Lincoln, the ridge becomes increasingly narrow, with dramatic drops on both sides. The trail is not very steep for the most part, and although it's narrow, rocks line both sides to make navigating easier, especially in bad weather. Krummholz and short alpine vegetation cling to the east side of the ridge as rocky outcrops fall away from the west side. Take the time to enjoy this stunning section of trail as you make the final short but steep ascent to the summit of Mount Lincoln at 3.9 miles.

You get a great view of the Cannon Cliffs, which rise steeply out of Franconia Notch to your west as the entire Pemigewasset Wilderness extends below to the east. From the top of both Mount Lincoln and Mount Lafayette, thirty-eight of the forty-eight 4,000-footers are visible. Can you identify them? What 4,000-footers are not visible?

Continue following the Franconia Ridge Trail north along the spine of the ridge, crossing over the hump informally called Mount Truman then making a short descent before climbing to the summit of Mount Lafayette at 4.9 miles. The tallest mountain in the Whites outside the Presidential Range, it is named for an American Revolutionary War hero from France, the Marquis de Lafayette. The remnants of rock walls

Milton poses on an outlook along the Old Bridle path above the Walker Brook valley.

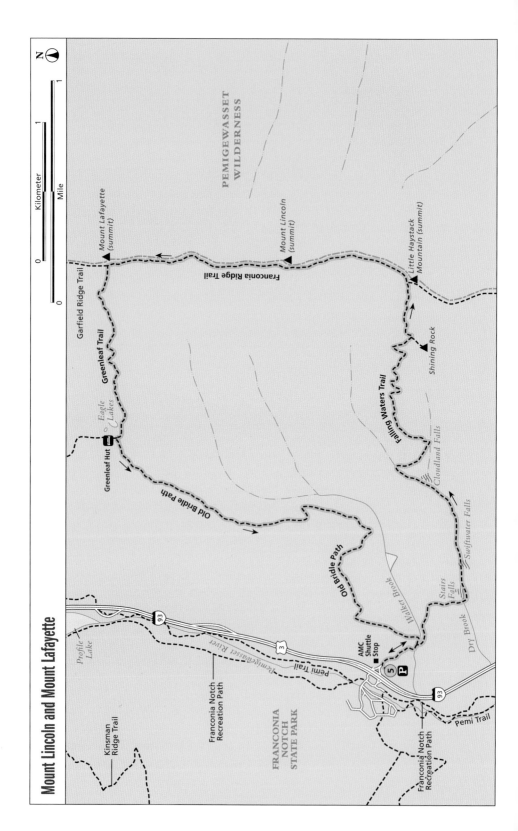

Mount Lincoln and Mount Lafayette

N

Kilometer

0   1

0   1

Mile

PEMIGEWASSET WILDERNESS

Mount Lafayette (summit) ▲

Garfield Ridge Trail

Greenleaf Trail

Eagle Lakes

Greenleaf Hut ■

Mount Lincoln (summit) ▲

Franconia Ridge Trail

Little Haystack Mountain (summit) ▲

Shining Rock ▲

Falling Waters Trail

Cloudland Falls

Old Bridle Path

Old Bridle Path

Swiftwater Falls

Stairs Falls

Dry Brook

Walker Brook

Profile Lake

93

Kinsman Ridge Trail

Franconia Notch Recreation Path

Pemigewasset River

3

Pemi Trail

AMC Shuttle Stop ■

5

P

FRANCONIA NOTCH STATE PARK

93

Franconia Notch Recreation Path

Pemi Trail

from an old summit house that was in use in the 1850s stand as a relic of a time when people had different ideas of how to enjoy these mountains.

From the summit of Mount Lafayette, turn left (west) to follow the Greenleaf Trail down to the Greenleaf Hut. The top half is above tree line, with great views down the ridge and into the valley. Wild grasses flutter in the wind, and lichen-covered rocks dot the landscape. The steepest part is near the top; as you descend, the grade eases a bit as the trail enters a wooded area, reaching a low point next to Eagle Lakes, which are tarns—lakes created from the scouring of glaciers. A brief climb leads to Greenleaf Hut at 6.0 miles.

Take the Old Bridle Path down from the hut as it heads along a ridge in a south-easterly direction. The path follows Agony Ridge, often on steep technical rock, passing over three big humps. Along the way there are multiple impressive viewpoints into Walker Brook Ravine and across the notch. By 7.3 miles you are back in the woods and the grade eases. At 8.7 miles you reach the junction with the Falling Waters Trail, returning to the trailhead at 8.9 miles.

Miles and Directions

0.0 Start at the parking lot and take the combined Falling Waters Trail / Old Bridle Path.

0.2 Turn right (southeast) onto the Falling Waters Trail.

0.7 Cross over Dry Brook.

0.8 Pass Stairs Falls.

0.9 Cross over Dry Brook below Swiftwater Falls.

1.3 Reach the base of Cloudland Falls.

2.8 Pass the junction with the spur trail to Shining Rock.

3.2 Reach the summit of Little Haystack and the junction with the Franconia Ridge Trail. Go left (east).

3.9 Reach the summit of Mount Lincoln.

4.9 Reach the summit of Mount Lafayette. Turn left (west) onto the Greenleaf Trail.

6.0 Reach Eagle Lakes and the Greenleaf Hut. Turn left (southwest) at the junction onto Old Bridle Path.

8.7 Reach the junction with the Falling Waters Trail.

8.9 Arrive back at the parking lot.

Other Routes

1. Pemigewasset Loop (hike 36)—distance: 38.5 miles (extended), 31.5 miles (basic); elevation gain: 12,500 feet (extended), 10,000 feet (basic)

2. Franconia Ridge Traverse (bonus hike 2)—distance: 13.7 miles point to point, 17.2-mile loop; elevation gain: 5,800 feet

APPALACHIAN MOUNTAIN CLUB

Those hardy folks who do the highly recommended hike up the Falling Waters Trail, along Franconia Ridge, and down the Bridle Path, will pass the Greenleaf Hut, operated by the Appalachian Mountain Club (AMC). The AMC runs eight huts throughout the White Mountains; most require a hike to get to. Each hut is staffed by energetic crews who serve family-style meals every morning and night throughout summer and early fall. Some huts are also open on a self-served basis through the winter.

In addition to running these mountain huts, AMC trail crews and thousands of volunteers maintain many trails all over the region. The organization also runs camps and educational programs and publishes many books and maps of the trails, all of which are highly recommended. According to their website, "AMC is the nation's oldest outdoor recreation and conservation organization," and its mission is to "promote the protection, enjoyment and understanding of the mountains, forests, waters and trails of the Appalachian Region."

You can find out more about everything the AMC does, and become a member, at outdoors.org.

Water streams down the multiple cascades of 80-foot-tall Cloudland Falls along the Falling Waters Trail.

6 | Mount Garfield

Mount Garfield, which rises along the northern edge of the Pemigewasset Wilderness, provides unparalleled views in every direction from the dramatic rocky promontory. You will truly get a sense of the ruggedness of the region and the sheer vastness of the wilderness. Although this hike is 5.0 miles each way, the trail follows the path of an old road built when there was a fire lookout on the summit; it is graded and only moderately steep, with easy footing.

Distance: 10.0 miles out and back
Summit elevation: 4,500 feet
4,000-footers rank: 17
Elevation gain: 3,150 feet
Difficulty: Moderate
Hiking time: About 5 hours
Trails used: Garfield Trail, Garfield Ridge Trail
Views: Excellent

Canine compatibility: Good
Special considerations: The road to the trailhead is closed in winter, requiring a 1.2-mile road walk in both directions.
Other: The graded path is a great option for speed-hikers or trail runners; only the last short section is steep, and footing is nice for most of the route.

Finding the trailhead: *From I-93 (from the south),* take exit 35 and continue onto US 3 North. Follow this for 4.9 miles and turn right onto Gale River Loop Road. In 1.1 miles take the 90-degree turn to the left; the trailhead will be on the right in a few hundred feet. *From I-93 (from the north),* take exit 36 and turn left onto NH 141 East toward US 3 North. In 0.8 mile join US 3 North for 4.1 miles then turn right onto Gale River Loop Road. In 1.1 miles take the 90-degree turn to the left; the trailhead will be on the right in a few hundred feet. *From the junction of US 302 and US 3 in Twin Mountain/Carroll,* head south on US 3 for 5.6 miles. Turn left onto Gale River Loop Road. In 1.1 miles take the 90-degree turn to the left; the trailhead will be on the right in a few hundred feet. **GPS:** N44 13.73' / W71 38.00'

The Hike

Although there is not much in the way of stunning views or notable features on the way up, the view from the summit into the Pemigewasset Wilderness is one of the best in the White Mountains and is well worth the effort. Mount Garfield was renamed from Franconia Haystack to Mount Garfield in 1881 after President James Garfield was assassinated. The Garfield Trail maintains a very consistent grade on the old road to the site of the former fire lookout, and once you get in a groove, you will find that the miles go by quickly.

The trail begins at a very mellow grade through a mixed forest that includes some nice hemlock stands. At 0.7 mile the trail makes a right turn then swings to the left to join the old road to the summit tower. At 1.1 miles you cross Thompson Brook, followed quickly by a crossing of Spruce Brook, and at 1.2 miles you make your final crossing of Spruce Brook. By this point you will have climbed only 250 feet. Over

The summit of Mount Garfield provides one of the best views into the heart of the Pemigewasset Wilderness. Owl's Head is on the left, with Franconia Ridge rising high to the west.

the next mile, the trail does begin to gain more elevation, with most of the climbing occurring in the last 3.0 miles.

The trail continues to wind its way up in a generally southward direction. At 3.0 miles you pop over a little ridge where the high point is known as Burnt Knoll. Make a short descent then begin climbing along a series of switchbacks, never having to go directly up this steeper terrain. You pass birch trees throughout the upper half of this hike. At 4.8 miles you reach the junction with the Garfield Ridge Trail.

This last little section before the summit is the only truly steep part. Turn right at the intersection and climb 0.2 mile on the Garfield Ridge Trail to the short spur on the left that will take you along open rock ledges to the summit. The foundation of the old fire lookout still remains and although not very aesthetic, can provide a nice wind block on blustery days. The fire lookout was built by the Civilian Conservation Corps (CCC) in 1940 but only operated until 1948.

There are views in all directions, but the view into the Pemigewasset Wilderness is breathtaking. The high peaks of the Franconia Range dominate the southwestern view, with a great view of Owl's Head due south. Here you see how Lincoln Brook on the west and Franconia Brook on the east wrap around that remote peak. To the east is Galehead Mountain, with North and South Twin Mountains rising beyond.

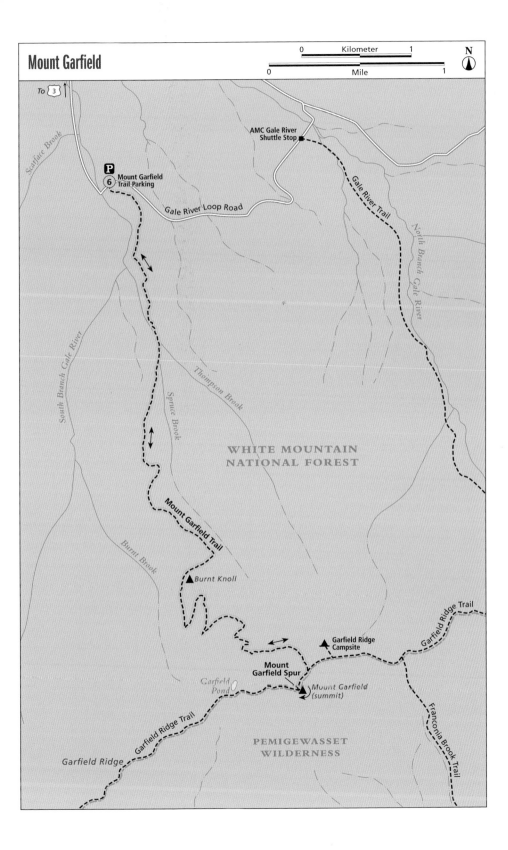

Mount Garfield

0 Kilometer 1
0 Mile 1

N

To 3

Scarface Brook

AMC Gale River
Shuttle Stop

P
6 Mount Garfield
   Trail Parking

Gale River Loop Road

Gale River Trail

North Branch Gale River

South Branch Gale River

Thompson Brook

Spruce Brook

WHITE MOUNTAIN
NATIONAL FOREST

Burnt Brook

Mount Garfield Trail

▲ Burnt Knoll

Garfield Ridge Trail

Garfield Ridge
Campsite ▲

Mount
Garfield Spur

Mount Garfield
(summit)

Garfield
Pond

Garfield Ridge Trail

Garfield Ridge

PEMIGEWASSET
WILDERNESS

Franconia Brook Trail

Mount Garfield's recognizable summit is viewed from the summit of South Twin Mountain.

Thirty 4,000-foot peaks are visible from the summit. See how many you can name. Return to the parking lot following the same route.

Miles and Directions

0.0   Start from the parking area and take the Garfield Trail.

0.7   The trail meets up with the original trail on an old logging road and heads right.

1.1   Cross Thompson Brook and Spruce Brook.

1.2   Cross Spruce Brook again.

3.0   Reach the small ridge crest called Burnt Knoll.

4.8   Turn right (south) onto the Garfield Ridge Trail.

5.0   Turn left (east) on to short spur to reach the summit of Mount Garfield. Return the way you came.

10.0   Arrive back at the trailhead.

Other Routes

1.   Pemigewasset Loop (hike 36)—distance: 38.5 miles (extended); 31.5 miles (basic); elevation gain: 12,500 feet (extended); 10,000 feet (basic)

2.   Galehead Garfield Loop (bonus hike 3)—distance: 15.6 miles; elevation gain: 4,400 feet

7 Galehead Mountain

Galehead Mountain may be a diminutive peak, barely qualifying as a 4,000-footer, but its location at the northern edge of the Pemigewasset Wilderness provides a nice perspective of the region, with good views of Galehead Hut below South Twin Mountain. The trip up the Gale River Trail is straightforward and beautiful, with impressive stone stairs. Galehead Hut has a nice view and is a good launching point for further adventures.

Distance: 10.4 miles out and back
Summit elevation: 4,024 feet
4,000-footers rank: 44
Elevation gain: 2,700 feet
Difficulty: Moderate
Hiking time: About 5 hours
Trails used: Gale River Trail, Garfield Ridge Trail, Frost Trail

Views: Okay; restricted views from ledge near summit and more views from Galehead Hut; no views from the summit
Canine compatibility: Good
Special considerations: The road to the trailhead is closed in winter, requiring a 1.6-mile road/snowmobile trail walk in each direction.

Finding the trailhead: *From I-93 (from the south),* take exit 35 and continue onto US 3 North. Follow this for 5.1 miles and turn right onto Gale River Trail (just past Gale River Loop Road). In 1.3 miles turn right at the junction; the parking lot will be on the left in about 0.25 mile. *From I-93 (from the north),* take exit 36 and turn left onto NH 141 East toward US 3 North. In 0.8 mile join US 3 North for 4.2 miles; turn right onto Gale River Trail (just past Gale River Loop Road). In 1.3 miles turn right at the junction; the parking lot will be on the left in about 0.25 mile. *From the junction of US 302 and US 3 in Twin Mountain/Carroll,* head south on US 3 for 5.2 miles. Turn right onto Gale River Trail. In 1.3 miles turn right at the junction; the parking lot will be on the left in about 0.25 mile. **GPS: N44 13.97' / W71 36.63'**

The Hike

Although the true summit of Galehead Mountain has no view, an overlook 0.2 mile before the summit provides a nice view over Twin Brook and down toward the Franconia Brook watershed. You get a great view of Galehead Hut, which offers a nice outlook into the Pemigewasset Wilderness as well. The first few miles are very easy as you follow the North Branch of the Gale River most of the way, although the trail is rarely next to the river.

The Gale River Trail begins very gently as you follow the path through the woods, crossing over a small stream at 0.2 mile, and continues along a very gentle climb to the southeast. The easy hiking provides an opportunity to admire the mixed forest and the prolific hobblebush. After about 1.0 mile the trail swings slightly to head more directly south, and at 1.4 miles you come close to the North Branch of

The top section of the Gale River Trail is rocky and steep.

the Gale River. The older trail used to cross the river a few times, but the new trail stays on the west side of the river for its entirety.

At 1.7 miles the trail takes a hard right then a hard left, following a newer section of trail as it climbs high above the river. At 2.3 miles you cross Garfield Stream and then finally start to climb at a decent rate. Not long after, at around 2,400 feet, the trail makes a short descent and then contours back over to the river, rejoining the old route. At 3.2 miles you reach an opening next to the river where you get a good view downstream as well as up toward the cliffs off North Twin.

Not long after this point, the trail begins to climb in earnest. There are some pretty steep stretches with great stonework. Think about the time and effort that went into creating these stone steps. The steepest section is right before the junction with the Garfield Ridge Trail at 4.1 miles.

▶ **DID YOU KNOW?** When Galehead Hut was rebuilt in 2000, the Appalachian Mountain Club was required to comply with the accessibility rules of the Americans with Disabilities Act. This meant they had to install a wheelchair ramp and handles in the bathrooms. Although some people initially questioned the need for this in a remote hut, that year a group of physically challenged hikers, including three in wheelchairs, set out to prove a point. With the help of friends and family, ropes, pulley systems, and lots of grit, they were able to make it all the way up the Gale River Trail to the hut!

Hikers enjoy a rest at Galehead Hut.

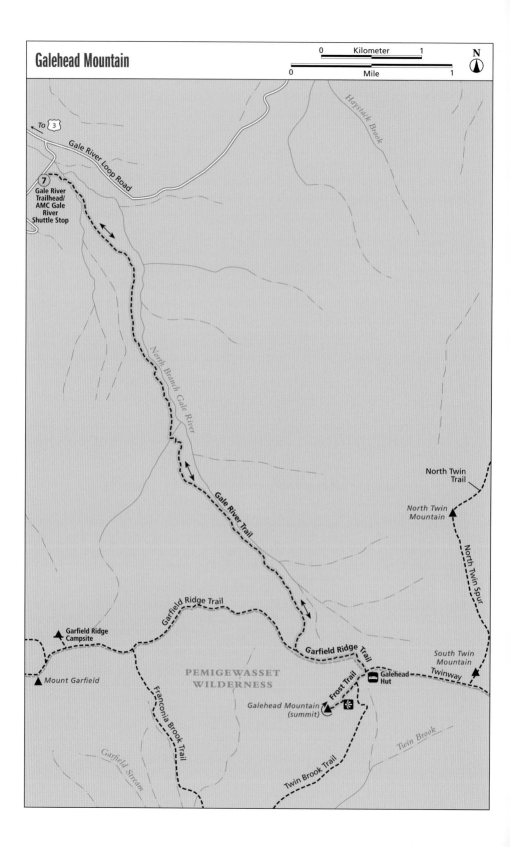

Galehead Mountain

0 Kilometer 1

0 Mile 1

N

To [3]

Gale River Loop Road

[7]
Gale River
Trailhead/
AMC Gale
River
Shuttle Stop

North Branch Gale River

Haystack Brook

Gale River Trail

North Twin
Trail

North Twin
Mountain

North Twin Spur

Garfield Ridge Trail

Garfield Ridge
Campsite

▲ Mount Garfield

PEMIGEWASSET
WILDERNESS

Garfield Ridge Trail

Galehead
Hut

South Twin
Mountain

Twinway

Franconia Brook Trail

Frost Trail

Galehead Mountain
(summit) ▲

Twin Brook Trail

Garfield Stream

Twin Brook

Turn left (west) onto the Garfield Ridge Trail, which climbs over some big boulders with a nice view during the contour over toward Galehead Mountain. After a sharp right turn (south), the trail climbs a short but steep pitch to a side trail leading to Galehead Hut at 4.7 miles. Enjoy the nice view from the opening near the hut, with the dramatic South Twin rising straight up to the east. The hump visible up and to the right (southwest) is Galehead Mountain, your destination.

The Frost Trail leaves from the (southwest) corner of the opening near the hut. Take this down, over some boulders, and quickly pass the junction with the Twin Brook Trail. Stay on the Frost Trail as it makes a short but steep climb. Near the top of the steepest pitch is the short spur to the overlook. There is no view from the summit, so take your time here and enjoy the view. You can see Galehead Hut and South and North Twin Mountains rising behind it. A 0.2-mile winding path through the woods takes you to the summit at 5.2 miles. Follow the same route back to the trailhead.

Miles and Directions

0.0 Start from the parking lot on the Gale River Trail.

0.2 Cross a small stream.

1.7 The trail takes a hard right onto the newer reroute.

2.3 Cross Garfield Stream.

3.2 Reach an opening next to river with views toward North Twin Mountain.

4.1 Turn left (west) onto the Garfield Ridge Trail.

4.7 Reach a short side trail and, soon after, the Galehead Hut. Continue on the Frost Trail.

4.8 Pass the junction with the Twin Brook Trail.

5.0 Reach a short side trail to the overlook.

5.2 Reach the summit of Galehead Mountain. Return the way you came.

10.4 Arrive back at the trailhead.

Other Routes

1. Pemigewasset Loop (hike 36)—distance: 38.5 miles (extended), 31.5 miles (basic); elevation gain: 12,500 feet (extended), 10,000 feet (basic)

2. Galehead Garfield Loop (bonus hike 3)—distance: 15.6 miles, elevation gain: 4,400 feet

3. Galehead and The Twins point-to-point (bonus hike 4)—distance: 12.2 miles; elevation gain: 4,200 feet

8 North Twin and South Twin Mountains

With multiple river crossings, a steep climb, and a beautiful ridge traverse ending on a peak with some of the best views of all the mountaintops in the White Mountains, this is certainly a memorable hike. Except for the summit of South Twin, it is likely that the only people you will run across are also doing their 4,000-footers.

Distance: 11.2 miles out and back
Summit elevation: North Twin, 4,761 feet; South Twin, 4,902 feet
4,000-footers rank: North Twin, 11; South Twin, 8
Elevation gain: 3,900 feet
Difficulty: Moderate
Hiking time: About 6.5 hours
Trails used: North Twin Trail, North Twin Spur

Views: Good from North Twin ledge; excellent from South Twin
Canine compatibility: Good in low water, but multiple river crossings will make this difficult in medium to high water.
Special considerations: The road to the trailhead is closed in winter, adding 2.5 miles each way.

Finding the trailhead: *From I-93 (from the south),* take exit 35 and continue onto US 3 North. Follow US 3 North for 7.8 miles. Turn right onto Haystack Road; the trailhead is at the end of the road in 2.5 miles. *From I-93 (from the north),* take exit 36 and turn left onto NH 141 East toward US 3 North. In 0.8 mile, join US 3 North for 7 miles. Turn right onto Haystack Road; the trailhead is at the end of the road in 2.5 miles. *From the junction of US 302 and US 3 in Twin Mountain/Carroll,* head south on US 3 for 2.5 miles. Turn left onto Haystack Road; the trailhead is at the end of the road in 2.5 miles. **GPS:** N44 14.28' / W71 32.85'

The Hike

There are many ways to bag these peaks, with benefits and drawbacks to each, so be sure to check the "Other Routes" in this chapter and the "Bonus Hikes" section toward the end of the book for other options. The route described here is the most straightforward out-and-back. You get a nice mellow walk through the woods with a few river crossings, a steep hike to the summit of North Twin, and a beautiful ridge walk to one of the most magnificent peaks in the Whites: South Twin Mountain. Due to the multiple stream crossings of the Little River, this hike is not recommended right after or during a big rain or during spring runoff.

From the parking lot the North Twin Trail heads southeast at a very mellow grade, mostly on an old railroad bed. The walking is smooth and pleasant, with an elevation gain of just over 500 feet in the first 2.0 miles. At 0.8 mile you come to your first river crossing. The Little River is not that little, and after a rain, it can be downright big. If you do hike this when the river is at or above your comfort level to cross, there is an informal trail that stays on the east side of the river, bypassing the first two crossings. If you take the alternate route, make sure to keep a close eye on your location with a

The North Twin Trail crosses the Little River multiple times.

map and compass or GPS device—the next crossing does not come back to the east side of the river for another 0.5 mile.

Trekking poles are highly recommended when crossing rivers, and be sure to follow the "three points of contact" concept by moving only one leg at a time with poles firmly planted. The main trail continues along the west side of the river until the second crossing at 1.3 miles. The forest here is a typical mixed forest where birch and beech intermingle with conifers. The final crossing, usually slightly easier, occurs at 1.9 miles.

After this final crossing the trail begins to climb, gently at first, soon crossing a small brook. The trail recrosses the often-dry brook at 2.5 miles, and from this point it gets steeper and steeper. After heading in a northwesterly direction, you will curve around to the west before making a sharp 90-degree turn at around 3.3 miles, where you contour to the south and make another 90-degree turn back to the west at around 3.5 miles.

The trail is steep, rocky, and lined with fir and birch trees. Notice the distinct layers in the forest, with young fir trees at a similar height growing beneath the more mature canopy. The trail is steepest between 3.5 and 4.0 miles, where it reaches the ridge, and at 4.2 miles you get a nice view to the southwest. The final more-level section takes you to the summit at 4.3 miles. Take the short spur to an open ledge for great views.

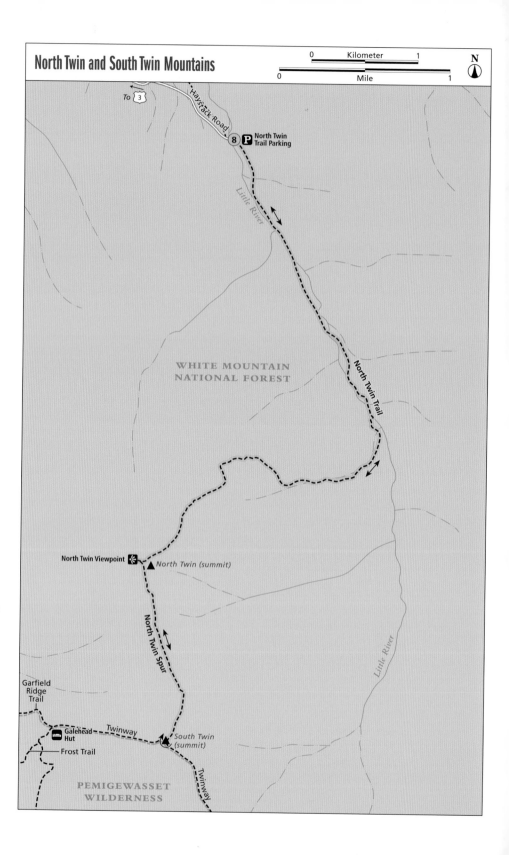

North Twin and South Twin Mountains

From the summit, continue straight (south) on the North Twin Spur, passing over one area with ledges, down to a low point, and up the easy trail to the summit of South Twin Mountain, with intermittent views along the way. The summit of South Twin Mountain affords breathtaking views in all directions. You can see Mount Garfield to the east, with Mounts Lafayette and Lincoln and the Franconia Range beyond to the southwest. The Presidential Range rises to the northeast, with Mounts Adams, Washington, Monroe, and Eisenhower clearly visible. In fact, you can see all but twelve of the 4,000-foot peaks from this high perch, so test yourself to see how many you can name.

Retrace your route to the trailhead.

Miles and Directions

0.0 Leave the parking area, following the North Twin Trail.

0.8 Cross the Little River.

1.3 Cross back over the river.

1.9 Cross the river again.

2.5 Cross a (usually) dry streambed.

3.5 Begin the steepest part of climb

4.2 Reach a viewpoint over to the left (southwest).

4.3 Reach the summit of North Twin and take the short spur to the right (west) to a great overlook. From the summit, continue straight (south) on the North Twin Spur toward South Twin Mountain.

5.6 Reach the summit of South Twin Mountain. Return the way you came.

11.2 Arrive back at the trailhead.

Other Routes

1. Pemigewasset Loop (hike 36)—distance: 38.5 miles (extended), 31.5 miles (basic); elevation gain: 12,500 feet (extended), 10,000 feet (basic)

2. Galehead and The Twins point-to-point (bonus hike 4)—distance: 12.2 miles; elevation gain: 4,200 feet

3. Bonds, Zealand, and Twins Traverse (hike 35)—distance: 23.1 miles; elevation gain: 6,800 feet

9 Bondcliff, Mount Bond, and West Bond

This long and challenging day hike rewards the intrepid adventurer with three stunning peaks, all with unique views deep within the Pemigewasset Wilderness. Walking along (and posing for photos on) the stunning cliffs of Bondcliff is an experience you are unlikely to forget. Although this out-and-back hike is long, 10 miles are basically flat and go by quickly.

Distance: 22.6 miles out and back
Summit elevation: Bondcliff, 4,265 feet; Mount Bond, 4,698 feet; West Bond, 4,540 feet
4,000-footers rank: Bondcliff, 30; Mount Bond, 14; West Bond, 16
Elevation gain: 3,850 feet
Difficulty: Difficult due to length
Hiking time: About 11 hours
Trails used: Lincoln Woods Trail, Bondcliff Trail, West Bond Spur

Views: Excellent from all three peaks
Canine compatibility: Okay. This is a long hike, and brook crossings can be difficult in high water; the steep scramble up ledges on Bondcliff may require some assistance.
Special considerations: The bridge at Lincoln Woods is the only bridge over the river. There is no safe crossing from the Pemi East Side Trail to the Lincoln Woods Trail and Bondcliff Trail other than this bridge. Older maps show a crossing that no longer exists.

Finding the trailhead: *From I-93 (from the south),* take exit 32 for NH 112 (Kancamagus Highway). Turn left onto NH 112 East, and in 5.1 miles turn left into the parking area for the Lincoln Woods Trail. *From I-93 (from the north),* take exit 32 for NH 112 (Kancamagus Highway). Turn left onto NH 112 East, and in 5.5 miles turn left into the parking area for the Lincoln Woods Trail. *From the junction of NH 16 and NH 112 in Conway,* take NH 112 West for 30 miles; turn right into the parking area for the Lincoln Woods Trail. **GPS:** N44 03.83' / W71 35.27'

The Hike

Much of this hike is on the Lincoln Woods and Bondcliff Trails, which are basically flat, making this 22.6 mile out-and-back easier than the mileage suggests. Give yourself plenty of time to enjoy the stunning views.

From the ranger's cabin near the parking at Lincoln Woods, head down the steps, go past the kiosk on the left, and cross the East Branch of the Pemigewasset River on the suspension bridge. Turn right onto the Lincoln Woods Trail. This trail, the bed of a logging railroad that was in use until 1948, is flat and allows bikes. This is one of the few trails that is wide enough to walk side by side; the only footing concerns are the sections where old hemlock railroad ties still stick out of the ground.

Head north on the Lincoln Woods Trail, past the junction with the Osseo Trail on the left in 1.4 miles and the junction with the trail to Black Pond in 2.6 miles. Not long after, you pass the junction with the Franconia Falls Trail at 2.9 miles and

The ridge along West Bond is visible from the summit of West Bond, directly in line with Mount Flume across the valley.

immediately cross over Franconia Brook on a bridge. Up to this point, the trail gains only 200 vertical feet.

After crossing the brook, stay to the right (northeast) on the Bondcliff Trail as the Franconia Brook Trail heads off to the left. You enter the Pemigewasset Wilderness here, and as if in sync with the wilderness designation, the trail becomes a bit rougher, although it still maintains a very level grade on the former railroad bed. (**Note:** Old maps may refer to this as the Wilderness Trail, back when there used to be a bridge over the East Branch of the Pemigewasset River. The bridge is no longer there, and the Franconia Brook Tentsite on the east side of the river must be accessed by following the East Side Trail from the Lincoln Woods parking area. Maps showing a line across the river at this junction refer to a rock hop across the river that is no longer feasible because the rocks are no longer there. Do not try to cross the river here.)

The Bondcliff Trail continues along the northwest side of the East Branch of the Pemigewasset River as it heads in a generally easterly direction crossing a small brook at 3.9 miles and an old campsite at 4.7 miles, at which point the trail veers to the left (north) and in a few hundred feet turns left again just before reaching Black Brook.

A short climb over a berm leads to an old logging road, which you leave quickly to begin ascending the lower slopes of the mountain. After 1.0 mile on this section, the trail makes a slight dip and begins climbing next to Black Brook on an old logging road grade. The forest transitions from mixed hardwood to a higher elevation

Mount Bond rises dramatically over the East Branch of the Pemigewasset River. West Bond is visible just to the left.

conifer forest and crosses the brook at 6.1 miles, 6.6 miles, and again at 7.2 miles. The trail zigzags a bit here, and after following an old streambed for a short while comes to a rockslide providing a nice view up toward Bondcliff at a spot around 3,000 feet in elevation.

After winding up to around 3,400 feet, the trail makes a turn to the south as it contours up the slope along an old logging road, eventually turning to the right (west) and finally north around 4,000 feet, where you join the main ridge. At 9.0 miles a short steep section requires a bit of scrambling where you may need to use your hands; at 9.1 miles you reach the open ledges that define the summit of Bond-cliff. One notable part of the cliff juts out and provides a dramatic view over the valley below. A little walking around here provides views in all directions, with both Mount Bond and West Bond visible to the north. From the summit of Bondcliff, you supposedly cannot see a human-made structure other than the tower atop Mount Carrigain.

The trail continues north as you dip down into the col between Bondcliff and Mount Bond. Shortly after beginning your climb up to Mount Bond, head back into the woods, climbing the rocky path up to the summit at 10.3 miles. One of the more impressive viewpoints, the summit of Mount Bond affords a view of thirty-eight 4,000-footers!

To get to West Bond, continue following the Bondcliff Trail north as it makes a quick down and up over the north knob of Mount Bond then heads down toward Mount Guyot. The West Bond Spur comes surprisingly quickly at just 10.8 miles

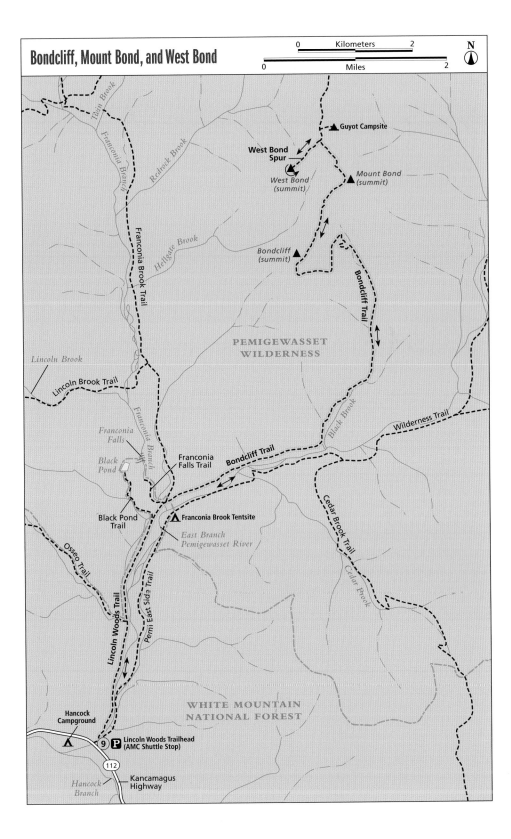

Bondcliff, Mount Bond, and West Bond

0 Kilometers 2
0 Miles 2

N

▲ Guyot Campsite

West Bond
Spur

West Bond
(summit)

Mount Bond
(summit)

Franconia Brook Trail

Redrock Brook

Ibin Brook

Franconia Branch

Hellgate Brook

Bondcliff
(summit)

Bondcliff Trail

PEMIGEWASSET
WILDERNESS

Lincoln Brook

Lincoln Brook Trail

Franconia Branch

Franconia
Falls

Black
Pond

Franconia
Falls Trail

Bondcliff Trail

Black Brook

Wilderness Trail

Black Pond
Trail

▲ Franconia Brook Tentsite

East Branch
Pemigewasset River

Cedar Brook Trail

Cedar Brook

Osseo Trail

Lincoln Woods Trail

Pemi East Side Trail

WHITE MOUNTAIN
NATIONAL FOREST

Hancock
Campground

Δ

9 P Lincoln Woods Trailhead
(AMC Shuttle Stop)

112

Hancock
Branch

Kancamagus
Highway

(around 4,400 feet). If you get to the spur trail on the right down to Guyot Shelter and campsite, you have gone about 0.2 mile too far.

Turn left onto the West Bond Spur as you head down to a col before making the final ascent to the summit at 11.3 miles. From here you get a great view of Bondcliff to the south, a close perspective of Owl's Head, and the eastern side of the Franconia Range. Return the way you came. *Note:* If you need water, you can make the 0.2-mile trek north on the Bondcliff Trail to the spur down to Guyot Shelter, which is also 0.2 mile, adding a total of 0.8 mile to your trip.

Miles and Directions

0.0 Start at the ranger station, head left, and cross the bridge over the East Branch of the Pemigewasset River; turn right onto the Lincoln Woods Trail.

1.4 Pass the junction with the Osseo Trail on the left.

2.6 Pass the junction with Black Pond Trail on the left.

2.9 Pass the junction with the Franconia Falls Trail on the left; cross the bridge and head straight/right (northeast) onto the Bondcliff Trail passing by the junction with the Franconia Brook Trail on the left.

4.7 The Bondcliff Trail turns left, away from the river.

6.1 Cross Black Brook.

6.6 Cross Black Brook again, often the last place for guaranteed water.

7.2 Cross Black Brook again (often dry). Shortly after this you get your first good view.

9.1 Reach the summit of Bondcliff.

10.3 Reach the summit of Mount Bond.

10.8 Turn left onto the West Bond Spur.

11.3 Reach the summit of West Bond. Return the way you came.

22.6 Arrive back at the trailhead.

Other Routes

1. Pemigewasset Loop (hike 36)—distance: 38.5 miles (extended), 31.5 miles (basic); elevation gain: 12,500 feet (extended), 10,000 feet (basic)

2. Bonds, Zealand, and Twins Traverse (hike 35)—distance: 23.1 miles; elevation gain: 6,800 feet

10 Mount Hancock (North Hancock) and South Hancock

The hike up massive Mount Hancock, with its multiple peaks, can be divided into two parts, with most of the hike a gentle climb (and descent) through a beautiful forest and along and across several nice streams. However, the final climb up Mount Hancock is one of the steepest sections of trail in the White Mountains; although it's short, you will be glad to take a break at the ledge with beautiful views near the peak. The ridge traverse is pretty straightforward, but the descent from South Hancock is only slightly less steep than the ascent up the other side.

Distance: 9.7-mile lollipop loop
Summit elevation: Mount Hancock, 4,420 feet; South Hancock, 4,319 feet
4,000-footers rank: Mount Hancock, 21; South Hancock, 26
Elevation gain: 3,000 feet
Difficulty: Difficult; most of hike is easy, but Mount Hancock slide is extremely steep; South Hancock slide is steep as well.
Hiking time: About 5.5 hours

Trails used: Hancock Notch Trail, Cedar Brook Trail, Hancock Loop Trail (includes North Link, Ridge Link, and South Link)
Views: Good but restricted from Mount Hancock; limited from South Hancock
Canine compatibility: Okay. Stream crossings in high water can be tough; climb up Mount Hancock is very steep.
Special considerations: Be careful crossing the Kancamagus Highway.

Finding the trailhead: *From I-93 (from the south),* take exit 32 for NH 112 (Kancamagus Highway). Turn left onto NH 112 East, and in 10.6 miles turn right into the parking area for the Hancock Overlook, immediately after a 180-degree hairpin turn. *From I-93 (from the north),* take exit 32 for NH 112 (Kancamagus Highway). Turn left onto NH 112 East, and in 11 miles turn right into the parking area for the Hancock Overlook immediately after a 180-degree hairpin turn. *From the junction of NH 16 and NH 112 in Conway,* take NH 112 west for 24.5 miles and turn left into the parking area for the Hancock Overlook. *Note:* Follow the short trail through woods at the northwest end of the parking area and cross the road carefully to get to the trailhead. **GPS:** N44 02.47' / W71 31.43'

The Hike

This interesting hike is almost two hikes because most of the hike is very mellow, with minimal elevation gain and rooty but not technical trail. The slide up Mount Hancock and the slide down South Hancock, however, are two of the steepest sections of trail in this book—and in the White Mountains—with the slide up Mount Hancock gaining 1,100 vertical feet in just over 0.5 mile!

The first, and most important, part of this hike is not getting run over while crossing the Kancamagus Highway. Named for John Hancock, the first signer of the Declaration of Independence, Mount Hancock, also known as North Hancock, lies on the southern boundary of the Pemigewasset Wilderness. The old route up the

Mount Chocorua is visible to the south from the South Hancock view on a beautiful autumn evening.

mountain used to climb Arrow Slide, an obvious Y-shaped slide visible at points along your route. The current trail, although not up a rockslide, is no less steep and showcases the ruggedness of the White Mountains.

Enter the woods and follow the nice gentle grade along an old railroad bed, paralleling the North Fork Hancock Branch, which is out of sight on the left, crossing over a small stream at 0.6 mile with views of the river at 1.2 miles. Cross a few small brooks and at 1.8 miles reach the junction with the Cedar Brook Trail.

Turn left onto the Cedar Brook Trail, where you make the first of numerous crossings of the North Fork. There are some rocky and rooty sections interspersed with easier sections; however, the grade is almost level. At 2.5 miles turn right at the junction onto the Hancock Loop Trail. After gaining only 600 vertical feet in the previous 2.5 miles, you cross the river one more time before beginning to climb, gently at first. The trail begins to get rocky at points, and at times the footing can be precarious due to the network of exposed roots now above surface on the eroded trail.

Continue climbing until you reach Loop Junction at 3.6 miles. To climb Mount Hancock first, take the North Link of the Hancock Loop Trail on the left and descend about 100 feet to a small stream. Here the fun begins! You will need to use your arms and all your strength to pull yourself up this extremely steep section, which alternates between large rocks and big stone steps. You get an obscured view of South Hancock on your right, not far from the top, and at 4.2 miles reach the Ridge Link.

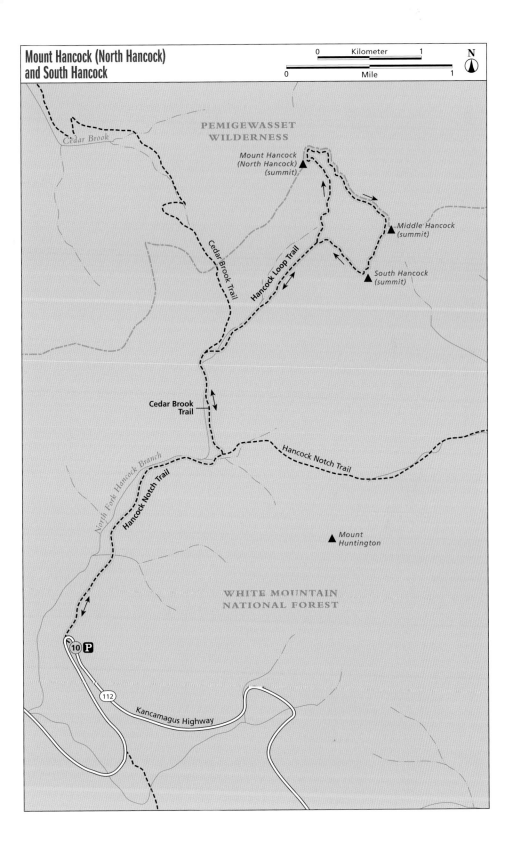

Mount Hancock (North Hancock) and South Hancock

0 Kilometer 1
0 Mile 1

N

Cedar Brook

PEMIGEWASSET
WILDERNESS

Mount Hancock
(North Hancock)
(summit)

Middle Hancock
(summit)

Cedar Brook Trail

Hancock Loop Trail

South Hancock
(summit)

Cedar Brook
Trail

Hancock Notch Trail

North Fork Hancock Branch

Hancock Notch Trail

Mount
Huntington

WHITE MOUNTAIN
NATIONAL FOREST

10 P

112

Kancamagus Highway

Although the lower section of the Hancock Loop Trail is not very steep, at times it is very rooty and requires careful foot placement.

A short spur to the left leads to a nice view to the south, with South Hancock nearby. The recognizable profile of Mount Chocorua is visible far to the southeast, with Mounts Passaconaway and Whiteface, the southernmost 4,000-footers, closer and just to the west of Mount Chocorua. The closest big peak to the south-southwest is Mount Osceola.

Head back to the trail junction and go straight (north) (or right from the top of North Link), following Ridge Link of the Hancock Loop Trail as it curves around the summit to head southwest toward South Hancock. The trail is fairly gentle as you pass through a fir wave, going up and down and up again to reach the summit of Middle Hancock at 5.1 miles. Continue straight to the low point; on your way back up, look for a rock on the right at 5.4 miles where you can get some obscured views to the west, including a good view of Arrow Slide. At 5.6 miles reach the summit of South Hancock.

A short spur to the left (southeast) leads to an overlook where you can see Mount Carrigain off to the left and Mount Passaconaway farther off to the right.

At the summit, head straight (northwest) (or right from the Ridge Link) as you make your way down the South Link of the Hancock Loop Trail. This trail is very steep, with much of it composed of unconsolidated dirt and gravel. Trekking poles help here, especially if you just pretend you are skiing. Take time during the descent to admire the views into the Pemigewasset Wilderness through the trees. After reaching Loop Junction at 6.1 miles, retrace your route back to the trailhead.

Miles and Directions

0.0 Start from trailhead across the Kancamagus Highway.

0.6 Cross over a stream.

1.8 Turn left onto the Cedar Brook Trail.

2.5 Turn right onto the Hancock Loop trail; shortly after, make a final crossing over the river.

3.6 Reach Loop Junction and head left (north) on the North Link of the Hancock Loop Trail, down a steep but short pitch to cross over a stream. Begin a very steep climb.

4.2 Reach the summit of Mount (North) Hancock. Take a left for a short side trail to views of the Osceolas and the Sandwich Range. Head right to go to South Hancock.

5.1 Reach Middle Hancock, a flat, wooded subpeak.

5.6 Reach South Hancock. Views are off to the left (southeast) down a very short side trail. The main trail heads right (northwest), back to the junction.

6.1 Reach Loop Junction. Follow the same route back to the trailhead.

9.7 Arrive back at the trailhead.

11 Owl's Head Mountain

For many, a trip up Owl's Head Mountain encapsulates much of what makes the goal of hiking the 4,000-foot peaks of New Hampshire so rewarding. You will enter deep into a remote wilderness, cross multiple rivers, climb an unofficial trail up an overgrown rockslide, and wander along an undefined ridge to a peak that just barely breaks the 4,000-foot mark. You will also experience true solitude, most likely only encountering other 4,000-foot peak-baggers along the way. And although the hike is long, 16 of the 18 miles are extremely flat, so this should be a doable day hike for most fit hikers.

Distance: 18.0 miles out and back
Summit elevation: 4,025 feet
4,000-footers rank: 43
Elevation gain: 3,400 feet
Difficulty: Difficult (due to length, river crossings, and climb up slide)
Hiking time: About 9 hours
Trails used: Lincoln Woods Trail, Franconia Brook Trail, Lincoln Brook Trail, Owl's Head Path

Views: Restricted views of the east side of Franconia Ridge from slide; no other real views
Canine compatibility: Not good for dogs due to length and multiple significant river crossings
Special considerations: Several river crossings make this hike dangerous when water levels are anything but low. Be careful on the rockslide, as it is an unmaintained trail. You will see few other hikers on your trip.

Finding the trailhead: *From I-93 (from the south),* take exit 32 for NH 112 (Kancamagus Highway). Turn left onto NH 112 East, and in 5.1 miles turn left into the parking area for the Lincoln Woods Trail. *From I-93 (from the north),* take exit 32 for NH 112 (Kancamagus Highway). Turn left onto NH 112 East, and in 5.5 miles turn left into the parking area for the Lincoln Woods Trail. *From the junction of NH 16 and NH 112 in Conway,* take NH 112 west for 30 miles; turn right into the parking area for the Lincoln Woods Trail. **GPS:** N44 03.83' / W71 35.27'

The Hike

Although this out-and-back hike to one of the most remote peaks on the list may be intimidating at first due to the length, it is actually easier than many of the much shorter hikes in this book. In fact, you gain only 1,400 vertical feet in the first 8.0 miles! The final ascent is a bit challenging, with a climb up a rockslide, a steep eroded stream, and dense growth on an unofficial trail. Do note, however, that there are some significant river crossings; during all but the lowest water levels, you will need to get your feet wet as you wade across. In high water these streams can be impassable.

From the ranger's cabin, head down the stairs, pass the kiosk on the left, and cross over the East Branch of the Pemigewasset River on the suspension bridge. Head right on the Lincoln Woods Trail, an extremely flat old railroad bed. A working logging railroad was in operation here until 1948. Bikes are allowed on this trail, and you may

Mount Liberty is clearly visible from the Owl's Head slide path.

see a lot of people using them to get to the trailhead for Franconia Falls. **Note:** It is imperative that you start your hike on the west side of the river, not on the Pemi East Side Trail. There is a campsite (Franconia Brook Tentsite) 2.9 miles up that trail, and maps showing a line across the river refer to a rock hop across the river that is no longer feasible because the rocks are no longer there. Do not try to cross the river anywhere but the bridge at Lincoln Woods.

Continue straight on the Lincoln Woods Trail. You pass a view opened by a washout, cross over Osseo Brook, and at 1.4 miles pass the junction with the Osseo Trail, which heads up toward Mount Flume. Continue straight and look for a nice view upstream at an opening where the trail nears the river. Cross another brook and at 2.6 miles pass the junction with the Black Pond Trail.

At 2.9 miles pass the junction with the Franconia Falls Trail, which leads to Franconia Falls, a popular destination on hot summer days; cross a bridge and shortly after reach the junction with the Franconia Brook Trail. Veer left at the junction to take the Franconia Brook Trail north as you enter the Pemigewasset Wilderness.

Although narrower, this trail is also an old railroad grade. A short climb takes you to the level trail where over the next 1.0 mile you will cross Camp 9 Brook twice and bypass a flooded area by veering off the old railroad bed. On the third crossing, at 4.2 miles (1.3 miles from the previous junction), it can get a little confusing. After crossing the brook, head left, up and over an embankment, and then right back onto the old trail. At 4.6 miles reach the junction with the Lincoln Brook Trail.

Turn left (west) onto the Lincoln Brook Trail. This trail alternates between some rougher sections and some nice smooth sections of old railroad grade. Along this trail you have numerous stream crossings, the first of which, Franconia Brook, you cross at 5.1 miles after a short descent. At 5.5 miles you cross a small brook then a big crossing of Lincoln Brook. The walking is beautiful around here as you head in a generally westerly direction. Most of the various local hardwood species are visible. Look for beech, paper birch, mountain maple, red maple, and sumac.

At 6.8 miles cross another stream as your path takes you north through the Lincoln Brook watershed between the high peaks of the Franconia Range on the left (west) and Owl's Head on the right (east). At 7.4 miles cross Liberty Brook, which pours down off the slopes of Mount Liberty and Little Haystack Mountain, and pass an open clearing. The final crossing of Lincoln Brook occurs 0.2 mile after this, at 7.6 miles, following a particularly muddy section, then the trail heads up to the east side of the river until you reach the junction with the unofficial Owl's Head Path.

At the time of this writing, the path was marked by a large rock cairn on the left and a smaller one on the right. As this is an unofficial trail, these cairns may or may not be there when you arrive, so look for a mossy flat area followed by a well-used path heading right (east) 0.4 mile after crossing Lincoln Brook.

The trail takes you through trees, quickly reaching the bottom of the slide. There is no correct way to ascend, so take the path that makes the most sense to you. There are rock cairns along the way to help guide you, but as long as you head up the slide, you are going in the right direction. Beautiful views of the Lincoln Brook Valley and the west side of the Franconia Ridge open behind you. Take your time to admire them, and catch your breath, as you scramble up the alternating gravel and ledgy slide. Around 3,000 feet in elevation there are some good ledges to take a break and enjoy the view.

The slide is steep but short, with the top portion partially covered by new tree growth. Around 3,300 feet, at the top of the slide, the informal path heads left into the woods. From here follow an eroded streambed that becomes a rough path. You will be dodging blowdowns, and eventually the grade will ease as you near the summit ridge.

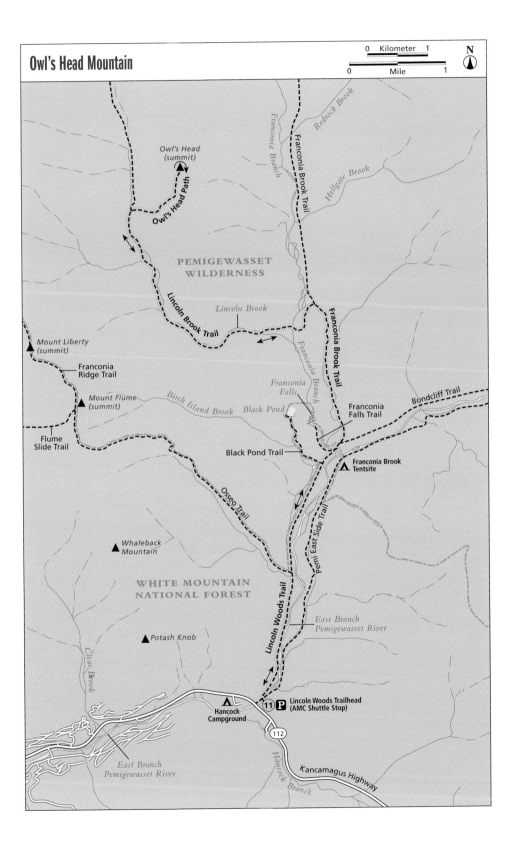

Owl's Head Mountain

0 Kilometer 1

0 Mile 1

N

Owl's Head
(summit)

Owl's Head Path

PEMIGEWASSET
WILDERNESS

Franconia Branch

Redrock Brook

Franconia Brook Trail

Hellgate Brook

Lincoln Brook Trail

Lincoln Brook

Franconia Brook Trail

Mount Liberty
(summit)

Franconia
Ridge Trail

Mount Flume
(summit)

Birch Island Brook

Black Pond

Franconia Branch

Franconia
Falls

Bondcliff Trail

Franconia
Falls Trail

Flume
Slide Trail

Black Pond Trail

Franconia Brook
Tentsite

Osseo Trail

Pemi East Side Trail

Whaleback
Mountain

WHITE MOUNTAIN
NATIONAL FOREST

Lincoln Woods Trail

East Branch
Pemigewasset River

Potash Knob

Clear Brook

Hancock
Campground

11 P Lincoln Woods Trailhead
(AMC Shuttle Stop)

112

East Branch
Pemigewasset River

Hancock Branch

Kancamagus Highway

A sharp left at the top takes you to a small clearing that used to be considered the summit, but the actual summit is 0.2 mile farther, so continue to follow the winding path over fallen logs until the obvious end, with a small clearing and a rock cairn marking the summit. Too bad there's no view, but the adventure is worth the effort, and you will get more views as you head back down the slide. Return to the trailhead along the same route.

Miles and Directions

0.0 Start from the ranger station. Cross the river on a bridge and turn right onto the Lincoln Woods Trail.

1.4 Pass the junction with the Osseo Trail on the left.

2.6 Pass the junction with the Black Pond Trail on the left.

2.9 Pass the junction with the trail to Franconia Falls on the left. Cross over Franconia Brook then turn left onto the Franconia Brook Trail.

4.2 Cross Camp 9 Brook (third time), being sure to stay left after crossing, followed by a quick up and down and right turn back onto old railroad grade trail.

4.6 Turn left (west) onto the Lincoln Brook Trail.

5.1 Cross Franconia Brook.

5.5 Cross Lincoln Brook.

6.8 Cross stream.

7.4 Cross Liberty Brook then pass through the Camp 12 clearing.

7.6 Cross Lincoln Brook.

8.0 Turn right at the rock cairn to begin ascent of Owl's Head Path.

8.1 Reach bottom of slide.

8.3 Reach top of slide

8.8 Reach top of the ridge near open area. Continue following the path to the north.

9.0 Reach the summit of Owl's Head Mountain. Return the way you came.

18.0 Arrive back at the trailhead.

Other Routes

Loop around Owl's Head, Lincoln Woods Trail to Franconia Brook Trail to Lincoln Brook Trail to Owl's Head slide path to Lincoln Brook Trail (north from slide path) to Franconia Brook Trail to Lincoln Woods Trail—distance: 21.6 miles; elevation gain: 4,200 feet

The last light of sunset reflects off the clouds above Franconia Ridge, as seen from the slide path on Owl's Head.

KANCAMAGUS HIGHWAY

The Kancamagus Highway (NH 112) is a beautifully scenic 35-mile stretch of road that travels through the White Mountains. Often referred to as the "Kanc," the road passes several beautiful White Mountain overlooks. Along the way there are six campgrounds and many waterfalls, including Sabbaday, Champney, and Lower Falls. (The last two are roadside and worth checking out.) This is a particularly nice road to travel during fall foliage season.

A highly recommended driving route that travels through some of the most impressive scenery involves taking the Kancamagus Highway east from Lincoln to NH 16 North to US 302, which goes through Crawford Notch. At Twin Mountain take US 3 South back to Lincoln, where you started the loop.

Kancamagus means "the Fearless One" and was the name of the grandson of Passaconaway, who united seventeen Indian tribes in central New England in the 1600s. The highway opened in 1959.

12 Mount Carrigain

With a dramatic walk along Signal Ridge and an observation tower on the summit, Mount Carrigain provides a straightforward and rewarding day hike. Due to its location on the southern edge of the Pemigewasset Wilderness, forty-three 4,000-footers are visible from the summit tower, a number equaled only by Mount Washington.

Distance: 10.4 miles out and back
Summit elevation: 4,700 feet
4,000-footers rank: 13
Elevation gain: 3,300 feet
Difficulty: Moderate

Hiking time: About 6.5 hours
Trails used: Signal Ridge Trail
Views: Excellent
Canine compatibility: Good

Finding the trailhead: *From the junction of US 302 and US 3 in Twin Mountain/Carroll,* follow US 302 East for 19 miles. Turn right onto Sawyer River Road; the parking area will be on the left in 2.0 miles. *From the junction of US 302 and NH 16 in Glen,* follow US 302 West for 10.1 miles. Turn left onto Sawyer River Road; the parking area will be on the left in 2.0 miles. **Note:** The trailhead is just across the road from the parking lot. **GPS:** N44 04.20' / W71 23.03'

The Hike

Although there are numerous reasons to love this hike, two factors make this a truly exceptional trip. First, Signal Ridge is stunning, and a traverse provides incredible treeless views over Carrigain Notch and beyond. Second, the observation tower on the summit, which sits right on the edge of the Pemigewasset Wilderness, will offer views of all but four of New Hampshire's 4,000-footers.

This is one of the more remote mountains in the Whites. There are two trails up the mountain, but the only reasonable day hike uses the Signal Ridge Trail for both ascent and descent. The trail begins just across the road from the parking area. You will start along Whiteface Brook as you wind gently up the mountain. Just under 1.0 mile in, you begin to head east as the trail climbs away from the brook and then levels out on a plateau and crosses a logging road at 1.4 miles.

The trail then turns right (north), and at 1.7 miles you cross Carrigain Brook. The trail continues following an old logging road, crosses another brook with a beaver pond on the left, and reaches the junction with the Carrigain Notch Trail on the right at 2.0 miles. You climb over a small ridge, followed by a sharp swing to the left (south) and a short descent before heading right (east) again as the trail begins to climb up the valley.

At 2.7 miles the trail leaves an old logging road, jigs to the left, and begins to climb in earnest. While the first 2.7 miles climbs just 850 feet, the next 1.9 miles goes up approximately 2,200 feet.

Three hikers with a total of eight legs check out the map on an overlook above Carrigain Notch on the Signal Ridge Trail.

Over the next 0.5 mile the trail makes another turn to the right, one to the left, and another to the right as the terrain gets steeper and steeper. From here you will climb steadily, turning right and crossing the upper part of Carrigain Brook then contouring north, with occasional restricted views. You pass through a beautiful birch forest and at 4.0 miles (3,700 feet) make a sharp left to follow a switchbacking route up to Signal Ridge.

After the long hike through the woods, the trail bursts out into the open on the ridge at 4.7 miles. Off to the right you will see Carrigain Notch, with the cliffs below Mount Lowell easily visible to the east and the unique Vose Spur, an interesting sub-peak on the near side of the notch to the northeast off the shoulder of Mount Carrigain. The summit and observation tower are visible straight ahead, 0.5 mile farther.

The views are incredible from the ridge, and the dramatically sloping east side feels unique among the hikes in the White Mountains. Crawford Notch and the Presidential Range beyond are visible to the northeast. You can also see the ski areas of Attitash and Cranmore to the east, and at certain spots iconic Mount Chocorua is visible to the south.

Continue along the ridge as it ducks back into the trees, makes a sharp left turn to the west, then turns north again as it climbs the summit cone, with some nice stone

A hiker descends from the observation tower atop Mount Carrigain.

steps before making a final right turn to reach the summit. It can be very windy on the platform, so use the opportunity in the sheltered area below to put on your jacket. The first lookout tower was built in 1910; the most recent observation tower was built in 1981.

From the summit you will be able to see the magnificent Pemigewasset Wilderness to the north and west, Crawford Notch and the entire southern Presidential Range to the northeast, the Hancocks just to the west, and the Sandwich Range to the south. In fact, the only 4,000-footers not visible from the summit are Cannon, North Kinsman, South Kinsman, and Galehead. Return to the trailhead along the same route.

Mount Carrigain

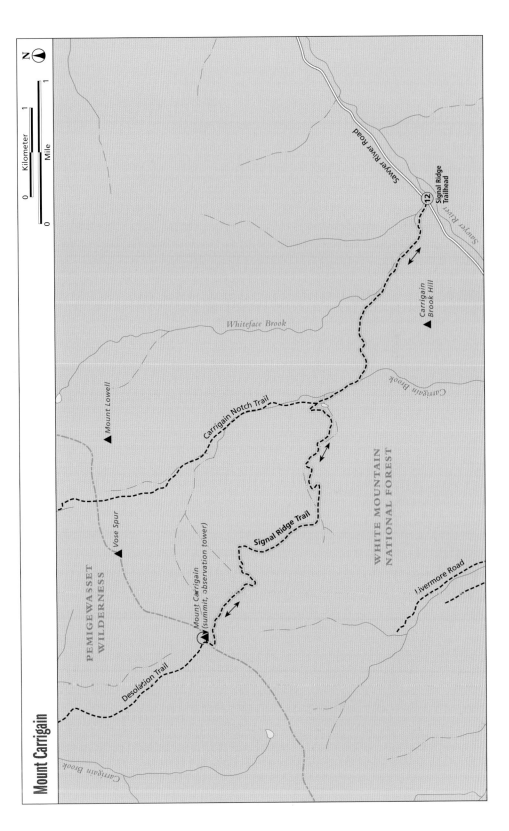

N

0   1   Kilometer
0   1   Mile

PEMIGEWASSET
WILDERNESS

Carrigain Brook

Desolation Trail

▲ Vose Spur

Mount Carrigain
(summit, observation tower)

Signal Ridge Trail

▲ Mount Lowell

Carrigain Notch Trail

Whiteface Brook

WHITE MOUNTAIN
NATIONAL FOREST

Livermore Road

Carrigain Brook

▲ Carrigain
Brook Hill

Sawyer River Road

12

Signal Ridge
Trailhead

Sawyer River

Miles and Directions

0.0 Start from the Signal Ridge Trailhead, across the road from the parking area.

1.4 Cross a logging road.

1.7 Cross Carrigain Brook.

1.9 Cross another brook with a beaver pond on the left.

2.0 Reach the junction with the Carrigain Notch Trail. Stay left on the Signal Ridge Trail.

2.7 The trail angles left (south) then right (east) as it begins a much steeper climb.

4.0 The trail makes a sharp left and climbs steeply with switchbacks to the ridge.

4.7 Reach the southern end of Signal Ridge, where the trail levels out and the summit is visible ahead.

5.2 Reach the observation tower on the summit of Mount Carrigain. Return the way you came.

10.4 Arrive back at the trailhead.

Other Routes

Signal Ridge Trail to Carrigain Notch Trail to Desolation Trail to Signal Ridge Trail—distance: 13.4 miles; elevation gain: 4,150 feet

Clouds fill the valley below Mount Carrigain.

Zealand and Crawford Notch Region

Pearl Cascade is one of two waterfalls on a short loop trail near the bottom of the Avalon Trail on the route up to Mounts Tom, Field, and Willey.

13 Mount Hale

The shortest hike in the book, Mount Hale is good option if the weather is bad and you don't want to go above tree line. As it's so short, you may be able to squeeze another hike in on the same day, or do it when you have limited time.

Distance: 4.4 miles out and back
Summit elevation: 4,054 feet
4,000-footers rank: 38
Elevation gain: 2,300 feet
Difficulty: Moderate (short)
Hiking time: About 2.5 hours

Trails used: Hale Brook Trail
Views: None
Canine compatibility: Good
Special considerations: The road to the trailhead is closed in winter, which adds 2.5 miles in each direction.

Finding the trailhead: *From the junction of US 302 and US 3 in Twin Mountain/Carroll,* follow US 302 East for 2.2 miles. Turn right onto Zealand Road; the small parking area will be on the right in 2.5 miles. *From the junction of US 302 and NH 16 in Glen,* follow US 302 West for 26.8 miles. Turn left onto Zealand Road; the small parking area will be on the right in 2.5 miles. **GPS:** N44 14.18' / W71 29.23'

The Hike

With basically no view and a straightforward and short trail, the reasons for climbing Mount Hale may seem to be lacking. However, with the prevalence of bad weather in the White Mountains, you will undoubtedly need a few hikes to do when going up into the alpine zone is not feasible. Since you are likely to encounter only other 4,000-foot peak-baggers on this trail, it often provides some nice solitude as well.

Short doesn't necessarily mean easy, as the trail climbs at a rate of more than 1,000 feet per mile, so be prepared for ample leg burn. From the trailhead the Hale Brook Trail quickly crosses the Spruce Goose Cross Country Ski Trail and gets slightly steeper as you go on. The lower portion of this hike passes through a nice birch forest. At 0.8 mile you cross Hale Brook. Downstream you'll see that the brook winds around short but steep rocky banks, creating a sort of mini-gorge.

After crossing the brook, the trail climbs steeply before contouring along the slope to the southeast above the brook, which is on your left. This stretch can make for some awkward sidehilling in winter. At 1.3 miles, around 3,000 feet in elevation, cross back over Hale Brook. The brook is small by this point, but it is a bit narrow with a steep drop-off, so be careful.

The trail then begins a series of switchbacks to avoid going straight up the steepest section, crosses another small stream around 1.7 miles, and then jogs to the right (southwest) as it follows the final ridge, making a small swing to the northwest just before reaching the summit clearing at 2.2 miles. On the short steep section near the summit, you may get an obscured view of Mount Willey off to the left.

Hale Brook winds its way down to the Zealand River.

In years past there was an obscured view from the summit as well, but over time the trees have grown up around the clearing and today there are no real views. The big rock pile marks the true summit; if you stand on it, you may be able to see some nearby peaks above the trees. In 1928 a fire tower was built on the summit and was in use until 1948. It was dismantled in 1972, but remnants are still visible.

Mount Hale is named for Edward Everett Hale, who was a late nineteenth- and early twentieth-century American writer from the Boston area, best known for his short story "The Man without a Country." He founded *Lend a Hand*, a periodical in which he advocated religious tolerance and social reforms. He was also known as an

Mount Hale

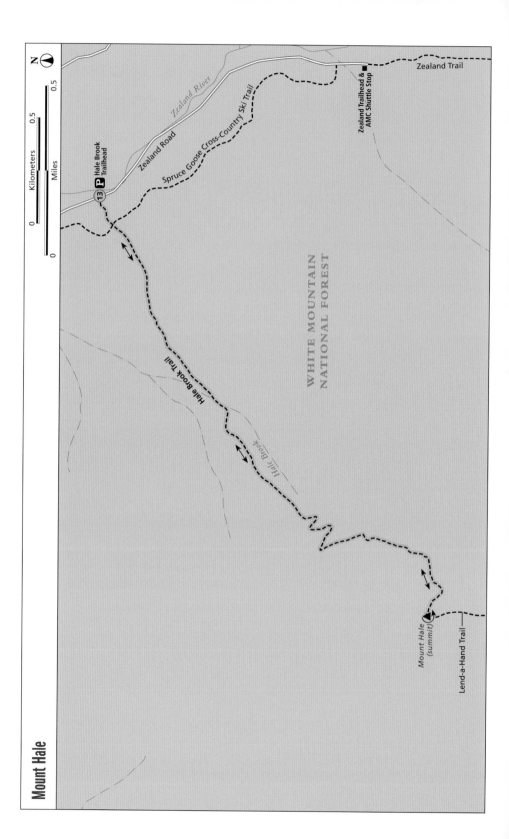

Zealand River

Zealand Road

Hale Brook Trailhead

13 P

Spruce Goose Cross-Country Ski Trail

Zealand Trailhead & AMC Shuttle Stop

Zealand Trail

WHITE MOUNTAIN NATIONAL FOREST

Hale Brook Trail

Hale Brook

Mount Hale (summit)

Lend-a-Hand Trail

N

Kilometers
0   0.5   0.5

Miles
0   0.5

If you stand on your toes atop the pile of boulders on the Mount Hale summit, you can catch some restricted views.

early conservationist. **Note:** The Lend-a-Hand Trail goes from the summit of Mount Hale to Zealand Hut and Zealand Falls.

Return back down the Hale Brook Trail to the trailhead.

Miles and Directions

0.0   Start climbing on the Hale Brook Trail from the small parking area.

0.8   Cross Hale Brook above a little water chute.

1.3   Cross Hale Brook again.

2.2   Reach the summit clearing. Return the way you came.

4.4   Arrive back at the trailhead.

Other Routes

1.   Zealand Trail to Twinway to Lend-a-Hand Trail to Hale Brook Trail to road walk on Zealand Road—distance: 8.7 miles; elevation gain: 2,450 feet

2.   Zealand Trail to Twinway to Zealand Spur (summit Zealand Mountain) to Twinway to Lend-a-Hand Trail to Hale Brook Trail to road walk on Zealand Road—distance: 14.5 miles; elevation gain: 4,300 feet

14 Zealand Mountain

Truly a hike where the journey is the reward, along the way you will cross over a gorgeous marsh and pond with long-range views, pass a dramatic waterfall, visit a unique hut with an interesting vista next to lounging spots along a river, and enjoy one of the most gorgeous clifftop views on the way to the peak. Who cares if the summit doesn't have any views?

Distance: 11.4 miles out and back
Summit elevation: 4,260 feet
4,000-footers rank: 31
Elevation gain: 2,700 feet
Difficulty: Moderate
Hiking time: About 6 hours
Trails used: Zealand Trail, Twinway

Views: Good from Zeacliff ledges and okay from Zealand Falls Hut; no view from the summit
Canine compatibility: Good
Special considerations: The road to the trailhead is closed in winter, adding 3.5 miles each way to the hike.

Finding the trailhead: *From the junction of US 302 and US 3 in Twin Mountain/Carroll,* follow US 302 East for 2.2 miles. Turn right onto Zealand Road; the parking lot will be at the end of this road in 3.5 miles. *From the junction of US 302 and NH 16 in Glen,* follow US 302 West for 26.8 miles. Turn left onto Zealand Road; the parking lot will be at the end of this road in 3.5 miles. **GPS:** N44 13.50' / W71 28.75'

The Hike

This hike is easier than the mileage suggests, as the early and latter portions of the hike traverse fairly level terrain with only minor elevation gain. The middle section between the hut and the ridge is the only section with significant climbing, and this is rewarded with a fantastic cliff-edge view at the top of the climb.

Start on the Zealand Trail, which gains only 450 feet over the first 2.5 miles. The path is smooth, quickly becomes very rooty and rocky, then gets smooth again as it travels along an old railroad grade, coming close to Zealand River at 0.8 mile. The trail leaves then rejoins the old railroad grade, eventually crossing the river on a bridge, crossing a brook, crossing another bridge over the river and then another small brook until at 1.8 miles you reach a boardwalk over a beaver pond with long-range views toward Zealand Ridge.

At 2.1 miles a beaver pond allows for great views over to Mount Tom; shortly after, at 2.3 miles, you reach the junction with the A-Z Trail, which heads up toward Mount Tom. Stay straight (south) on the Zealand Trail until you reach the junction with the Twinway at 2.5 miles.

Turn right onto the Twinway. Notice the white blazes? You are now on the Appalachian Trail. A side path on the left will take you to Zealand Falls, a unique series of

Guests of the Zealand Falls Hut enjoy reading—and napping—on the ledges above the falls.

waterfalls where the water cascades in various directions over large granite blocks. The Twinway will take you to Zealand Falls Hut at 2.7 miles. One of the smallest of the AMC huts, it is also one of the oldest, originally built in 1932. The hut is open for self-service in winter and sits right next to open ledges on Whitewall Brook that provide great views from the top of the falls out over Zealand Pond and toward Mount Tom. From the hut you get a great view through Zealand Notch out toward Mount Carrigain.

The trail heads up to the right, passing some nice cascades and over a few branches of Whitewall Brook. Just after Lend-a-Hand Trail comes in on the right, turn left (south) and cross Whitewall Brook. In high water this can be treacherous, so be careful. From here the real climbing begins, with some steep sections as the Twinway heads south up toward Zealand Ridge. You'll pass through a nice birch forest, and as the trail levels out at just over 3,600 feet, a spur to the ledges atop Zeacliff heads to the left.

The view here is incredible, and since there is no view from the summit of Zealand Mountain, this is the place to stop, enjoy lunch, and relax. Mounts Tom, Field, and Willey are visible across Zealand Notch, with the high Presidential Range and Mount Washington rising behind them. The cliffs across the notch are on the side of Whitewall Mountain, and you get a good look at the flat Ethan Pond Trail, which cuts through it, following the old Zealand Valley logging railroad. To the right is Mount Carrigain and the deep V of Carrigain Notch, and far to the right is Mount Hancock. Between the two, far in the distance, is Mount Whiteface. Without a doubt, the Zeacliff Overlook provides one of the best views of the eastern half of the Pemigewasset Wilderness.

Alas, you still have a peak to bag. A short side trail on the right leads back to the Twinway, making a short loop. (The short bit of the Twinway that you bypass on this loop has a nice open outlook with some westerly views toward the Twins.) After heading left (west) on the Twinway, you quickly come to the junction with the Zeacliff Trail at 4.0 miles. Continue straight on the Twinway and at 4.4 miles come to a short but steep side trail down to Zeacliff Pond. Some interesting views can be had by taking the side trails around the pond, but it's often very muddy down there.

The Twinway rolls up and down with a few short steep sections, finally coming to a sign for Zealand Mountain at 5.6 miles. Turn right here and take the 0.1-mile

The cliffs on Whitewall Mountain and the flat Ethan Pond Trail are clearly visible from the Zeacliff ledges across Zealand Notch.

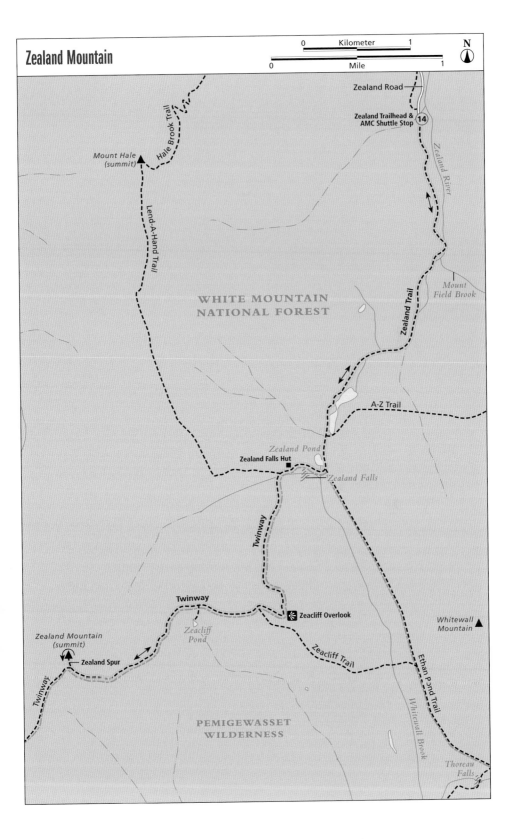

Zealand Mountain

0 Kilometer 1
0 Mile 1

N

Zealand Road

Zealand Trailhead &
AMC Shuttle Stop

14

Hale Brook Trail

Zealand River

Mount Hale
(summit)

Lend-A-Hand Trail

WHITE MOUNTAIN
NATIONAL FOREST

*Mount
Field Brook*

Zealand Trail

A-Z Trail

Zealand Pond

Zealand Falls Hut

Zealand Falls

Twinway

Twinway

Zeacliff Overlook

*Whitewall
Mountain*

Twinway

*Zeacliff
Pond*

Zealand Mountain
(summit)

Zealand Spur

Zeacliff Trail

Ethan Pond Trail

Whitewall Brook

Twinway

PEMIGEWASSET
WILDERNESS

*Thoreau
Falls*

spur to the summit of Zealand Mountain, marked by a sign in a small opening in the woods and a rock cairn. Return to the trailhead on the same route.

Miles and Directions

0.0 Start on the Zealand Trail from the parking area at the end of Zealand Road.

1.8 Reach a beaver pond on boardwalk with views to Zealand Ridge. Cross the boardwalk.

2.1 Reach a pond with a view of Mount Tom.

2.3 Reach the junction with the A-Z Trail. Stay right/straight (south) on the Zealand Trail.

2.5 Turn right onto Twinway.

2.7 Reach Zealand Falls and the Zealand Falls Hut a few hundred feet beyond. The trail continues past hut on the right (north) side of the brook.

2.9 Reach the junction with the Lend-a-Hand Trail on the right. Stay left on Twinway; shortly after, cross a small brook then the main brook.

3.9 A spur to the left heads to the outstanding Zeacliff Overlook.

4.0 Pass the junction with the Zeacliff Trail.

4.4 Reach the junction on left for short spur down to Zeacliff Pond.

5.6 Turn right at the junction onto the short spur trail to the summit.

5.7 Reach the summit of Zealand Mountain. Return the way you came.

11.4 Arrive back at the trailhead.

Other Routes

1. Pemigewasset Loop (hike 36)—distance: 38.5 miles (extended); elevation gain: 12,500 feet (extended)

2. Bonds, Zealand, and Twins Traverse (hike 35)—distance: 23.1 miles; elevation gain: 6,800 feet

3. Zealand Trail to Twinway to Zealand Spur to Twinway to Lend-a-Hand Trail (summit Mount Hale) to Hale Brook Trail to road walk on Zealand Road—distance: 14.5 miles; elevation gain: 4,300 feet

4. Zealand Trail to Ethan Pond Trail to Zeacliff Trail to Twinway to Zealand Spur to Twinway to Zealand Trail—distance: 12.6 miles; elevation gain: 3,100 feet

15 Mount Tom, Mount Field, and Mount Willey (and Mount Avalon)

Mounts Tom, Field, and Willey rise up on the western side of Crawford Notch. Although none of these peaks are above tree line, there are numerous views, including a fantastic view from ledges just off the summit of Mount Willey. Although these peaks can be climbed on separate hikes, bagging all three at once is efficient, as the dips between these peaks along the ridge aren't very large. The side trip to Mount Avalon on your descent from the ridge is a worthy hike itself, with incredible views down through Crawford Notch and over to the Presidential Range.

Distance: 10.2-mile lollipop loop with spurs
Summit elevation: Mount Tom, 4,051 feet; Mount Field, 4,340 feet; Mount Willey, 4,285 feet
4,000-footers rank: Mount Tom, 40; Mount Field, 23 (tied); Mount Willey, 29
Elevation gain: 3,750 feet
Difficulty: Moderate

Hiking time: About 6 hours
Trails used: Avalon Trail, Cascade Loop, A-Z Trail, Mount Tom Spur, Willey Range Trail
Views: Restricted views from Mount Tom; good views from Mount Field; great views from Mount Willey and Mount Avalon
Canine compatibility: Good

Finding the trailhead: *From the junction of US 302 and US 3 in Twin Mountain/Carroll,* follow US 302 East for 8.5 miles. Park in the lot on the right for the Crawford Depot, which is just past the entrance to the AMC Highland Center. *From the junction of US 302 and NH 16 in Glen,* follow US 302 West for 20.6 miles. Turn left into the lot for the Crawford Depot, which is just before the entrance to the AMC Highland Center. **GPS:** N44 13.08' / W71 24.70'

The Hike

There are a few ways to bag these peaks, and many folks do them on separate hikes. The most efficient way is to hike them together, and with a nice ridge walk and a trip to Mount Avalon, you can pack in a lot on this reasonable day hike. You can save 1.4 miles by making this a point-to-point by dropping off a car at the bottom of the Kedron Flume Trail in Crawford Notch. However, by doing the hike described here, you return to your car and get the bonus of stopping by Mount Avalon while avoiding the steep descent off Mount Willey.

Start up the Avalon Trail, which begins across the train tracks from the Macomber Family Information Center. Continue straight (west) on the Avalon Trail, past the junction with the Mount Willard Trail on the left. *Note:* The Mount Willard Trail is a nice short but popular day hike that leads to Mount Willard, which affords a stunning view down through Crawford Notch—a great alternative for folks who want a dramatic view accessed via a short climb.

From the west side of the Mount Avalon, you get a great view of Mount Willey rising high above to the south.

After crossing Crawford Brook at 0.2 mile, take the short Cascade Loop on the left to pass the beautiful Beecher and Pearl Cascades and rejoin the Avalon Trail at 0.3 mile. At 0.7 mile you cross back over the brook, where the water cascades down through an interesting little gorge. The trail climbs steadily, getting slightly steeper before reaching the junction with the A–Z Trail. Head straight/right (southwest) on the A–Z Trail. After crossing a gully, the trail contours up along the mountain, dipping a final time to cross the upper portion of Crawford Brook at 1.9 miles. Reach the junction with the Mount Tom Spur at 2.2 miles.

The section of the Avalon Trail from Mount Avalon to the junction with the A-Z Trail is steep and rocky.

Turn right (north) onto the Mount Tom Spur and follow the trail through areas of blowdowns to the summit of Mount Tom at 2.9 miles, marked by a little clearing with a big rock cairn. Stand-up views are possible from the summit clearing, but better views can be had on a short side trail just off the spur trail below the main summit, where there is a bench. Heading back down the trail, you can get some decent views through blowdowns back toward Mount Field. Don't worry, you'll get better views later in the hike. Head back down to the trail junction and at 3.5 miles turn right (southwest) onto the A–Z Trail. A few hundred feet later, reach the junction of the Willey Range Trail on the left.

Turn left (southeast) onto the Willey Range Trail and make a nice gradual ascent. At 4.4 miles the Avalon Trail merges on the left; just beyond, at 4.5 miles, you reach the summit of Mount Field. The trees obscure a view, but there are still a few viewpoints near the summit. Just to the north of the summit, before you reach the peak, there are views over the Pemigewasset Wilderness toward the Bonds and the Franconia Range beyond. A very short side path on the left leads to further views north and northeast, where you get a view of Mount Tom, with Bretton Woods and the Mount Washington Hotel below. Better views can be had from Mount Willey.

Continue on the Willey Range Trail. Occasional views open up as you head down; there are a few steep sections. After reaching the col just below 4,000 feet in elevation, make the final ascent to Mount Willey, reaching the summit at 5.8 miles. Just before the summit you get incredible views to the west. After topping out on the peak, marked by a large cairn, continue for a few dozen yards and take the short side trail on the left to the beautiful eastern viewpoint high above Crawford Notch.

Directly across the Saco River valley are the slabs and slides on the side of Mount Webster. From this vantage point you can see the southern peaks of the Presidential Range, with the high peaks of Mounts Washington, Jefferson, and Adams rising in the distance. Looking to the southeast you can see many of the more southern mountains, including Stairs Mountain and Mount Resolution, framing the southern end of the valley with Kearsarge North rising beyond.

Head back north, retracing your steps along the ridge, but just after Mount Field at 7.2 miles, turn right (northeast) onto the Avalon Trail. The trail begins descending gently but gets steep before bottoming out in a col just below Mount Avalon. After a brief climb, at 8.2 miles take the short but steep side trail to the ledgy summit of Mount Avalon, which affords extensive views to the south, east, and north. Just behind the summit ledges you also get a good view of Mount Tom and the eastern sides of Mounts Field and Willey. Head back to the Avalon Trail and make the very steep descent back down to the junction with the A–Z Trail at 8.9 miles, where you turn right and head back to the parking area for a total of 10.2 miles.

Miles and Directions

0.0 Start hiking up the Avalon Trail, which starts across the railroad tracks behind the information center.

0.1 Continue straight as the Willard Trail joins on the left.

0.2 Cross Crawford Brook. Just beyond, you can take the short loop to the left, Cascade Loop, which passes Beecher and Pearl Cascades and rejoins the trail at 0.3 mile.

0.7 The trail crosses back over the brook.

1.3 Continue right/straight (southwest) onto the A-Z trail as the Avalon Trail comes in from the left.

2.2 Turn right (north) onto the Mount Tom Spur.

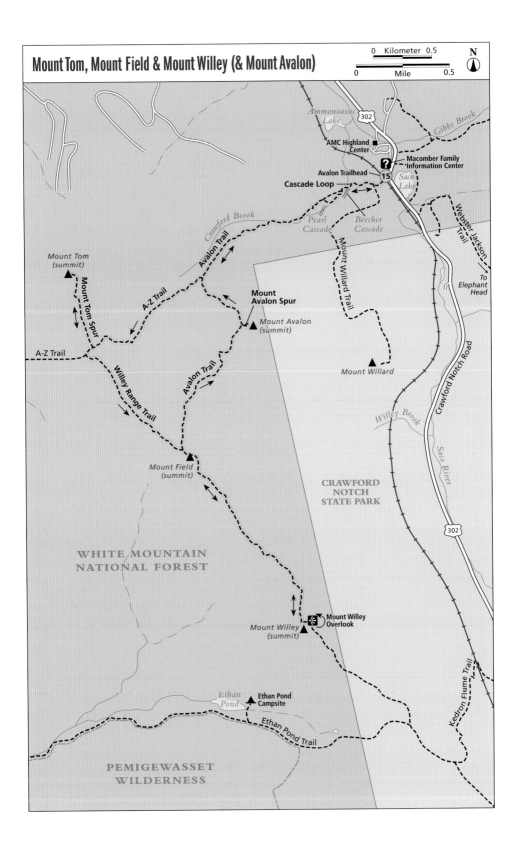

Mount Tom, Mount Field & Mount Willey (& Mount Avalon)

0   Kilometer   0.5

0   Mile   0.5

N

Ammonoosuc Lake

302

Gibbs Brook

AMC Highland Center

Macomber Family Information Center

Avalon Trailhead

Cascade Loop

15

Saco Lake

Crawford Brook

Pearl Cascade

Beecher Cascade

Avalon Trail

Webster Jackson Trail

To Elephant Head

Mount Tom (summit)

Mount Tom Spur

A-Z Trail

Mount Avalon Spur

Mount Willard Trail

Mount Avalon (summit)

A-Z Trail

Willey Range Trail

Avalon Trail

Mount Willard

Crawford Notch Road

Mount Field (summit)

Willey Brook

Saco River

CRAWFORD NOTCH STATE PARK

302

WHITE MOUNTAIN NATIONAL FOREST

Mount Willey Overlook

Mount Willey (summit)

Ethan Pond

Ethan Pond Campsite

Kedron Flume Trail

Ethan Pond Trail

PEMIGEWASSET WILDERNESS

A crescent moon shines high above the Willey Range.

2.9   Reach the summit of Mount Tom. Turn around and head back down to the junction with the A-Z Trail.

3.5   Reach the junction with the A-Z Trail. Head right (southwest) for a few hundred feet to the junction with the Willey Range Trail; turn left (southeast) onto the Willey Range Trail.

4.4   Reach the junction of the Willey Range and Avalon Trails. Continue straight on the Willey Range Trail.

4.5   Reach the summit of Mount Field. Continue straight on the Willey Range Trail.

5.8   Reach the summit of Mount Willey. Notice the beautiful views to the right (west) just before reaching the summit. Be sure to take the short spur to the left (east) just after the summit to get amazing views over Crawford Notch. Head back (northeast) on the Willey Range Trail to the junction with the Avalon Trail.

7.2   Turn right (northeast) onto the Avalon Trail.

8.2   Turn right (southeast) onto the short steep side trail to Mount Avalon.

8.3   Reach the summit of Mount Avalon.

8.4   Return to the Avalon Trail and head straight/right down to the junction with the A-Z Trail.

8.9   Turn right (east), following the Avalon Trail at the junction with the A-Z Trail.

10.2   Arrive back at the parking area.

Other Routes

1.   Willey Range point-to-point: Kendron Flume Trail to Ethan Pond Trail to Willey Range Trail to A-Z Trail to Mount Tom Spur to Avalon Trail—distance: 8.5 miles; elevation gain: 4,000 feet

2.   Mount Willey only out-and-back: Kendron Flume Trail to Ethan Pond Trail to Willey Range Trail—distance: 5.4 miles; elevation gain: 3,300 feet

3.   Mount Tom and Mount Field only (with Mount Avalon): Avalon Trail to A-Z Trail to Mount Tom Spur to A-Z Trail to Willey Range Trail to Avalon Trail—distance: 7.3 miles; elevation gain: 2,950 feet

Waterville Valley and the Sandwich Range

A hiker descends on the steep bypass of the chimney between Mount Osceola and East Osceola.

16 Mount Osceola and East Osceola

A relatively easy hike to the summit of Mount Osceola rewards you with dramatic clifftop views as it rises high above Waterville Valley. The short but challenging trip over to East Osceola provides partial views to the north and includes a traverse through the chimney—a short technical scramble through a steep narrow chute that is fun in both directions.

Distance: 8.4 miles out and back
Summit elevation: Mount Osceola, 4,340 feet; East Osceola, 4,156 feet
4,000-footers rank: Mount Osceola, 23 (tied); East Osceola, 34
Elevation gain: 3,200 feet
Difficulty: Moderate, with one difficult section (chimney) between the two peaks
Hiking time: About 5 hours
Trails used: Mount Osceola Trail

Views: Great views from Mount Osceola; restricted views from East Osceola
Canine compatibility: Good except for one steep section (chimney) between two peaks.
Special considerations: Tripoli Road is closed in winter. If doing this hike in winter, either snowshoe or ski to the trailhead from the gate near Waterville Valley or take the much more difficult route over East Osceola from the Kancamagus Highway.

Finding the trailhead: *From I-93 North,* take exit 31 and turn right onto Tripoli Road. Follow this for 6.6 miles; the parking lot will be on the left. *From I-93 South,* take exit 31 and turn left onto Tripoli Road. Follow this for 6.6 miles; the parking lot will be on the left. *Note:* If you're staying in Waterville Valley, follow Tripoli Road 4.5 miles from the junction of NH-49 and Tripoli Road. **GPS:** N43 59.02' / W71 33.53'

The Hike

With an elevation gain of just over 2,000 feet in 3.0 miles, the hike to the summit of Mount Osceola is fairly easy, but the mile between Osceola and East Osceola is fairly challenging. A relatively short hike, and dramatic clifftop view can make the summit downright crowded on nice weekends but far fewer people make the journey out to East Osceola.

Mount Osceola was named for Chief Osceola of the Seminoles, who in the 1830s warred against the United States when the government tried to forcefully relocate the tribe to Oklahoma. He died in prison in 1837. The mountain is the dominant peak on the ridge that divides Lincoln and Waterville Valley. It is possible to summit these peaks from Tripoli Road (hike described here) as well as from the Kancamagus Highway. Although the hikes are roughly similar in length, the northern part of the Mount Osceola Trail is steep, eroded, and somewhat technical, making the route from Tripoli Road easier and more enjoyable.

The trail begins at Thornton Gap, the high point on Tripoli Road. The Mount Osceola Trail starts out fairly flat before beginning to climb at a steady rate. Unlike

The sun sets behind Mount Osceola and Mount Moosilauke farther to the west.

many other hikes, the most difficult section is actually near the beginning, where even though the climb is very moderate, the trail starts out very rocky, with uneven footing caused by old landslides.

You will cross a stream shortly after beginning. Around 1.0 mile or so into the hike, the trail begins to become less rocky. At first it contours to the east then to the north as it climbs up to Breadtray Ridge. The forest begins with mixed hardwoods and quickly transitions into one of birch and fir. Reach a switchback at 1.3 miles and another at 1.6. The walking in this middle section is nice and smooth as you travel through a fir forest. This is the lower portion of Breadtray Ridge, which you leave for a short while before rejoining on the last 0.5 mile to the summit of Osceola.

At 2.1 miles, cross a small brook as the trail turns to the right (southeast). After a slightly steeper climb, begin a series of longer switchbacks at 2.3 miles until you reach the summit ridge at 2.8 miles. During this section, you traverse a series of angled bedrock slabs, which may require you to walk in the crease where the rock dives into the ground. Although awkward, these are fairly easy to traverse, but you may need to take extra caution when it is wet and use nearby trees as handholds.

When you reach the anchors of the original fire tower at 3.2 miles, you have reached the true summit. A short spur trail to the north leads to a small opening that,

Mount Osceola is easily recognizable by the giant scar on the north side of the mountain.

with the aid of a nicely placed boulder, affords great views into the Pemigewasset Wilderness and toward the Franconia Range.

Continue on the trail, pass the foundation of a newer fire tower and reach the clifftop view for which Mount Osceola is famous. Three fire towers were erected here in the early part of the twentieth century, the final one in 1942. The tower was last manned in 1955 and completely removed in 1985.

The view is stunning. From the ledges, the most prominent peak is your next destination, East Osceola. From here you get a great view of the route along the dramatic ridgeline, which drops off precipitously to the south. Amazingly, even though the view to the west is obscured, the location of Osceola as one of the more southwestern of the 4,000-foot peaks affords it one of the most expansive views in the White Mountains. With a little walking around and a trip to the aforementioned viewpoint on the short spur trail, forty-one 4,000-footers are visible. See what peaks you can make out. The Presidential Range should be obvious, but can you identify the northernmost peaks of Mount Cabot and Mount Waumbek in the distance? From here you also get a great view of the slide on North Tripyramid, one of the toughest and most breathtaking hikes in the Whites.

Mount Osceola & East Osceola

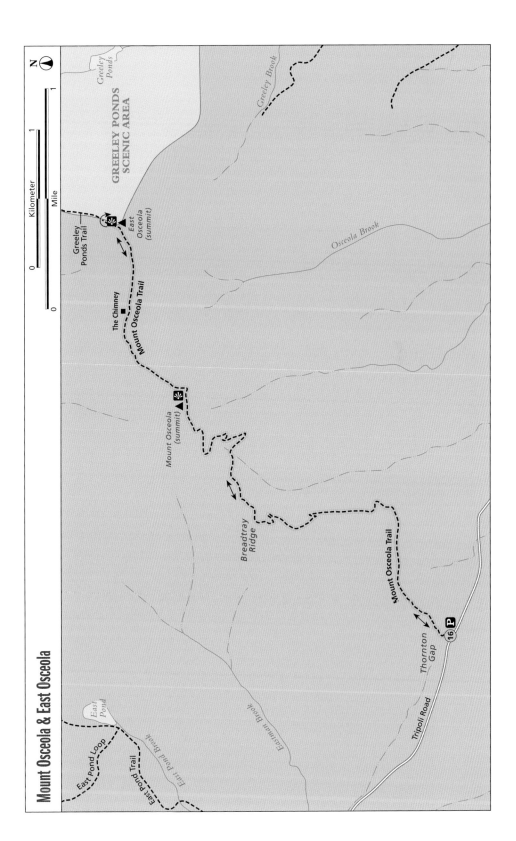

To get to East Osceola, follow the trail that leaves just to the left of the cliffs and the old tower foundation. Descend alternately easy and rough sections before reaching the crux of the route, the chimney, at 3.8 miles. This short but extremely steep series of narrow ledges is pretty straightforward when dry, but head to the left above the chimney to take a more moderate, albeit also very steep, slanted detour. Many hikers chose to take the detour on the way over to East Osceola and climb up the chimney on the way back.

From here, the route climbs fairly steeply up to the summit of East Osceola. At 4.0 miles there is a nice ledge from which great views can be had to the north and west. Although the summit at 4.2 miles doesn't have much in the way of views, if you continue along the trail past the summit for about 75 yards, you'll get to a nice overlook with views to the east. Return the way you came to get back to the trailhead.

Miles and Directions

0.0 Start on the Mount Osceola Trail from the trailhead on Tripoli Road.

3.2 Reach the main summit ledges. Follow the trail on the left toward East Osceola.

3.8 Reach the chimney, a steep chute just above the low point between the two peaks. You can downclimb this or go around down a detour on the left, which is steep and angled but easier than the chimney.

4.0 Reach a view to left (north).

4.2 Reach the summit of East Osceola. Continue a few hundred feet past the summit to a spot with views to the east. Turn around to head back over to Mount Osceola.

8.4 Arrive back at the parking area on Tripoli Road.

Other Routes

Greely Ponds Trail to Mount Osceola Trail out-and-back (from Kancamagus Highway)— distance: 7.6 miles; elevation gain: 3,250 feet

17　Mount Tecumseh

Entirely below tree line, this is one of the shortest hikes in the book. Climbing the lowest of New Hampshire's 4,000-footers, the trail's consistent grade makes it a perfect hike to dip your toes in the peak-bagging waters. It is also a great hike if you have limited time or want to see how you like hiking in winter; the start from the Waterville Valley ski area makes it extremely accessible.

Distance: 5.0 miles out and back with summit loop
Summit elevation: 4,003 feet
4,000-footers rank: 47 (tied)
Elevation gain: 2,250 feet
Difficulty: Easy to moderate
Hiking time: About 3 hours

Trails used: Mount Tecumseh Trail, Sosman Trail
Views: Good but limited
Canine compatibility: Good
Special considerations: During winter or on busy summer weekends, you may need to park in a lower lot and follow the road up to the trailhead.

Finding the trailhead: *From I-93 (from the south),* take exit 28 and turn right onto NH 49 East. Keep straight and follow this for 10.2 miles. Turn left onto Tripoli Road and continue for 1.2 miles. Head left/straight onto Ski Area Road and park in a lot close to the base lodge. The trail begins on the right side of the upper parking lot. *From I-93 (from the north),* take exit 28 and turn left onto NH 49 East. Keep straight and follow this for 10.4 miles. Turn left onto Tripoli Road and continue for 1.2 miles. Head left/straight onto Ski Area Road and park in a lot close to the base lodge. The trail begins on the right side of the upper parking lot. **GPS: N43 58.00' / W71 31.62'**

The Hike

The route roughly follows Tecumseh Brook, crossing it a few times. The trail is on the north side of the Waterville Valley ski resort, and you will both hear (when open) and see parts of the ski area on your way up. The mountain is named for a Shawnee Chief from Ohio who fought against white settlers and even coordinated a multi-tribe victory against US soldiers in 1811 at the Battle of Tippecanoe.

After stepping into the woods from the base of the ski area, the Mount Tecumseh Trail crosses a small stream then stays to the left (south) side of the brook. After crossing Tecumseh Brook at 0.3 miles, the trail begins to climb a bit more steeply. Climb steadily along a small ridge on the north side of the brook. Just over 1.0 mile in, make a short descent back to the brook, which you cross at 1.1 miles. This crossing also approximately coincides with the elevation where hardwood forest transitions to conifer forest.

A short but steep section of switchbacks leads to a short spur (signed) at 1.2 miles to a ski trail, where you get a nice view of Waterville Valley and the surrounding peaks, including Mount Osceola and the Tripyramids. From the spur junction, take a

Mount Tecumseh's southwest side is wild and remote, as seen from the cliffs on the Welch and Dickey Loop.

sharp right turn onto an old logging road as it heads up a consistent, fairly steep and rocky grade to the east, followed shortly by a jog to the southeast.

The trail continues to narrow and at 1.9 miles gets very steep. At 2.1 miles it quickly levels out, reaching the junction with the Sosman Trail at 2.2 miles. Turn right (north), following the combined Sosman/Mount Tecumseh Trail; at 2.3 miles

Mount Tecumseh

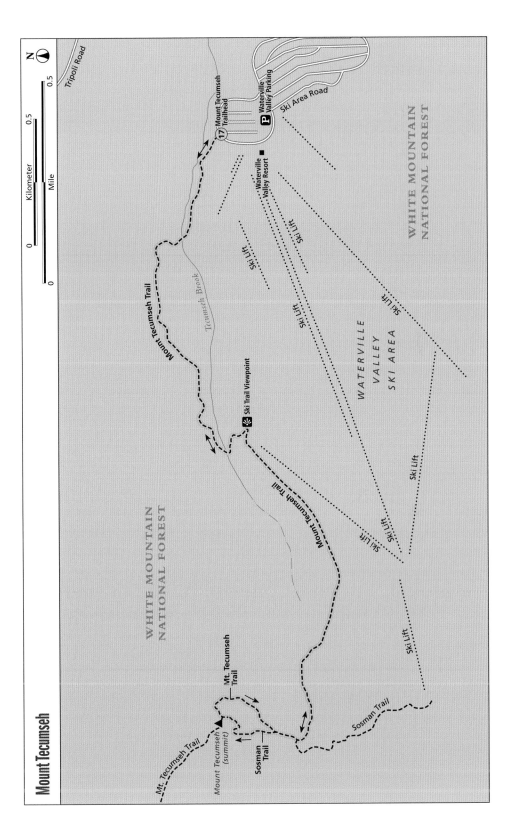

N

Kilometer
0   0.5   0.5

Mile
0   0.5

Tripoli Road

Mount Tecumseh Trailhead

(17)

Waterville Valley Parking

P

Ski Area Road

Waterville Valley Resort

Tecumseh Brook

Ski Lift

Ski Lift

Ski Lift

WATERVILLE VALLEY SKI AREA

Ski Lift

Ski Lift

Ski Lift

Ski Lift

WHITE MOUNTAIN NATIONAL FOREST

Ski Trail Viewpoint

Mount Tecumseh Trail

Mount Tecumseh Trail

WHITE MOUNTAIN NATIONAL FOREST

Mt. Tecumseh Trail

Mt. Tecumseh Trail

Mount Tecumseh (summit)

Sosman Trail

Sosman Trail

turn left onto the Sosman Trail up a short, winding, and fairly steep ascent to the summit at 2.5 miles.

The summit ledge provides nice views to Mount Osceola, East Osceola, and the Sandwich Range. In the distance through the notch between Mount Osceola and East Osceola, you get a glimpse of Mount Hancock, a long but nice view of Mount Washington and the Presidential Range, and the recognizable peak of Mount Carrigain can be seen just to the left of East Osceola. In the far distance to the right of East Osceola, you can even make out the Carter Range.

From the summit, continue straight then to the right, making sure to follow the Mount Tecumseh Trail back toward Waterville Valley. This can be a little confusing, as the northern half of the Mount Tecumseh Trail continues to the northwest, down to Tripoli Road. Your trail is on the right, and it makes a 180-degree turn back around to the southwest. Look for a nice view of the slides on the Tripyramids. Continue following this trail down as it levels out and meets up with the Sosman Trail at 2.7 miles. Continue straight on the combined trail; turn left (east) at at 2.8 miles back onto the Mount Tecumseh Trail which takes you back to the trailhead.

Miles and Directions

0.0 Start from the parking area at the Waterville Valley ski resort on the Mount Tecumseh Trail.

0.3 Cross Tecumseh Brook.

1.1 Cross back over Tecumseh Brook.

1.2 Reach a short spur trail on the left out to a ski trail with decent views.

2.2 Turn right (north) at the intersection with the Sosman Trail. The Mount Tecumseh Trail and Sosman Trails join here for a short section.

2.3 At the junction where the two trails split again, turn left onto the Sosman Trail on a short but steep ascent to the summit of Mount Tecumseh.

2.5 Reach the summit of Mount Tecumseh. Stay right (east) then turn to the south on the Mount Tecumseh Trail back around the summit cone. Do not follow the Mount Tecumseh Trail left (northwest), as this will take you to Tripoli Road on the other side of the mountain.

2.7 At the junction, go straight (west) on the combined Sosman/Mount Tecumseh Trail.

2.8 At the next junction where the two trails split, turn left (east), back onto the Mount Tecumseh Trail.

5.0 Arrive back at the trailhead.

Other Routes

Mount Tecumseh Trail out-and-back (from Tripoli Road)—distance: 6.2 miles; elevation gain: 2,550 feet

18 North Tripyramid and Middle Tripyramid

The Pine Bend Brook Trail begins very gradually but gets steep as it nears the summit ridge. This route is shorter and easier than the more widely known loop up the North Slide and down the South Slide from Waterville Valley; you may even find you have the trail to yourself. A short "must-do" side trip from the summit of North Tripyramid takes you to the top of the North Slide, where you will be treated to expansive views to the west with Mount Moosilauke rising between the nearby peaks of Mount Tecumseh and Mount Osceola.

Distance: 9.6 miles out and back
Summit elevation: North Tripyramid, 4,180 feet; Middle Tripyramid, 4,140 feet
4,000-footers rank: North Tripyramid, 32; Middle Tripyramid, 35
Elevation gain: 3,500 feet
Difficulty: Moderate (*Note:* The alternate route using North and South Slides is very difficult.)
Hiking time: About 5.5 hours
Trails used: Pine Bend Brook Trail, Mount Tripyramid Trail

Views: Good but restricted views from peaks; excellent view from top of North Slide
Canine compatibility: Good, but some stream crossings can be difficult in high water. The alternate route over North and South Slides is tough but doable for athletic dogs.
Special considerations: The alternate route up North Slide and down South Slide is highly recommended.

Finding the trailhead: *From I-93 (from the south),* take exit 32 for NH 112 (Kancamagus Highway). Turn left onto NH 112 East and go 18.7 miles; parking is on the right. *From I-93 (from the north),* take exit 32 for NH 112 (Kancamagus Highway). Turn left onto NH 112 East and go 19.1 miles; parking is on the right. *From the junction of NH 16 and NH 112 in Conway,* take NH 112 West for 16.5 miles; parking is on the left. **GPS:** N44 00.12' / W71 24.80'

The Hike

This is the most straightforward route to climb these two peaks. However, if you want a challenge with a climb up an incredibly picturesque slide, the slightly longer (11.0 miles round-trip) route from Waterville Valley up the slide on North Tripyramid and down the slide on South Tripyramid is one you won't forget. This route is very nice; a very short side trip to the top of the slide on North Tripyramid will get you similar views and is really the only option if weather conditions are not ideal. Also note that although this route is easier, it is by no means "easy," with two fairly significant climbs on the route up from the Kancamagus Highway.

The first few miles of this route are indeed easy, gaining just 600 vertical feet. The Pine Bend Brook Trail initially heads to the east then turns toward the south as it gains elevation slowly, often following the route of old logging roads and crossing

The sun sets over Mount Moosilauke between Mounts Tecumseh and Osceola, as seen from partway up the north slide (other route 1).

branches of Pine Bend Brook numerous times. On these lower elevations you pass through a beautiful hemlock forest as you follow the brook.

The trail swings to the right (west) around 1.3 miles in and shortly after makes numerous crossings of various branches of the brook, with the final crossing after a short descent around 1.7 miles in. The trail then swings back toward the left (southwest) and continues climbing at a moderate grade. Just below 2,200 feet in elevation, at 2.1 miles, you pass a sign indicating that you are entering the Sandwich Range Wilderness.

As if in response to this designation, in short order the trail swings left (south) and the real climbing begins. The trail crosses a rocky streambed and heads up along the north side of the valley on very steep and rocky footing. Climb up the side of an old streambed, hopping from one big moss-covered boulder to another. Around 2.5 miles in, the trail turns to the left (east) before turning again toward the south to climb up along a wooded ridge.

Just when you think the steep climb will never end, you pop out onto the Scaur Ridge at 3.0 miles, where the trail completely flattens out. At 3.2 miles the Scaur Ridge Trail comes in from the right (west) and the trail continues for another 0.5 mile along the narrow ridge, with a slight descent followed by a very gradual ascent.

If you don't mind hiking down at night with a headlamp, you can get a great sunset from the top of the North Tripyramid slide.

The final 0.25 mile gets very steep again, climbing almost 500 feet in a short burst. At 4.0 miles you reach the junction with the Mount Tripyramid Trail on the right. The summit is just a few dozen yards farther ahead.

For incredible views, the short steep descent 0.2 mile right (northeast) down the Mount Tripyramid Trail to the top of the North Slide is a must. If you head down the slide a short bit, the views open up even more. You can see Mount Moosilauke in the distance rising up between Mount Tecumseh and Mount Osceola. You also see numerous peaks in the Pemigewasset Wilderness, including the high peaks of the Franconia Range, and the Hancocks much closer to the north, with the obvious bulk of Mount Carrigain just to the right of these. Far to the northeast are the high peaks of the Presidential Range. From the actual summit of North Tripyramid you can get a decent view from a short side path.

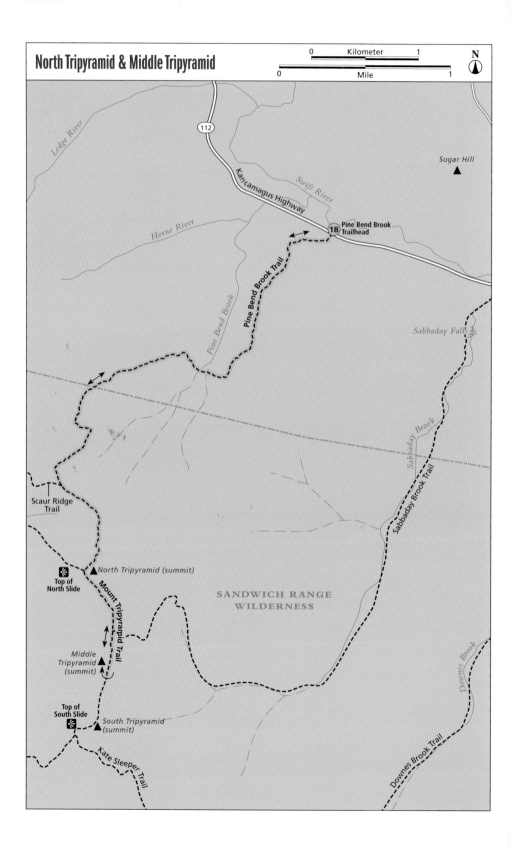

North Tripyramid & Middle Tripyramid

0   Kilometer   1

0   Mile   1

N

Ledge River

112

Sugar Hill

Kancamagus Highway

Swift River

Horne River

Pine Bend Brook Trailhead

18

Pine Bend Brook Trail

Pine Bend Brook

Sabbaday Falls

Sabbaday Brook

Sabbaday Brook Trail

Scaur Ridge Trail

North Tripyramid (summit)

Top of North Slide

Mount Tripyramid Trail

SANDWICH RANGE WILDERNESS

Middle Tripyramid (summit)

Downes Brook

Top of South Slide

South Tripyramid (summit)

Kate Sleeper Trail

Downes Brook Trail

From the junction of the Pine Bend Brook and Mount Tripyramid Trails, head left (southeast) down off the summit of North Tripyramid, where a 0.5-mile 300-foot descent to the col between North Tripyramid and Middle Tripyramid takes you to the junction with the Sabbaday Brook Trail on the left at 4.5 miles. A short but steep ascent south along the Mount Tripyramid Trail takes you to the summit of Middle Tripyramid, the other official 4,000-footer on the ridge, at 4.8 miles. Just before the summit you get a view to the west of Waterville Valley and Mount Moosilauke beyond, and from the summit a ledge provides a nice view to the east. You can see the rocky summit of Mount Chocorua, with Mount Passaconaway and Mount Whiteface very close to the southeast. For more nice views, another 0.6 mile takes you to the summit of South Tripyramid with the top of the South Slide just beyond, providing a unique vista to the south.

From the summit of Middle Tripyramid, head back to North Tripyramid and down Pine Bend Brook Trail to return to the parking area.

Miles and Directions

0.0   Follow the Pine Bend Brook Trail from the parking area on the Kancamagus Highway.

1.5–1.7   Cross numerous branches of Pine Bend Brook. (There are numerous crossings before this as well.)

1.7   Take a sharp turn to the left (west) and begin to climb more.

2.1   Enter the Sandwich Range Wilderness.

2.2   Cross a streambed and begin to ascend more steeply.

3.2   Reach the junction with the Scaur Ridge Trail. Stay left (southeast) on the Pine Bend Brook Trail.

4.0   Reach the summit of North Peak. Just ahead, reach the junction with the trail from North Slide. (Head right down this trail for a few hundred feet to get incredible views from the top of the North Slide.) At the junction near the summit, head left (south) on the Mount Tripyramid Trail toward Middle Tripyramid.

4.5   Pass the Sabbaday Brook Trail on the left; continue on the Mount Tripyramid Trail.

4.8   Reach the summit of Middle Tripyramid. (**Option:** For more good views, continue another 0.6 mile over South Tripyramid to the top of South Slide.) Retrace your route to the trailhead.

9.6   Arrive back at the parking area.

Other Routes

1.   Tripyramids Loop up North Slide, down South Slide (bonus hike 5)—distance: 11.1 miles; elevation gain: 3,200 feet

2.   Sabbaday Brook Trail out-and-back: Sabbaday Brook Trail to Mount Tripyramid Trail (south to Middle Tripyramid, north to North Tripyramid, then back south to Sabbaday Brook Trail)—distance: 11.4 miles; elevation gain: 3,300 feet

3.   Sabbaday Brook Trail to Mount Tripyramid Trail (south to Middle Tripyramid, north to North Tripyramid) to Pine Bend Brook Trail then road walk on the Kancamagus Highway—distance: 11.1 miles; elevation gain: 3,250 feet

19 Mount Whiteface and Mount Passaconaway

This hike up Mount Whiteface over to Mount Passaconaway and down through The Bowl takes you up and over steep ledges, around a dramatic ridge, and through an old-growth forest. Because these are the southernmost of New Hampshire's 4,000-footers, they afford truly exceptional views and allow you to see down to the lakes region and provide an interesting perspective of the White Mountains to the north.

Distance: 13.0-mile double loop (includes trip to north overlook off Mount Passaconaway)
Summit elevation: Mount Whiteface, 4,020 feet; Mount Passaconaway, 4,043 feet
4,000-footers rank: Mount Whiteface, 45; Mount Passaconaway, 42
Elevation gain: 4,600 feet (includes spur to north overlook off Mount Passaconaway)
Difficulty: Moderate to difficult; some ledge scrambling
Hiking time: About 7 hours

Trails used: Blueberry Ledge Trail, Rollins Trail, Dicey's Mill Trail, East Loop, Walden Trail, spur to north overlook
Views: Excellent from south ledges on Mount Whiteface and north overlook from Mount Passaconaway; no views from summits
Canine compatibility: Good, but there's a tough ledge scramble on Mount Whiteface on the Blueberry Ledge Trail.
Special considerations: This route passes through private property and involves a bit of road walking, so be respectful and don't wander off-route.

Finding the trailhead: *From I-93 (from the south),* take exit 24 and turn right onto NH 25 East. In 4.5 miles turn left onto NH 113, and in 11.7 miles turn left to stay on NH 113 East. In 3.7 miles stay straight and continue onto NH 113A. In 6.7 miles go straight/left onto Ferncroft Road where NH 113A makes a sharp turn to the right. In 0.5 mile turn right to park at the Ferncroft Trailhead parking lot, just 0.1 mile ahead. *From I-93 (from the north),* take exit 25 and turn left onto NH 175A East, which becomes NH 175 South. In 5.2 miles turn left onto US 3 South and in 1.1 miles turn left onto NH 113. In 11.7 miles turn left to stay on NH 113 East. In 3.7 miles stay straight and continue onto NH 113A. In 6.7 miles go straight/left onto Ferncroft Road where NH 113A makes a sharp turn to the right. In 0.5 miles turn right to park at the Ferncroft Trailhead parking lot, just 0.1 mile ahead. *From NH 16,* turn (left from the south, right from the north) onto NH 113 West in the town of Chocorua. Follow this for 1.1 mile and turn right onto Gardner Hill Road. In 1.8 miles turn right onto NH 113A East, and in 5.6 miles turn right onto Ferncroft Road. In 0.5 mile turn right to park at the Ferncroft Trailhead parking lot, just 0.1 mile ahead. *Note:* Directions to the trailhead are provided in "The Hike" section below. **GPS:** N43 54.85' / W71 21.45'

The Hike

This natural loop hike has a bit of everything and summits the southernmost two of New Hampshire's 4,000-footers. You get to climb open slabs with views, hoist yourself up dramatic ledges, traverse a stunning ridgeline, and descend one of the few

Mount Washington can be seen in the distance from the ledges near the summit of Mount Whiteface.

forests in the region that has never been logged. The Bowl Research Natural Area encompasses a 1,556-acre watershed of virgin forest, which itself is completely surrounded by the Sandwich Range Wilderness. Due to the location, this hike has a very different feel than many others in this guide, offering unique views and a different type of ruggedness.

A bit of road walking begins this hike, and as you will be traveling through private property, it is very important to be respectful by parking at the Ferncroft Trailhead and staying on the road. From the parking lot, head back down the curving road, then go right on Ferncroft Road. At 0.3 mile from the parking area, turn left to cross Squirrel Bridge. Follow a gravel road (signed) before the trail heads off to the left at 0.5 mile from the parking. Stay straight as the Pasture Path comes in from the left (south); pass the Blueberry Ledge Cutoff on the right at 0.6 mile and enter the Sandwich Range Wilderness.

Over the next 1.0 mile the trail is very flat, but as you start to climb and head in a more northeasterly direction, you reach the first ledge at 1.6 miles. These open ledges are covered with myriad lichen as maple and pine trees grasp the rock, seemingly growing out of nothing. In late summer or early fall, you may be lucky enough to find some nice blueberries.

At 2.0 miles the Blueberry Ledge Cutoff comes in on the right and the grade of the climb lessons. Back in the woods, the trail eventually steepens, with a good climb up to a crest around 3.0 miles in; at 3.2 miles the Tom Wiggin Trail comes in from the right (east). After another short crest, the trail becomes very steep. Starting around 3.5 miles, you are rewarded with incredible views off steep ledges as you climb the rock slabs. If it's wet, this can be dangerous, so take your time and use your hands when needed.

Just as you near 4,000 feet in elevation, the climb relents. After a turn to the left, climb the rocky ledge on the left for expansive views from the south summit of Mount Whiteface at 3.9 miles. Since the true summit does not have a view, treat yourself to a break and enjoy the best vista on the mountain. You can see the distinct shape of Mount Chocorua to the east and Mount Passaconaway across The Bowl to the northeast. As this is the southernmost 4,000-footer, you can even see big Squam Lake and even bigger Lake Winnipesaukee to the south.

Climb off the ledge. The McCrillis Trail comes in from the left (west). Take the Rollins Trail straight (northwest) as you begin to follow the ridge that joins Mount Whiteface and Mount Passaconaway and surrounds The Bowl. Pass the junction with the Kate Sleeper Trail on the left at 4.0 miles, and at 4.2 miles reach the true summit of Mount Whiteface, marked by a small rock cairn.

The Rollins Trail continues with several difficult sections as it stays along the ridge. There are a few nice views into The Bowl. After a short climb around 5.0 miles, the trail makes a few turns as it descends fairly steeply to the col between Mount Whiteface and Mount Passaconaway. A rolling traverse of the col followed by a short climb over the shoulder of Mount Passaconaway takes you to the junction with Dicey's Mill Trail at 6.4 miles.

Turn left to follow Dicey's Mill Trail north toward Mount Passaconaway, reaching the junction with East Loop at 6.6 miles. For a nice loop of the summit, continue straight/right (east) on East Loop; at the junction with the Walden Trail at 6.8 miles, head left (north) and follow the Walden Trail toward the summit at 7.4 miles. You pass a nice outlook to the east, and just before reaching the true summit, a signed spur trail on the right takes you down 200 vertical feet in 0.3 mile to an incredible northward-looking view at 7.7 miles.

From here you can see many of the biggest peaks in the region, from the Tripyramids to the left (west); most of the peaks in the Pemigewasset Wilderness to the north, including Mount Carrigain straight ahead; and the dramatic peaks of the Presidential Range farther to the northeast.

Climb back up the spur trail, turn right, and in a few hundred feet reach the junction with Dicey's Mill Trail. A spur to the left takes you to the true summit at 8.0 miles, marked by a rock cairn. Mount Passaconaway's interesting name comes from a chief of the Penacook tribe who lived in the region during the seventeenth century.

Continue on Dicey's Mill Trail as it switchbacks down the summit cone, reaching the junction with East Loop at 8.7 miles on the left and Rollins Trail at 8.9 miles on the right. Stay straight and follow Dicey's Mill Trail through The Bowl, fairly steeply at first then becoming more gradual before crossing a stream at 10.3 miles and passing

Mount Chocorua is easily recognizable from the steep ledges near the top of the Blueberry Ledge Trail.

the junction with the Tom Wiggin Trail on the right at 10.7 miles. At 11.8 miles you leave the wilderness and pass a path with a bridge over the river on the right to the Blueberry Ledge Cutoff. At 12.6 miles you reach the road; follow this back to the parking area at 13.0 miles.

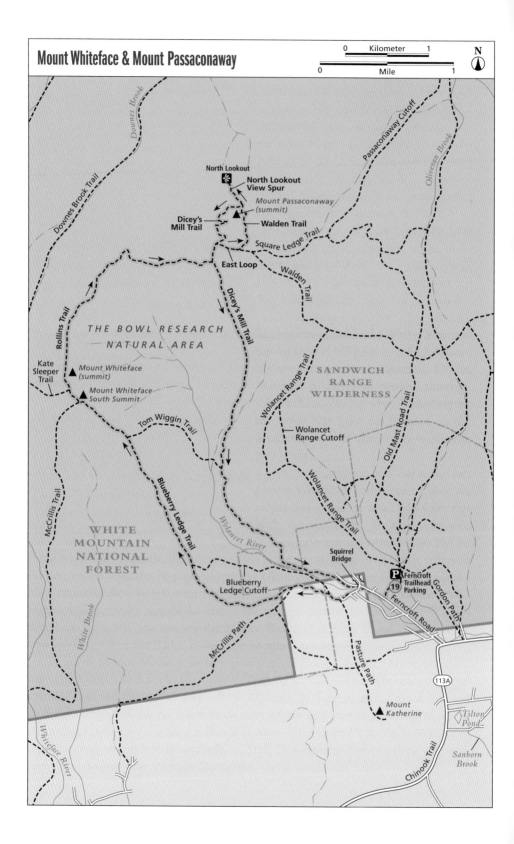

Mount Whiteface & Mount Passaconaway

0   Kilometer   1

0   Mile   1

N

North Lookout

North Lookout
View Spur

Mount Passaconaway
(summit)

Dicey's
Mill Trail

Walden Trail

Square Ledge Trail

East Loop

Walden Trail

Downes Brook

Passaconaway Cutoff

Oliverian Brook

Downes Brook Trail

Rollins Trail

THE BOWL RESEARCH
NATURAL AREA

Dicey's Mill Trail

Kate
Sleeper
Trail

Mount Whiteface
(summit)

Mount Whiteface
South Summit

Tom Wiggin Trail

McCrillis Trail

Wolancet Range Trail

SANDWICH
RANGE
WILDERNESS

Old Mast Road Trail

Wolancet
Range Cutoff

Wolancet Range Trail

Blueberry Ledge Trail

WHITE
MOUNTAIN
NATIONAL
FOREST

Wolancet River

Squirrel
Bridge

P Ferncroft
Trailhead
Parking
19

Gordon Path

Blueberry
Ledge Cutoff

White Brook

McCrillis Path

Ferncroft Road

Pasture Path

Mount
Katherine

113A

Tilton
Pond

Whiteface River

Chinook Trail

Sanborn
Brook

Miles and Directions

0.0 Start from the Ferncroft Trailhead and head back down the road.

0.1 Turn right onto Ferncroft Road

0.3 Turn left to cross Squirrel Bridge at the sign for Blueberry Ledge Trail.

0.5 Stay straight/right as Pasture Path enters from the left (south).

0.6 Stay straight/left as the Blueberry Ledge cutoff enters from the right (east).

0.9 Stay straight/right as McCrillis Path enters from the left (southwest).

2.0 Stay on Blueberry Ledge Trail as the Blueberry Ledge Cutoff enters from the right.

3.2 Reach the junction with the Tom Wiggin Trail. Continue straight on the Blueberry Ledge Trail.

3.6 Reach the first open ledge.

3.8 Reach a nice open ledge with a view to The Bowl.

3.9 Reach the south summit and junction of the Rollins and McCrillis Trails. Head straight (north) on the Rollins Trail.

4.0 Go straight (north), past the Kate Sleeper Trail on the left.

4.2 Reach the summit of Mount Whiteface; continue on the Rollins Trail.

6.4 At the junction turn left (north) onto the Dicey's Mill Trail.

6.6 Stay straight/right (east) onto the East Loop.

6.8 Turn left (northeast) at the junction onto the Walden Trail.

7.4 Turn right (north) onto the North Lookout spur trail near the summit of Passaconaway.

7.7 Reach North Lookout.

8.0 Return to the summit area. Turn right (west) onto the Walden Trail, and at the junction with the Dicey's Mill Trail, follow the short spur left to the true summit.

8.7 Take the Dicey's Mill Trail down from the summit cone. Stay right at the junction with East Loop.

8.9 Pass the junction with the Rollins Trail on the right, continuing on the Dicey's Mill Trail.

10.3 Cross a stream.

10.7 Pass the junction with the Tom Wiggin Trail on the right.

11.8 Leave the wilderness and pass the connector trail to Blueberry Ledge Cutoff on the right.

12.6 Reach the road; continue straight (southeast).

13.0 Arrive back at the parking area.

Other Routes

1. Wonalancet Range Trail to Walden Trail to Dicey's Mill Trail to Rollins Trail to Blueberry Ledge Trail to Tom Wiggin Trail to Dicey's Mill Trail to Ferncroft Road—distance: 12.6 miles; elevation gain: 5,050 feet

2. Mount Whiteface only: Ferncroft Road to Blueberry Ledge Cutoff to Blueberry Ledge Trail to Rollins Trail (turnaround) to Blueberry Ledge Trail to Tom Wiggin Trail to Dicey's Mill Trail to Ferncroft Road—distance: 8.5 miles; elevation gain: 3,100 feet

3. Mount Passaconaway only: out and back on Dicey's Mill Trail—distance: 9.8 miles; elevation gain: 3,050 feet

The Presidential Range and Mount Isolation

Hikers climb up the steepest part of the Tuckerman Ravine Trail from the base of the headwall.

20 Mount Jackson (with Mount Webster Loop)

Though the shortest in stature of the Presidential Range 4,000-footers, Mount Jackson rises high above Crawford Notch, providing outstanding views in all directions. With spurs to nice overlooks, a high elevation forested ridge-walk, 360-degree views from the summit, a clifftop overlook from Mount Webster, and a nice waterfall and pool, this short hike packs a big punch and is a great entrance to hiking in the Presidential Range.

Distance: 6.5-mile lollipop loop
Summit elevation: Mount Jackson, 4,052 feet; Mount Webster, 3,910 feet
4,000-footers rank: 39
Elevation gain: 2,500 feet
Difficulty: Moderate
Hiking time: About 4 hours

Trails used: Webster-Jackson Trail (Jackson and Webster branches), Webster Cliff Trail, Elephant Head Spur Trail (optional)
Views: Excellent
Canine compatibility: Good, with one steep ledgy section coming off Mount Jackson

Finding the trailhead: *From the junction of US 302 and US 3 in Twin Mountain/Carroll,* follow US 302 East for 8.7 miles. Parking is on the right just past Saco Lake and right before the sign for Crawford Notch State Park. The trailhead is across the road. *From the junction of US 302 and NH 16 in Glen,* follow US 302 West for 20.3 miles. Parking is on the left just after you pop out of the notch at the top of the hill. If you pass Saco Lake on the right, you have gone too far. The trailhead is across from the parking area. **GPS:** N44 12.90' / W71 24.50'

The Hike

Named for Charles T. Jackson, a geologist who was responsible for the first geological survey of New Hampshire, Mount Jackson is the only official 4,000-foot peak in the range that is not named for a US President.

The Webster-Jackson Trail begins climbing right from the outset. Typical of hikes in the range, much of the footing requires climbing up steep sections of weathered rocks alternating with sections of nice dirt trail and bedrock slabs. At 0.1 mile you reach the junction with the spur to Elephant Head on the right. If you have the time, this short 0.25-mile spur takes you to an outstanding clifftop view right above the narrow Gateway entrance to Crawford Notch State Park. The hike to Elephant Head is a great option for those with just an hour to spare or for young intrepid hikers not yet ready for a longer adventure.

Continue up the trail, which goes another 0.1 mile along Elephant Head Brook then heads right (southeast) as it contours up the side of the mountain. At 0.6 mile a short spur on the right leads to Bugle Cliff, a dramatic overlook above Crawford Notch with a good view of the railroad tracks on the west side of the notch above the road.

A sign atop Mount Jackson lets you know you're on the Appalachian Trail.

On the northern side of this trail, extending toward Mount Clinton Road, lies an old forest of red spruce that somehow avoided the extensive logging of the White Mountains that began in the late 1870s. Keep your eye out for these trees as well as fine old yellow birch specimens on the lower portion of the hike to get a glimpse into the past, when mature trees dominated a virgin forest.

At 0.9 mile you pass over Flume Cascade Brook. The big falls on the lowest part of this brook are visible from US 302 and are a popular tourist attraction. Continue to contour up the slope, alternating between relatively smooth sections and steep rocky sections with a few short drops until you reach the junction where the Webster-Jackson trail splits into two branches. Take the trail to the left (east) and climb up along Silver Cascade Brook, crossing three small branches at 1.8 miles, eventually turning southeast toward the summit of Mount Jackson.

As you near the summit, the trail turns first to the north and then zigzags to the east near a fir wave. There are some short sections where you may need to use your hands to scramble over the rocks. Pop out onto the broad, mostly open slabs that signify you're almost at the top, and at 2.6 miles reach the summit and the junction with the Webster Cliff Trail, which is also the Appalachian Trail.

Although the summit isn't above tree line, the open ledges provide great views to the south and west. By following the Webster Cliff Trail left (north) for 100 yards or so, you get a fantastic view north along the ridge to the higher peaks. You can

A brief squall creates a nice rainbow over Mount Crawford, as seen from Mount Jackson.

see Mizpah Hut, tucked under Mount Pierce, and the whole southern Presidential Range and even Mount Jefferson poking up behind Mount Eisenhower. The Boott Spur extends off to the right (east) from Mount Washington. The Presidential Range–Dry River Wilderness abuts the entire eastern side of Mount Jackson, with Mount Isolation and the Montalban Ridge visible to the east.

Directly to the south you can see the Sandwich Range and Mount Carrigain. Across Crawford Notch and Saco River Valley, Mounts Tom, Field, and Willey rise up to the west, with most of the major peaks in the Pemigewasset Wilderness visible beyond.

If you are just interested in bagging Mount Jackson, head back down the way you came for a total hike of 5.2 miles. However, the lollipop loop over to Mount Webster and back down adds only 1.3 miles and makes for a much more compelling journey when the weather is decent.

Head right (south) on the Webster Cliff Trail (also the Appalachian Trail) and quickly descend a short series of steep rock ledges. The trail follows the ridge then dips off the northeast side as it travels through beautiful high-elevation forest, crossing a few moss-covered, boggy areas. Reach the saddle at 3.6 miles (1.0 mile from the Mount Jackson summit) then climb an easy 0.3 mile to reach the Webster branch of

Mount Jackson (with Mount Webster Loop)

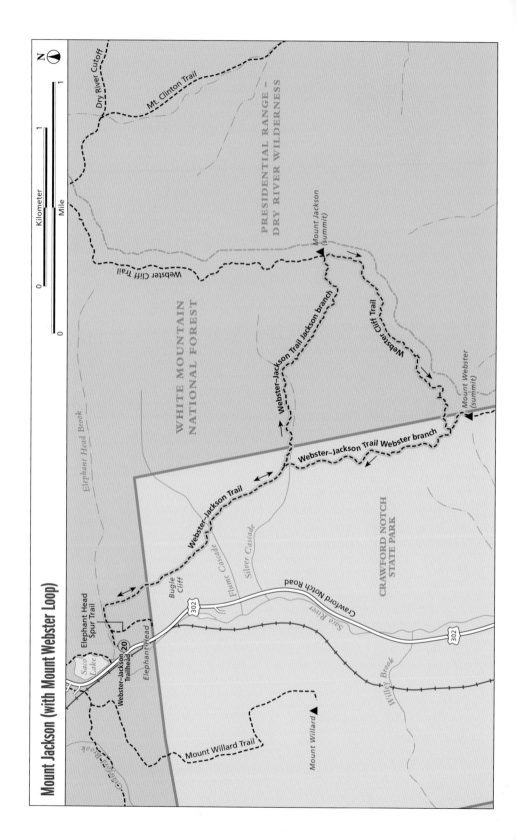

N

Kilometer

Mile

PRESIDENTIAL RANGE –
DRY RIVER WILDERNESS

WHITE MOUNTAIN
NATIONAL FOREST

CRAWFORD NOTCH
STATE PARK

Dry River Cutoff

Mt. Clinton Trail

Webster Cliff Trail

Mount Jackson
(summit)

Webster–Jackson Trail Jackson branch

Webster Cliff Trail

Mount Webster
(summit)

Webster–Jackson Trail Webster branch

Webster–Jackson Trail

Elephant Head Brook

Bugle Cliff

Flume Cascade

Silver Cascade

Crawford Notch Road

Saco River

302

Elephant Head
Spur Trail

Elephant Head

Webster–Jackson
Trailhead

20

Saco
Lake

Mount Willard Trail

Mount Willard

Willey Brook

302

the Webster-Jackson Trail. Continue straight/left (south) on the Webster Cliff Trail to reach the summit and the dramatic clifftop perch on Mount Webster.

Turn around and head north, back up the trail, and at the junction turn left (north) down the Webster branch of the Webster-Jackson Trail. This is a steep, rocky, rooty, and often very wet section of trail, so take your time. At 5.1 miles (1.0 mile from junction), cross Silver Cascade Brook next to a beautiful waterfall and pool. This brook plunges down the valley, with beautiful cascades visible from US 302. A short steep climb of 50 feet takes you to the junction with the other branch of the Webster-Jackson Trail. Head left (northwest) back down to the road.

Miles and Directions

0.0 Start hiking up the Webster-Jackson Trail from the trailhead on the east side of NH 302

0.1 Reach the junction of the 0.25-mile side trail to Elephant Head on the right. (Well worth the trip, with incredible views down the notch.)

0.6 Reach the junction with the short spur to Bugle Cliff on the right.

0.9 Cross Flume Cascade Brook.

1.4 Reach the trail junction of the two Webster-Jackson Trail branches. Stay to the left and follow the Jackson branch of the Webster-Jackson Trail to the east.

1.8 Begin the ascent (southeast), away from the stream.

2.6 Reach the summit of Mount Jackson. To get to Mount Webster, turn right (south) onto the Webster Cliff Trail.

3.6 Cross a low point between peaks.

3.9 Head straight/left at the junction with the Webster branch of the Webster-Jackson Trail on a short spur to the summit of Mount Webster.

4.0 Reach the summit of Mount Webster. Turn around and head back (northwest) to the junction with the Webster-Jackson Trail.

4.1 Head left (northwest) at the junction to descend the Webster branch of the Webster-Jackson Trail.

5.1 Cross Silver Cascade Brook, with a nice pool and waterfall. The junction with the Jackson branch of the Webster-Jackson Trail is just over the rise on the other side of the stream. Turn left (northwest) to follow the Webster-Jackson Trail back to the trailhead.

6.5 Arrive back at the trailhead.

Other Routes

1. Webster-Jackson Trail to Webster-Jackson Trail (Jackson branch) out-and-back—distance: 5.2 miles; elevation gain: 2,550 feet

2. Presidential Traverse (full) (hike 33)—distance: 22.9 miles; elevation gain: 10,050 feet

3. Mount Monroe to Mount Jackson point-to-point (bonus hike 7)—distance: 12.5 miles; elevation gain: 4,650 feet

21 | Mount Pierce

Mount Pierce is an unassuming rounded summit on the southern arm of the Presidential Range. You get beautiful views accessed by a relatively moderate hike up the Crawford Path, one of the most historically important trails in the White Mountains. An optional loop to Mizpah Spring Hut adds a hundred feet of climbing and 0.25 mile to the hike.

Distance: 6.4 miles out and back
Summit elevation: 4,312 feet
4,000-footers rank: 27
Elevation gain: 2,400 feet
Difficulty: Moderate
Hiking time: About 4.5 hours

Trails used: Crawford Connector, Crawford Path, Webster Cliff Trail
Views: Excellent
Canine compatibility: Good
Special considerations: The last 0.1 mile can be difficult to find in winter; use GPS.

Finding the trailhead: *From the junction of US 302 and US 3 in Twin Mountain/Carroll,* follow US 302 East for 8.2 miles. Turn left onto Mount Clinton Road just before a big curve in the road and the AMC Highland Center. The parking lot is on the left in 0.1 mile. *From the junction of US 302 and NH 16 in Glen,* follow US 302 West for 20.8 miles. Turn right onto Mount Clinton Road, which is just past the entrance to the AMC Highland Center. The parking lot is on the left in 0.1 mile. **GPS:** N44 13.42' / W71 24.68'

The Hike

Although Franklin Pierce may not be one of the most instantly recognizable of the US presidents, it makes sense that a mountain in the Presidential Range is named for the fourteenth president, a native of New Hampshire. The hike starts from the parking lot on Mount Clinton Road, using the Crawford Connector, because there is no parking for day hikers at the AMC Highland Center, the actual terminus of the Crawford Path, unless you are a paying guest.

The Crawford Connector starts at the end of the parking area. Almost immediately, cross the Mount Clinton Road and make a gentle ascent to the southeast. Since the trail begins at almost 2,000 feet, the first part of your hike takes you through a typical transition zone where the mixed hardwood forest has begun to give way to one of birch, fir, and spruce. At 0.4 mile the trail, in quick succession, passes the spur trail to Crawford Cliff, crosses Gibbs Brook, and intersects the Crawford Path. Head left at this junction to follow the Crawford Path up along Gibbs Brook to the northeast.

At 0.6 mile a short spur trail leads to a nice view of Gibbs Falls. Just past this junction you enter the Gibbs Brook Scenic Area. Along the way in this lower section you will see outstanding examples of old-growth forest that somehow escaped the

The Crawford Path, from higher up on the ridge, provides a nice view down to Mount Pierce.

logging of previous centuries. You may see some massively wide yellow birch, red spruce, and balsam fir. Gibbs Brook Scenic Area, created in 1961, is 900 acres and provides a glimpse into what the forest may have looked like before settlement, logging, and development. Keep your eye out for spruce grouse and black-backed woodpeckers here. You will be inside the Gibbs Brook Scenic Area for the next 0.75 mile.

The trail climbs fairly consistently and moderately as it follows high above Gibbs Brook, beginning to veer away to the south at 1.5 miles. At 1.9 miles you reach the junction of the Mizpah Cutoff. Continue left (northeast) on the Crawford Path as it contours up the slopes below the summit cone of Mount Pierce. As the size of the trees shrink, you begin to get glimpses of Mount Washington and Mount Eisenhower. The trail levels out just before you reach the junction of the Crawford Path and the Webster Cliff Trail at 3.1 miles. Turn right (south) onto the Webster Cliff Trail and reach the summit at 3.2 miles.

Looking north from the summit you can see Mount Washington, with Mount Eisenhower jutting up nearby. Just to the left of Mount Eisenhower, Mount Jefferson rises high in the distance. Many peaks are visible to the south, with Mount Passaconaway and Mount Whiteface due south and Mount Carrigan just to the west. The ridgeline of Mounts Tom, Field, and Willey are obvious across Crawford Notch to

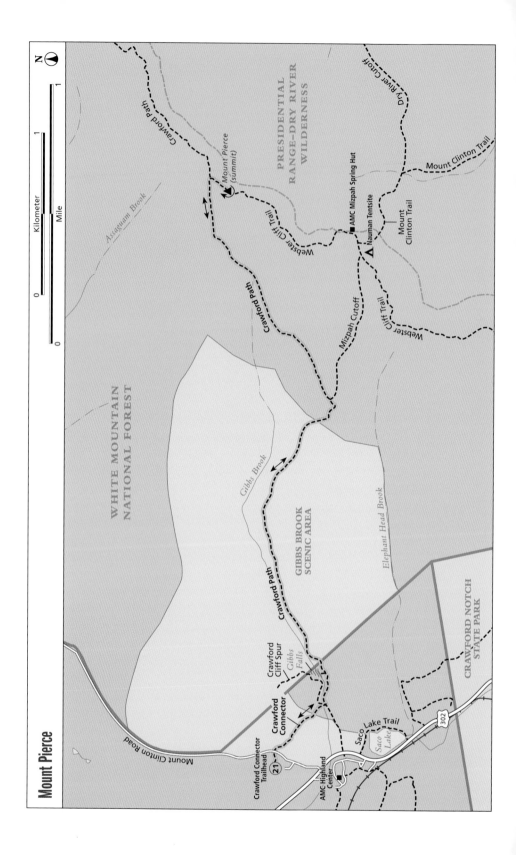

Mount Pierce

WHITE MOUNTAIN NATIONAL FOREST

PRESIDENTIAL RANGE-DRY RIVER WILDERNESS

GIBBS BROOK SCENIC AREA

CRAWFORD NOTCH STATE PARK

Crawford Path

Mount Pierce (summit)

Assaquam Brook

Webster Cliff Trail

AMC Mizpah Spring Hut

Nauman Tentsite

Mount Clinton Trail

Mount Clinton Trail

Dry River Cutoff

Mizpah Cutoff

Webster Cliff Trail

Cliff Trail

Crawford Path

Gibbs Brook

Elephant Head Brook

Crawford Cliff Spur

Gibbs Falls

Crawford Connector

Crawford Path

Saco Lake Trail

Saco Lake

302

Mount Clinton Road

Crawford Connector Trailhead

21

AMC Highland Center

N

Kilometer

Mile

0   1

0   1

the southeast, and beyond you can just catch the tops of some of the higher peaks in the Pemigewasset Wilderness.

Return back down the Crawford Path. (You can also make a slightly longer loop by following the Webster Cliff Trail south past the AMC Mizpah Spring Hut to the Mizpah Cutoff, which intersects the lower portion of the Crawford Path, as noted in "Other Routes" below.)

Miles and Directions

0.0 Start at the parking lot on the Crawford Connector and quickly cross Mount Clinton Road.

0.4 Pass the spur trail on the left to Crawford Cliff. Cross the bridge over Gibbs Brook and join the Crawford Path; turn left (west) onto the Crawford Path.

0.6 Reach the junction of the short spur trail to a viewpoint overlooking Gibbs Falls.

1.9 Reach the junction with the Mizpah Cutoff. Head straight/left (northeast) staying on the Crawford Path.

3.1 Take a sharp right (south) at the junction with the Webster Cliff Trail.

3.2 Reach the summit of Mount Pierce. Turn around, following same route back to the trailhead. (**Option:** Continue straight/south to the Mizpah Hut then take the Mizpah Cutoff back to Crawford Path for a slightly longer loop.)

6.4 Arrive back at the parking lot.

Other Routes

1. Crawford Connector to Crawford Path to Webster Cliff Trail to Mizpah Cutoff to Crawford Path to Crawford Connector—distance: 6.6 miles; elevation gain: 2,600 feet

2. Pierce and Eisenhower out-and-back (bonus hike 6)—distance: 9.6 miles; elevation gain: 3,700 feet

3. Pierce and Eisenhower Loop: Crawford Connector to Crawford Path to Webster Cliff Trail to Crawford Path to Mount Eisenhower Loop to Edmands Path to Mount Clinton Road (road walk)—distance: 10.5 miles; elevation gain: 3,400 feet

4. Presidential Traverse (full) (hike 33)—distance: 22.9 miles; elevation gain: 10,050 feet

5. Mount Monroe to Mount Jackson (bonus hike 7)—distance: 12.5 miles; elevation gain: 4,650 feet

22 Mount Eisenhower

This classic route in the southern Presidentials takes you up a historic trail to a giant domed peak with 360-degree views, and is a straightforward day hike. This is the lowest peak in the Presidential Range that still rises high enough to extend into the true alpine zone. The reward-to-work ratio is high for this hike.

Distance: 6.6 miles out and back
Summit elevation: 4,760 feet
4,000-footers rank: 12
Elevation gain: 2,900 feet
Difficulty: Moderate

Hiking time: About 4.5 hours
Trails used: Edmands Path, Mount Eisenhower Loop
Views: Excellent
Canine compatibility: Good

Finding the trailhead: *From the junction of US 302 and US 3 in Twin Mountain/Carroll,* follow US 302 East for 4.4 miles. Turn left onto Base Station Road; you'll see a sign for the cog railway. In 4.5 miles turn right onto Mount Clinton Road; the parking lot is on the left in 1.3 miles. *From the junction of US 302 and NH 16 in Glen,* follow US 302 West for 20.8 miles. Turn right onto Mount Clinton road, just past the entrance to the AMC Highland Center. The parking lot is on the right in 2.3 miles. **GPS: N44 14.93' / W71 23.48'**

The Hike

Built under the direction of J. Rayner Edmands in 1909, Edmands Path remains mostly unchanged since its creation, showcasing trail-building at its finest. Although this trail is by no means easy, it nonetheless shows how a well-built trail that focuses on a consistent grade can withstand the test of time. Only the final section of the hike is above tree line, and with views in every direction from the bald, sloping summit, this hike makes for an extremely rewarding adventure that fit individuals can do in an afternoon.

When the trail was originally built, well before Eisenhower became president, the mountain was named Mount Pleasant. An effort led by Sherman Adams, a New Hampshire native who was Eisenhower's chief of staff, got the name changed to Mount Eisenhower. He is the most modern president to have a peak named for him in the White Mountains.

From the trailhead, which is right around 2,000 feet in elevation, Edmands Path begins as a gentle walk through a hardwood forest. In just under 0.4 mile, cross Abenaki Brook on a small bridge, after which the trail begins to turn upward. This forest is filled with fine examples of beautiful yellow birch. At about 1.0 mile the trail begins to steepen, and at 1.2 miles (around 2,600 feet) the real climbing begins. Along the way, be sure to admire the nice trail work, including numerous examples of stone steps.

Hikers descend heading north off the summit on the Mount Eisenhower Loop.

Above this point, most of the hardwoods are gone and the typical high elevation boreal forest of spruce and fir trees dominates along the trail. Over the next mile, from 1.2 to 2.2 miles, you climb 1,300 feet in elevation. Along the way there are numerous spots where the bare bedrock is visible due to years of erosion. When wet, these slabby sections may take extra care to traverse safely.

Hikers make the final ascent along Edmands Path.

At 2.5 miles you cross a small streambed, which you follow for a short while before the trail finally begins to relent as it contours to the northeast before popping around a ridge to head east. Shortly after, the small stunted trees become small enough to allow nice views to the north and northeast, where Mount Franklin (not an official 4,000-footer) is visible just ahead with Mount Jefferson rising to the north. Although the trail levels out just below tree line, care should be taken as you cross a rocky talus slope, which can be very slippery with ice or a little snow.

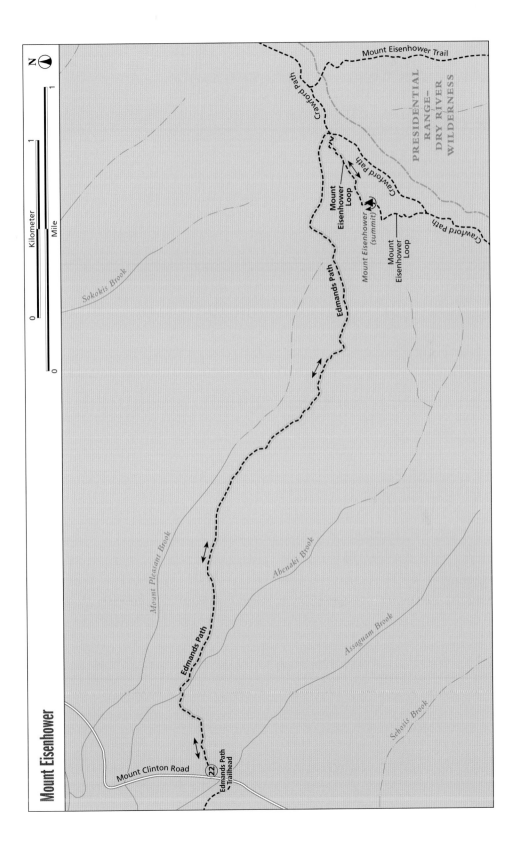

Mount Eisenhower

N

Kilometer

Mile

Mount Eisenhower Trail

Crawford Path

PRESENTIAL RANGE- DRY RIVER WILDERNESS

Mount Eisenhower Loop

Crawford Path

Mount Eisenhower (summit)

Mount Eisenhower Loop

Crawford Path

Edmands Path

Sokokis Brook

Mount Pleasant Brook

Edmands Path

Abenaki Brook

Assaquam Brook

Sebosis Brook

Mount Clinton Road

22

Edmands Path Trailhead

At 2.9 miles reach the junction with the Eisenhower Loop. Just beyond is the junction with the Crawford Path (also the Appalachian Trail), which heads north to Mount Washington and south to the northern end of Crawford Notch. To maintain a reasonable grade, the Crawford Path does not summit Mount Eisenhower (or Mount Monroe to the north), so at the junction turn right (southwest) onto the Eisenhower Loop.

From this point the trail remains above tree line, climbing the northeast side of the evenly shaped summit dome. Head past a small boggy area then switchback a few times before following the ridge to the southwest on the final leg to the summit. Reach the giant rock cairn marking the summit at 3.3 miles.

Looking north you will see Mount Franklin nearby, with the giant Mount Washington looming above everything farther north. Mount Jefferson is easily visible as well, and turning around you can see Mount Pierce and Mount Jackson south along the ridge. The incredibly rugged and remote Presidential Range–Dry River Wilderness lies to the east and south, with Mount Isolation clearly visible, if you know what to look for. Across the Saco River Valley to the southwest, you can make out the distinctive shape of Mount Carrigain.

As the summit is so wide open, it's tempting to walk around, but please stay on the trail to avoid damaging the fragile alpine vegetation. You can continue down the other side of the loop trail for a short bit to get better views to the south and east. Retrace your steps and take Edmands Path back down to the parking area.

Miles and Directions

- **0.0**   Start from the parking area on Mount Clinton Road and follow Edmands Path.
- **0.4**   Cross the bridge over Abenaki Brook.
- **2.5**   Reach a small stream flowing over ledges.
- **2.9**   Turn right onto the Mount Eisenhower Loop.
- **3.3**   Reach the summit of Mount Eisenhower. Return the way you came.
- **6.6**   Arrive back at the parking area.

Other Routes

1. Pierce and Eisenhower out-and-back (bonus hike 6)—distance: 9.6 miles; elevation gain: 3,700 feet
2. Pierce and Eisenhower Loop: Crawford Connector to Crawford Path to Webster Cliff Trail to Crawford Path to Mount Eisenhower Loop to Edmands Path to Mount Clinton Road (road walk)—distance: 10.5 miles; elevation gain: 3,400 feet
3. Presidential Traverse (full) (hike 33)—distance: 22.9 miles; elevation gain: 10,050 feet
4. Mount Monroe to Mount Jackson (bonus hike 7)—distance: 12.5 miles; elevation gain: 4,650 feet

THE APPALACHIAN TRAIL

Numerous hikes in this book travel along the Appalachian Trail (AT), which goes straight through the White Mountains and includes along its route traverses of the Kinsman, Franconia, Presidential, and Wildcat-Carter-Moriah Ranges.

Approximately 2,200 miles long, the AT runs a continuous path from Springer Mountain in Georgia to the summit of Mount Katahdin in Maine, following the spine of the Appalachian Mountain chain. Along its path the AT travels through Georgia, North Carolina, Tennessee, Virginia, West Virginia, Maryland, Pennsylvania, New Jersey, New York, Connecticut, Massachusetts, Vermont, New Hampshire, and Maine. There are public shelters along the whole route, spaced a day's hike or less apart.

After years of effort, the Appalachian Trail (officially the Appalachian National Scenic Trail) is now protected for almost its entire length through the National Park Service. The NPS has tried to maintain at least a 1,000-foot-wide corridor for the trail, even in populated areas.

In 1948 Earl Shaffer was the first person to hike the entire Appalachian Trail in one straight shot. Every year, thousands of people attempt to hike the AT from end to end and these hardy souls are called "through-hikers." A through-hike usually takes from five to seven months. Hundreds finish every year, and almost 90 percent are "north-bounders," who hike from south to north. The trail is marked with white blazes along its entirety; trails that intersect the Appalachian Trail are marked with blue blazes.

The Appalachian Trail traverses the Presidential Range, although the official route doesn't summit all of the peaks.

23 Mount Monroe and Mount Washington

The Ammonoosuc Ravine Trail to Jewell Trail Loop is a classic hike up Mount Washington. At the top of Ammonoosuc Ravine, a quick out-and-back takes you up Mount Monroe right next to the Lakes of the Clouds Hut. The lakes are gorgeous, and with much of this hike above tree line, the views are extensive. The walk on the Gulfside Trail takes you along the edge of the Great Gulf, one of the most dramatic and impressive ravines in the White Mountains. *Note:* If you just want to summit Mount Monroe, you can go up and down the Ammonoosuc Ravine Trail instead of making the full loop.

Distance: 10.5-mile loop (7.0 miles out and back for Monroe only)
Summit elevation: Mount Monroe, 5,372 feet; Mount Washington, 6,288 feet
4,000-footers rank: Mount Monroe, 4; Mount Washington, 1
Elevation gain: 4,450 feet (2,900 feet if only doing Mount Monroe)
Difficulty: Difficult

Hiking time: About 6.5 hours
Trails used: Ammonoosuc Ravine Trail, Crawford Path, Mount Monroe Loop, Trinity Heights Connector, Gulfside Trail, Jewell Trail
Views: Excellent
Canine compatibility: Good, but tough due to a few steep sections and some stream crossings

Finding the trailhead: *From the junction of US 302 and US 3 in Twin Mountain/Carroll,* follow US 302 East for 4.4 miles. Turn left onto Base Station Road; you'll see a sign for the cog railway. The parking lot for the Ammonoosuc Ravine Trail is on the right in 5.6 miles. *From the junction of US 302 and NH 16 in Glen,* follow US 302 West for 24.6 miles. Turn right onto Base Station Road; you'll see a sign for the cog railway. The parking lot for the Ammonoosuc Ravine Trail is on the right in 5.6 miles. **GPS:** N44 16.03' / W71 21.68'

The Hike

Depending on your time and fitness level, you may want to hike only Mount Monroe. However, by the time you get to Monroe, you're pretty close to Mount Washington, which is why the hike described summits both, making for an aesthetic and rewarding loop. If you just want to climb Mount Monroe, follow the directions from that summit in reverse to head back down the Ammonoosuc Ravine Trail.

This trail is the shortest route to climb both Mount Monroe and Mount Washington from the west side of the range. Although it is possible to start from a higher parking area near the cog railway base station, it saves less than a mile and requires paying (more). For the sake of simplicity, this hike description begins at the actual trailhead for the Ammonoosuc Ravine Trail.

From the parking area, follow the Ammonoosuc Ravine Trail into the woods and climb gently, crossing Franklin Brook at around 0.3 mile and some pipes in the

The Jewell Trail makes a beautiful winding descent down a ridge due west of Mount Clay.

ground shortly after. At about 1.0 mile you begin following the Ammonoosuc River, right where the Ammonoosuc Link to the cog railway base station comes in from the left. The trail climbs gently but steadily, crossing Monroe Brook at 1.7 miles before continuing along the main valley. Shortly after, you will pass by an avalanche track and get your first views up toward the ridge.

At 2.1 miles you cross the Ammonoosuc River at Gem Pool below some beautiful cascades. At this point the trail changes from a gentle walk with occasional rough footing to a steep rocky trail, which starts out with some incredible stone steps. In fact, over the next 0.4 mile you will gain 750 feet in elevation! At 2.3 miles a side path on the right descends a few hundred feet to a cool viewpoint at the foot of the gorge. Continue climbing up the steep trail, crossing a few streams, with another nice view around 2.4 miles. Just beyond, at 2.5 miles, cross the main brook on ledges near the top of a waterfall, with beautiful cascades above as well.

Continue climbing as the grade eases a bit. You cross the streams a few more times. Be careful—the ledges surrounding the streams can be very slippery early in the morning or after a rain. Soon you get a magnificent view of Mount Washington directly above to the northeast as you pop out among the alpine vegetation just below the AMC Lakes of the Clouds Hut (around 5,000 feet in elevation) at 3.1 miles from the trailhead.

To get to the top of Mount Monroe, the peak just to the south of the hut, follow signs for the Crawford Path and take this south for 0.1 mile before reaching the junction with the Mount Monroe Loop on the right. After a gentle start, the trail climbs steeply to the summit ridge, with the true summit at the south end 0.3 mile from the Crawford Path junction and 3.5 miles from the trailhead.

The views from the summit of Mount Monroe are stunning. You can stand on a clifftop perch (which makes for dramatic photos!) and peer up to Mount Washington. As the closest peak to the big one, the view is impressive. Between Boott Spur directly to the east and the summit of Monroe lies Oakes Gulf, a broad but steep valley down which the Dry River Trail descends. To the south-southeast across the Dry River Valley lies Mount Isolation, identified by the slab summit at the north end of the long ridge extending south to Mount Davis.

Incredible views to the southwest extend toward Mount Eisenhower, with the other southern Presidential peaks just beyond Eisenhower to the left. Across Crawford Notch Mounts Willey, Field, and Tom (left to right) poke up above Eisenhower; mountains in the Pemigewasset Wilderness are visible beyond. Although not very prominent, if you know what you are looking for, you can see the northernmost 4,000-footers, Mount Waumbek and Mount Cabot, directly to the north. Just to the west of Mount Washington, almost due north, are Mounts Clay and Jefferson.

To continue the loop, head back down the way you came to the Lakes of the Clouds Hut (3.9 miles), where you will follow the Crawford Path north to the summit of Mount Washington. As you leave the hut, pass the junction of the Dry River Trail on your right. You will pass the two lakes, with the larger lake on your right (south) and the smaller lake ahead on your left, with dramatic views over the water to the north.

Just over 0.1 mile from the hut, pass the Camel and Tuckerman Crossover Trails on your right and continue a gentle climb along the east side of the ridge in a northeasterly direction toward the summit of Mount Washington. At 0.9 mile from the hut (4.8 miles from the trailhead) you pass the Davis Path on your right, followed shortly by the Westside Trail on your left. From here the Crawford Path makes a winding, rocky ascent up the summit cone; at 5.2 miles the Gulfside Trail enters from the left. After a short climb, follow the "Crawford Path to Summit" sign, passing the Yankee Building and Tip Top House on your left and the Stage Office and cog railway on the right. The summit of Mount Washington is the signed high point next to the Tip Top House at 5.5 miles.

As the highest point in the northeast, the views are incredible, at least on the somewhat rare day when the summit is not immersed in clouds. Walk around and see what other 4,000-footers you can identify. Forty-three are visible from the summit. Beyond the visit to the Sherman Adams Visitor Center with interactive displays and hot food from a cafeteria, you can also check out the historic Tip Top House. You can also arrange for a tour of the weather observatory. Needless to say, there is a lot to do and learn about at Mount Washington State Park and the Mount Washington

A hiker enjoys a clifftop view near the summit of Mount Monroe.

Observatory on the summit. However with a road and railway to the top, the majority of people you will encounter on the summit will have a less intimate relationship with the mountain.

From the summit you can take the Trinity Heights connector. This leaves from a sign just to the right of the Tip Top House, a short walk to the east from the summit. This will take you 0.2 mile to the Gulfside Trail (5.7 miles), where you turn right (north) to follow it down and across the cog railway tracks. After crossing the tracks, you shortly reach the intersection with the Great Gulf Trail. The Gulfside Trail heads

Mount Monroe rises above the lakes of the clouds and the Lakes of the Clouds Hut.

left (east) with the cog railway tracks on your left and the stunningly dramatic Great Gulf on your right.

The Gulfside Trail traverses the upper edge of the dramatic Great Gulf, a beautifully shaped glacial cirque. The Great Gulf Wilderness is a wild and stunning area that drains multiple brooks and streams into the Peabody River from the northern Presidential Range. It stretches all the way from Mount Washington to Mount Madison.

From the junction with the Great Gulf Trail, follow the Gulfside Trail as it descends gradually to the col between Mount Clay and Mount Washington, passing the Westside Tail on your left at 6.4 miles and reaching the junction with the Mount Clay Loop on your right at 6.5 miles. Continue on the Gulfside Trail; after a short climb on the west side of Mount Clay, followed by a short descent on big boulders, you arrive at the junction with the Jewell Trail on the left (west) at 6.8 miles.

The Jewell Trail descends to the northwest in the alpine zone then begins to head west around 5,200 feet as it switchbacks first through alpine terrain, then krummholz, and eventually through small conifers, which become tall enough to obscure views below 4,500 feet. This is one of the gentlest trails in the northern Presidentials, and you can make good time on the descent. Great views off the ridge allow you to see the southern Presidentials rising up to the south and Mount Jefferson just to the north.

The trail continues to ease a bit as you descend, passing through a fir wave around 3,800 feet that provides more views. At 9.4 miles (2.6 miles from junction with the Gulfside Trail), the Jewell Trail crosses Clay Brook, makes a short ascent on the other side, and passes the Jewell Link to the cog railway base station on the right before descending through an easy but rooty and sometimes muddy section. At 10.1 miles,

Mount Monroe & Mount Washington

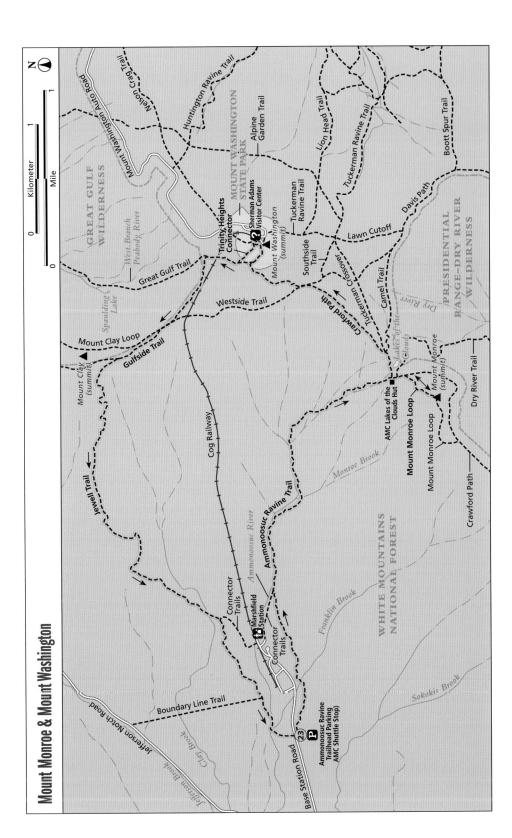

pass the Boundary Line Trail on the right. After a short descent, you cross Franklin Brook on a bridge and head up to the road across from the Amonoosuc Ravine Trail parking area at 10.5 miles.

Miles and Directions

0.0 Start from the parking area and take the Ammonoosuc Ravine Trail.

0.3 Cross Franklin Brook.

1.7 Cross Monroe Brook.

2.1 Cross the Ammonoosuc River at the Gem Pool. Begin a steep climb.

2.3 A side path leads to a viewpoint.

2.5 Cross over the main brook at the top of the falls.

3.1 Reach the Lakes of the Clouds Hut. Turn right (south) onto the Crawford Path.

3.2 Turn right (southwest) onto the Mount Monroe Loop.

3.5 Reach the summit of Mount Monroe. (**Option:** Turn around here for a 7.0 mile out-and-back hike.)

3.9 Return to the Lakes of the Clouds Hut. Head right (east) onto the Crawford Path, passing between both lakes.

4.0 Pass Camel Trail and Tuckerman Crossover on the right. Stay straight on the Crawford Path.

4.8 Pass Davis Path on the right, followed shortly by the Westside Trail on the left. Stay straight (north) on the Crawford Path.

5.2 Reach the Gulfside Trail. Head right (east) where the Gulfside Trail and Crawford Path become one. Look for the "Crawford Path to Summit" sign.

5.5 Reach the summit of Mount Washington. Take the Trinity Heights Connector from the back corner of the Tip Top House.

5.7 Turn right (north) onto the Gulfside Trail.

5.9 After crossing the cog railway tracks, reach the junction with the Great Gulf Trail. Head left (west) to continue following the Gulfside Trail.

6.4 Pass the junction with the Westside Trail on the left. Stay straight.

6.5 Reach the junction with the Mount Clay Loop. Stay left on the Gulfside Trail.

6.8 Reach the junction with the Jewell Trail. Turn left (northwest) onto the Jewell Trail.

9.4 Cross Clay Brook and shortly pass the Jewell Link.

10.1 Pass the Boundary Line Trail on the right.

10.5 Arrive at the road across from the parking lot.

Other Routes

1. Monroe only (similar loop with no Mount Washington): Ammonoosuc Ravine Trail to Crawford Path to Monroe Loop to Crawford Path to Westside Trail to Gulfside Trail to Jewell Trail—distance: 9.8 miles; elevation gain: 3,950 feet

2. Presidential Traverse (full) (hike 33)—distance: 22.9 miles; elevation gain: 10,050 feet

3. Mount Monroe to Mount Jackson (bonus hike 7)—distance: 12.5 miles; elevation gain: 4,650 feet

24 Mount Jefferson

Short in mileage but big in challenge, this hike up the third tallest peak in the White Mountains climbs along a rocky ridgeline with dramatic "caps" that provide fun scrambles over rocky ledges. Starting from the highest trailhead in the Whites, most of the hike is above tree line and provides dramatic views for much of the route.

Distance: 5.0 miles out and back
Summit elevation: 5,716 feet
4,000-footers rank: 3
Elevation gain: 3,000 feet
Difficulty: Difficult; short but steep
Hiking time: About 3.5 hours

Trails used: Caps Ridge Trail
Views: Excellent
Canine compatibility: Very tough for dogs due to steep ledge scrambling on the "caps" and some boulder hopping near the top

Finding the trailhead: *From the junction of US 302 and US 3 in Twin Mountain/Carroll,* follow US 302 East for 4.4 miles. Turn left onto Base Station Road; you'll see a sign for the cog railway. In 4.5 miles turn left onto Jefferson Notch Road. The parking lot is on the right in 3.2 miles. *From the junction of US 302 and NH 16 in Glen,* follow US 302 West for 24.6 miles. Turn right onto Base Station Road; you'll see a sign for the cog railway. In 4.5 miles turn left onto Jefferson Notch Road. The parking lot will be on the right in 3.2 miles. *From the junction of US 2 and NH 16 in Gorham (western junction),* follow US 2 West for 9.4 miles then turn left onto Valley Road. In 1.2 miles turn left onto Jefferson Notch Road. The parking lot will be on the left in 5.3 miles. **Note:** Jefferson Notch Road is a winding, narrow dirt road that, due to its elevation, can remain snow-covered and be closed fairly late into the season. The southern portion of this road is often in better shape than the northern portion. **GPS:** N44 17.78' / W71 21.22'

The Hike

Short, steep, and breathtaking, the Caps Ridge Trail that traverses the Ridge of the Caps on the western side of Mount Jefferson provides an incredible bang for your buck. Starting from the highest trailhead in New Hampshire—in fact, the highest point reached by a public road in the state—you quickly ascend above tree line and become immersed in the steep rock scrambling and boulder hopping that characterize any high-ridgeline traverse in the northern Presidentials. But don't treat this like any other 5-mile hike in the Whites; plan for a full half-day adventure.

You can create several short loops off the summit to get different perspectives of the unique geography, but this hike description focuses solely on the Caps Ridge Trail.

The trail was built in 1920 by an AMC crew. You are only going to want to hike this classic route in good weather. With so much of the route above tree line, and lots of exposure, falls in slippery conditions can have severe consequences.

A hiker enjoys the view from one of the "caps."

The first little bit from the parking lot is gentle enough as you walk through a muddy section before ascending a moderately steep trail lined by moss-draped rocks in a forest of birch, spruce, and fir. At the 1.0-mile mark you come to a granite out-crop where you get your first view, a good one down Jefferson Brook and along the northern side of the southern Presidentials. Turn around from the viewpoint and you can see your route and the first cap up ahead.

At 1.1 mile you pass the Link Trail on your left and at 1.5 miles reach the first cap. As you traverse the caps, remember to look up to make sure you are following the blazes painted on the rocks. Take your time and use the "three points of contact" method to make sure you are secure before making your next technical move. No part of this route is difficult, but it's easy to make mistakes when rushing.

If you look left (north), the next ridgeline has another classic route, the Castle Trail, which traverses the big rock outcrops known as The Castles; over your right shoulder to the southeast you can see Mount Washington rising high above. After cresting the third and highest cap at 1.9 miles, the trail has a few short sections of dirt but mainly becomes a boulder hop through ever-shrinking high-alpine krummholz.

At 2.1 miles the Cornice Trail crosses your path; make sure to stay straight, as there will be signs on both sides. The final 0.4 mile is tough as you climb 700 vertical feet over boulders and on steep winding paths through high-alpine grasses.

From the summit you get a magnificent 360-degree view, with forty 4,000-foot-ers visible. Mount Adams rises to the northeast, separated by Edmonds Col high above the steep Jefferson Ravine. To the south, Mount Washington towers above

Mount Jefferson

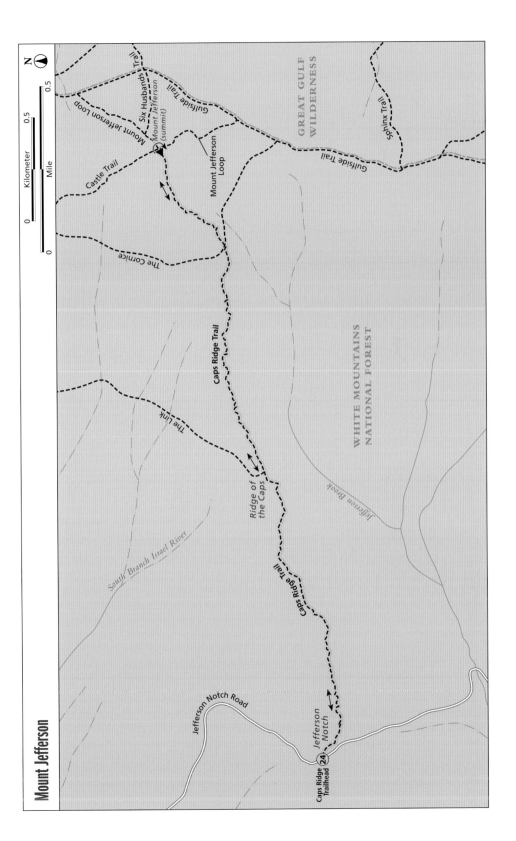

N

Kilometer
0   0.5   0.5

Mile
0   0.5

Six Husbands Trail

Mount Jefferson Loop

Castle Trail

Mount Jefferson (summit)

Gulfside Trail

Mount Jefferson Loop

The Cornice

GREAT GULF WILDERNESS

Sphinx Trail

Gulfside Trail

The Link

Caps Ridge Trail

WHITE MOUNTAINS NATIONAL FOREST

Jefferson Brook

Ridge of the Caps

South Branch Israel River

Caps Ridge Trail

Jefferson Notch Road

Jefferson Notch

Caps Ridge Trailhead

24

Mount Washington provides one of the only views of Mount Jefferson from above.

nearby Mount Clay as the dramatic southern wall of the Great Gulf faces you. If it's windy, you can hop over the top knob of the summit and tuck just behind in the sheltered level(ish) area below. Return down the trail, or create a loop using one of the many side trails, making sure to traverse back to the Caps Ridge Trail.

Miles and Directions

0.0 Start the Caps Ridge Trail from the high point at Jefferson Notch.

1.0 Reach the first viewpoint.

1.1 Stay straight/right at the junction with the Link Trail.

1.5 Reach the top of the first cap.

1.9 Reach the third (highest) cap.

2.1 Pass through the junction with the Cornice Trail, which will be on both sides. Stay straight, heading northeast.

2.5 Reach the summit of Mount Jefferson. Return the way you came.

5.0 Arrive back at the trailhead.

Other Routes

There are many more hiking options for the northern Presidential peaks, including long trips through the Great Gulf. Below are just a few reasonable options.

1. Jefferson summit loop: Caps Ridge Trail to The Cornice to Gulfside Trail to Mount Jefferson Loop (over peak) to Gulfside Trail (north) to Randolph Path to The Cornice to Caps Ridge Trail—distance: 7.2 miles; elevation gain: 3,250 feet

2. Castle Trail to Israel Ridge Path to Castle Ravine Trail to Randolph Path to Gulfside Trail to Mount Jefferson Loop to Castle Trail—distance: 10.25 miles; elevation gain: 4,300 feet

3. Presidential Traverse (full) (hike 33)—distance: 22.9 miles; elevation gain: 10,050 feet

THE GRID

For most people, hiking all the New Hampshire 4,000-footers is a major accomplishment. Many people take it one step further and try to get their "Winter 4,000-footers"—completing all forty-eight peaks during the three months of winter, although usually over the course of many years.

Achieving the "White Mountain Grid," however, is an order of magnitude more difficult and involves hiking each of New Hampshire's 4,000-footers in every month of the year. You read that correctly: *every month of the year.* Although it could take many years, by the time a grid is completed, a hiker will have completed 12 × 48 mountains. (A grid of 12 × 48, get it?) That's 576 mountains. Now *that's* impressive.

In 2016 Sue Johnston, an incredible ultra-runner and hiker, did the unthinkable. She completed the Grid in a calendar year! Every month of the year, with rain, wind, snow, and probably every conceivable weather condition, she hiked all forty-eight peaks. (She also threw in some other hikes for good measure.)

She gives a lot of credit to the full support of her husband. Over the course of the year, she climbed more than a million vertical feet and more than 3,000 miles. One more interesting fact: This was her second time completing the grid!

Mounts Washington and Monroe catch the last light of the day, which comes very early during the heart of winter.

25 | Mount Adams and Mount Madison

With a climb up the dramatic Air Line to the second highest peak in New England, you are treated to impressive views into King Ravine; and from the summit of Mount Adams, the 360-degree panorama is breathtaking. After the big ascent up Mount Adams, the extra 600 vertical feet to climb Mount Madison is almost an afterthought; and from the summit of Mount Madison, you get one of the best views of the Wildcat-Carter-Moriah Ridge and the dramatic Carter Notch. You pass the Madison Spring Hut as well, which sits high above Snyder Brook Ravine. If you have enough time, the waterfalls near the Appalachia Trailhead and parking area are just a minute or two side trip from your descent route on Valley Way.

Distance: 10.1-mile loop with spurs
Summit elevation: Mount Adams, 5,799 feet; Mount Madison, 5,366 feet
4,000-footers rank: Mount Adams, 2; Mount Madison, 5
Elevation gain: 5,200 feet
Difficulty: Very difficult

Hiking time: About 7 hours
Trails used: Air Line, Gulfside Trail, Osgood Trail, Valley Way, Fallsway (optional)
Views: Excellent
Canine compatibility: Doable but very difficult; there is a lot of boulder hopping.

Finding the trailhead: *From the junction of US 2 and NH 16 in Gorham (western junction),* follow US 2 West for 5.4 miles. Parking for the Appalachia Trailhead will be on the left. *From I-93,* take exit 40 and head right on US 302 East for 11.1 miles. Turn left onto US 3 North and then turn right onto NH 115 North in 2.0 miles. Continue for 9.7 miles to the intersection with US 2. Turn right and on US 2 East and go 7.1 miles. Parking for the Appalachia Trailhead will be on the right. **GPS:** N44 22.28' / W71 17.37'

The Hike

Mount Adams and Mount Madison are the second and fifth highest peaks, respectively, in the White Mountains. Although many people hike these separately, the mountains are very close, and adding Madison to a hike up Adams adds only about 600 vertical feet of gain and creates a fantastic loop. As you can see from any map of the northern Presidentials, there are countless ways to summit these peaks. The route up Air Line provides a stunning journey up the spine of Mount Adams, and returning via Valley Way allows for a straightforward, quick descent with the option of checking out some cool waterfalls not far from the Appalachia Trailhead and parking area.

Although taking Airline from the Appalachia Trailhead is the shortest route to the summit of Adams, this hike (with Madison) climbs more than 5,000 vertical feet. This is a full-day hike, and because of the large section in the alpine zone, it is important to do this hike only when the forecast is clear. If it gets foggy, it's very easy to get

Both Mount Adams (left) and Mount Madison (right) look no less dramatic when covered in a blanket of snow.

disoriented and lost. As this trailhead is a major launching point for many hikes in the northern Presidential Range, parking fills up quickly on a nice weekend. To avoid having to park alongside US 3, it's recommended that you arrive fairly early.

From the Appalachia Trailhead, follow the main trail into the woods, crossing the Presidential Rail Trail and into a clearing for a power line. At a sign marking the trail, Valley Way splits to the left as Air Line goes right. Continue to follow Air Line at a moderate grade as it passes Sylvan Way at 0.2 mile, Beechwood Way at 0.6 mile, and Short Line at 0.8 mile. At 0.9 mile, join the Randolph Path for a few yards before continuing straight (south) on Air Line.

Just after reaching 1.5 miles, the trail begins to ascend much more steeply, with rough footing as it climbs up to Durand Ridge. The ascent eases off a bit before the Scar Trail joins from the left at 2.5 miles. Continue up along the ridge as the trees continue to shrink until, at just above 4,300 feet in elevation (around 3.0 miles into your hike), you pop out of the trees and are greeted by expansive views. To the right (west) the steep cliffs on the headwall of King Ravine drop away to the valley below.

Soon the Upper Bruin Trail comes in from the left (east); just beyond, at 3.2 miles, the Chemin des Dames Trail comes in from the right (west), out of King Ravine. This section, where the steep sides of Durand Ridge drop away, is called the Knife Edge. King Ravine is a fine example of a glacial cirque, with a steep, rounded shape that was formed by the massive power and weight of ice during previous ice ages.

Continue climbing along the ridge as Air Line Cutoff comes in from the Madison Spring Hut on the left (east) at 3.5 miles; at 3.7 miles the King Ravine Trail climbs up out of King Ravine and joins Air Line on the right (west) through big slabs, the Gateway of King Ravine. Just beyond this you reach the junction with the Gulfside Trail.

Air Line and the Gulfside Trail join for a hundred yards before Air Line cuts left (south) at 3.8 miles as it begins the final ascent up the boulder field that defines the summit cone of Mount Adams. You pass the minor peak of John Quincy Adams on the left as you carefully hop from boulder to boulder. It's important to stop frequently to keep your eye on the rock cairns that mark the path; it is very easy to go off-route here. The final rocky, steep climb takes you to the summit of Mount Adams at 4.3 miles, where Lowe's Path joins from the west and the Star Lake Trail joins from the southeast.

It's appropriate that the second-highest mountain in the Whites is named for the second US president, John Adams. To the east, your next summit, Mount Madison, is clearly visible; and although the Madison Spring Hut is blocked by the ridge, Star Lake can be seen on the southern edge of the col between the two peaks.

To the northwest you can make out Mount Waumbek and Mount Cabot on ridges that appear as small hills from this high vantage point. To the southwest, Mount Jefferson and Mount Clay rise up along the ridge. Dramatic cliffs drop off the ridge, creating the wall above Jefferson Ravine, which separates Mount Adams and Mount Jefferson. The Great Gulf is the huge ravine to the south between Mount Clay, Mount Jefferson, and Mount Washington, and the entire area to the east of the ridge is part of the Great Gulf Wilderness. Directly south, you can see the Mount Washington Auto Road as it winds its way up along Chandler Ridge toward the Mount Washington summit.

To get to Mount Madison, retrace your steps, following the blue blazes and rock cairns back down Air Line to the Gulfside Trail. At 4.9 miles turn right (east) onto the Gulfside Trail and follow this down to the Madison Spring Hut at 5.3 miles. Perched in the north part of the col between Mount Adams and Mount Madison, Madison Spring Hut overlooks the Snyder Brook Ravine. The original hut was built in 1888 with the most recent iteration rebuilt in 2011. This modern hut can sleep fifty-two guests and is open June through September.

The Madison Spring Hut sits just 550 vertical feet below the summit of Mount Madison.

You can fill up your water containers at the hut if it is open. Since you will be taking Valley Way back down to the trailhead, you can leave your pack at the hut while you make your jaunt up to the summit of Madison, which is about 550 feet and 0.5 mile above the hut.

Follow signs for the Osgood Trail, which begins next to the hut. Pass the junction for Pine Link on the left and follow the Osgood Trail up the ridge, staying on the north side of the ridge before moving slightly south of the highest line, finally popping out on rocks just to the west of the actual summit. Reach the summit at 5.8 miles.

From the summit, the Wildcat-Carter-Moriah Ridge rises up across the valley where NH 16 and the Peabody River head north from Pinkham Notch. You can clearly see the ski trails on Wildcat Mountain and the dramatic Carter Notch between Wildcat A and Carter Dome. At the summit of Madison, the Watson Path comes in from the north, and the Osgood Trail (which is also the Appalachian Trail) heads straight east before it curves around to the south to Pinkham Notch. To the north you can see the towns of Gorham and Berlin beyond.

Head back down the way you came along Osgood Trail to the hut, enjoying the views of Mount Washington over to your left through some interesting rock formations. From the hut, at 6.3 miles, follow signs down the Valley Way

You stay on the west side of Snyder Brook as it drops into the valley, passing the Upper Bruin Trail on your right at 6.8 miles and the Valley Way Tentsite spur trail at 6.9 miles. This top section is steep and rough. Valley Way stays higher up along the west side of the valley as Snyder Brook continues to drop below. Lower Bruin comes in from the right (east) at 7.3 miles; the Watson Path crosses the Valley Way at

An Appalachian Trail through-hiker traverses the Gulfside Trail above King Ravine on his way toward the Madison Spring Hut.

7.7 miles. The Valley Way continues, reaching a steeper section around 7.9 miles as it heads north then curves around to the west and crosses a few small brooks before heading north again. At 9.1 miles you cross the Randolph Path and shortly after pass junctions with the Brookside Trail and Beechwood Way.

At 9.4 miles the Fallsway Trail comes in on the right. It makes a short loop back to Valley Way as it passes beautiful Tama Falls. The falls are well worth the very short diversion. Just below where the Fallsway Trail meets up with Valley Way again, it heads back off the Valley Way for more falls, including Salroc Falls, just a bit off Valley Way in the Snyder Brook Scenic Area, and also worth the short diversion.

Continue to follow Valley Way past the intersections with Sylvan Way and Maple Walk before returning to the trailhead at 10.1 miles.

Miles and Directions

0.0 Start from the Appalachia Trailhead, following signs for Air Line. Pass over the Presidential Rail Trail and, at the opening for the power line, turn right onto Air Line at the junction with the Valley Way.

0.2 Pass through the junction with Sylvan Way.

0.6 Pass through the junction with Beechwood Way.

0.8 Pass the junction with Short Line on the right.

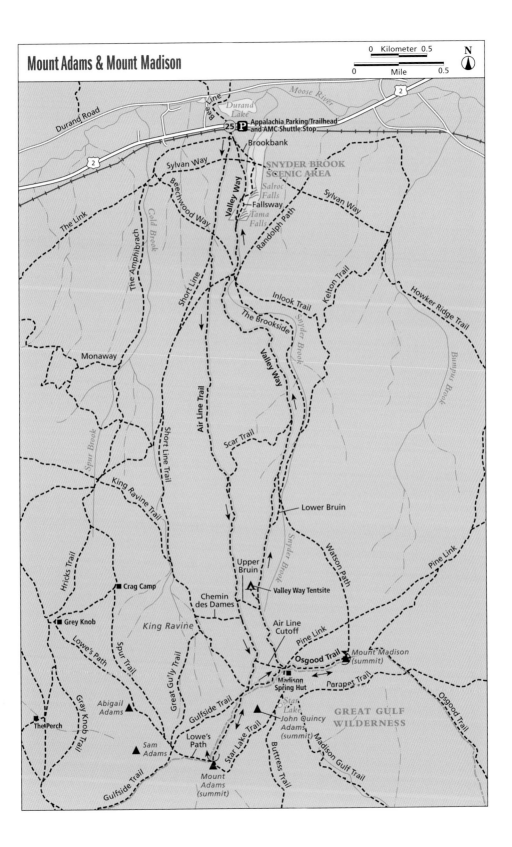

Mount Adams & Mount Madison

0   Kilometer   0.5

0   Mile   0.5

N

Moose River

Durand Road

Bee Line

Durand Lake

25 P Appalachia Parking/Trailhead and AMC Shuttle Stop

2

Brookbank

Sylvan Way

SNYDER BROOK SCENIC AREA

Salroc Falls

Beechwood Way

Valley Way

Fallsway

Sylvan Way

Tama Falls

2

The Link

Randolph Path

The Amphibrach

Cold Brook

Short Line

Inlook Trail

Kelton Trail

Howker Ridge Trail

Snyder Brook

The Brookside

Bumpus Brook

Monaway

Valley Way

Air Line Trail

Scar Trail

Short Line Trail

Spur Brook

Lower Bruin

Snyder Brook

King Ravine Trail

Hricks Trail

Crag Camp

Upper Bruin

Watson Path

Pine Link

Grey Knob

Valley Way Tentsite

Lowe's Path

Chemin des Dames

King Ravine

Air Line Cutoff

Spur Trail

Great Gully Trail

Pine Link

Osgood Trail

Mount Madison (summit)

Gray Knob Trail

Abigail Adams

Gulfside Trail

Madison Spring Hut

Parapet Trail

Osgood Trail

The Perch

Star Lake

GREAT GULF WILDERNESS

Sam Adams

Lowe's Path

John Quincy Adams (summit)

Madison Gulf Trail

Star Lake Trail

Buttress Trail

Mount Adams (summit)

Gulfside Trail

0.9 At the junction with the Randolph Path, join Randolph Pass and head right for a few yards before heading left back onto Air Line.

2.4 Pass the junction with the Scar Trail on the left.

3.1 Pass the junction with the Upper Bruin Trail on the left.

3.2 Pass the junction with the Chemin des Dames Trail on the right.

3.5 Continue on Air Line as the Air Line Cutoff heads left to the Madison Spring Hut.

3.7 Pass the junction with the King Ravine Trail on the right; shortly after, reach the Gulfside Trail. Turn right (west) onto the Gulfside Trail where Air Line and Gulfside intersect.

3.8 Turn left (south) to follow Air Line.

4.3 Reach the summit of Mount Adams. Head back down Air Line.

4.9 Turn right (east) onto Gulfside Trail.

5.3 Reach the Madison Spring Hut. Follow signs for the Osgood Trail, which heads east from the hut. Take the Osgood Trail to the summit.

5.8 Reach the summit of Mount Madison.

6.3 Arrive back at the Madison Spring Hut. Follow signs for Valley Way.

6.8 Pass the junction with the Upper Bruin Trail on the left.

6.9 Pass the junction with the Valley Way Tentsite spur trail on the left.

7.3 Pass the junction with the Lower Bruin Trail on the right.

7.7 Cross the Watson Path.

9.1 Cross the Randolph Path; shortly after, pass junctions with the Brookside Trail and Beechwood Way.

9.4 The Fallsway Trail comes in from right. (**Option:** This is a good short loop back to Valley Way with nice waterfalls. Take it if you have the time.)

9.5 The Fallsway Trail rejoins Valley Way then shortly after heads right again. (**Note:** There are more waterfalls just off this trail that are worth visiting.)

9.8 Pass through the junction with Sylvan Way.

10.0 Pass the junction with Maple Walk, immediately followed by the junction with Air Line.

10.1 Arrive back at the Appalachia Trailhead and parking.

Other Routes

There are many more options for the northern Presidential peaks, including long trips through the Great Gulf. Below are some reasonable options.

1. Mount Adams only: Air Line out-and-back—distance: 8.6 miles; elevation gain: 4,550 feet

2. Mount Adams only: Air Line to Randolph Path to Short Line to King Ravine Trail to Air Line to summit, back down Air Line—distance: 8.8 miles; elevation gain: 4,550 feet

3. Mount Madison only: Air Line to Air Line Cutoff to Osgood Trail (out-and-back from hut) to Valley Way—distance: 8.5 miles; elevation gain: 4,200 feet

4. Mount Madison only: Pine Link Trail to Howker Ridge Trail to Osgood Trail out-and-back—distance: 7.4 miles; elevation gain: 4,100 feet

5. Presidential Traverse (full) (hike 33)—distance: 22.9 miles; elevation gain: 10,050 feet

26 Mount Washington

The classic, and most popular, route up New England's highest peak takes you through Tuckerman Ravine, a steep glacially scoured cirque known as the hotbed of big mountain skiing in the East, but it is equally celebrated for a trail that gracefully ascends around and over a giant headwall to the massive summit cone of Mount Washington. On the way down, you will enjoy the views as you traverse the northern edges of the ravine and over Lion Head, a prominent feature that soars above the valley below.

Distance: 8.5-mile lollipop loop
Summit elevation: 6,288 feet
4,000-footers rank: 1
Elevation gain: 4,400 feet
Difficulty: Difficult
Hiking time: About 6 hours
Trails used: Tuckerman Ravine Trail, Lion Head Trail

Views: Excellent
Canine compatibility: Doable, but there are some very steep sections.
Special considerations: Parking can fill up quickly on busy weekends. Tuckerman Ravine Trail can become a conga line with a lot of people, reducing your pace to whatever people in front of you are hiking.

Finding the trailhead: *From the junction of US 2 and NH 16 in Gorham (eastern junction),* follow NH 16 South for 10.6 miles to the parking lot at the Pinkham Notch Visitor Center on the right. *From the junction of US 302 and NH 16 in Glen (just south of Storyland),* take NH 16 North for 12 miles to the parking lot at the Pinkham Notch Visitor Center on the left. **GPS:** N44 15.43' / W71 15.17'

The Hike

This extremely popular route up New England's most famous mountain is challenging, often crowded, extremely exposed to inclement weather—and absolutely stunning. Give yourself plenty of time, and if hiking on a weekend, the earlier you can start the better, as both the parking lot and the trail itself get very crowded. As a large portion of this hike is well above tree line and on exposed terrain, make sure to carry rain and wind gear and prepare for temperatures that can be much colder than at the parking area. Stop by the Pinkham Notch Visitor Center to get the latest forecast and to talk to a ranger if you have any questions before hitting the trail.

From the visitor center, follow signs for the Tuckerman Ravine Trail, immediately passing the Old Jackson Road (a ski trail) on the right. The bottom part of this hike, up to Hermit Lake, is along a very wide tractor trail. Climb steadily, cross the Cutler River on a solid bridge, and reach the viewing platform for Crystal Cascade at 0.3 mile. Pass the junction with the Boott Spur Trail on the left at 0.4 mile, and after a series of switchbacks and a long straight section, pass the Huntington Ravine Trail on the right in 1.3 miles.

Not far up the Tuckerman Ravine Trail, you come across beautiful Crystal Cascade.

Soon you cross back over the river, past the Huntington Ravine Fire Road on the right at 1.7 miles and past the junction with the Raymond Path on the right at 2.1 miles. Lion Head Trail enters from the right at 2.3 miles, just below Hermit Lake and the Hermit Lake Shelters at 2.4 miles. In addition to the shelters, there are numerous buildings for avalanche rescue and are used by rangers in winter. There are outhouses and a communal area with a big deck to enjoy the view and eat and drink. Hermit Lake is just to the north of the trail and shelters.

The Tuckerman Ravine Trail heads west from the Hermit Lake area, immediately passes a small pond, and climbs a short steep pitch over the Little Headwall. The grade then eases as you climb up through the wide ravine. At around 3.1 miles you reach the base of the headwall, where the trail turns right and climbs very steeply. The footing is secure, but watch out for rockfall and be especially careful if the trail is at all wet. Beautiful wildflowers line the trail here in summer, and butterflies flutter around as rivulets of water course down the headwall.

After the steepest section, the trail cuts back left (southwest) as it traverses both above and below cliffs then climbs up a wide, rocky path to the junction with the Alpine Garden Trail at 3.4 miles, more than 700 feet above the base of the headwall. Continue straight ahead on the Tuckerman Ravine Trail to Tuckerman Junction at 3.6 miles. This is on the lower edge of Bigelow Lawn, the broad plateau where alpine flowers proliferate during summer.

At Tuckerman Junction, the Lawn Cutoff heads left (south) and Tuckerman Crossover heads straight (southwest). Take a sharp right, heading north to continue following the Tuckerman Ravine Trail. The trail climbs steeply up the summit cone on big boulders. Make you are following the cairns by stopping and looking ahead; it is easy to get off-route up here. Pass the Lion Head Trail on the right at 3.8 miles, and finally, at 4.2 miles, you reach the auto road and parking lot. Wooden stairs take you to the summit area, with the true summit in the middle between all the buildings.

Although the summit can be overwhelming at times with the sheer number of tourists, most of whom either drive or take the cog railway up, make sure to walk around to get views in all directions. As the highest peak in the Northeast, the summit of Mount Washington provides jaw-dropping views, provided you are there during one of the rare clear days. Test your knowledge of New Hampshire's 4,000-footers—all but four peaks (Cannon Mountain, North and South Kinsman, and Galehead) are visible from the summit.

Return by descending the wooden steps and heading back down the Tuckerman Ravine Trail. At 4.6 miles (0.4 mile from the summit), head left (east) at the junction with the Lion Head Trail. Follow the rocky trail as it angles down across the summit cone. The grade lessens as you reach the junction with the Alpine Garden Trail at 5.1 miles. The Alpine Garden Research Natural Area extends north for almost a mile from this junction, spanning hundreds of yards on both sides of the Alpine Garden Trail, all the way to where it meets the Huntington Ravine Trail. In summer this is a fantastic area to enjoy the displays of wildflowers that proliferate during the short growing season in the alpine zone.

The mellow pitch continues as you head east on the Lion Head Trail, the unique high-alpine vegetation flourishing on the plateau. As you approach the prominent feature of Lion Head, you follow the northern edge of Tuckerman Ravine. From this

The cog railway takes hundreds of visitors up and down the mountain . . . the easy way.

vantage point, you really get an idea of how powerful the ice must have been to have carved out the glacial cirque, with its steep and smooth sides.

At 5.3 miles you reach Lion Head, which provides a stunning dramatic view with an almost sheer drop-off down to the floor of the ravine. From here you can see the headwall to the right, Boott Spur across on the other side of the ravine, and Hermit Lake almost directly below. Looking east across Pinkham Notch, you get a dramatic view of Wildcat Ridge, the deep recess of Carter Notch, and the Carter Range extending to the north.

Lion Head Trail swings to the left as it descends around the promontory, making a sharp turn to the right (south) as it passes the Lion Head Winter Route on the left at 5.8 miles. Continue down through the forest to the junction with the Tuckerman Ravine Trail at 6.2 miles. Turn left and follow the Tuckerman Ravine Trail to the trailhead at Pinkham Notch at 8.5 miles.

Miles and Directions

0.0 Start behind the Pinkham Notch Visitor Center and follow signs for the Tuckerman Ravine Trail.

0.3 Reach the viewing platform for Crystal Falls.

0.4 Pass the Boott Spur Trail on the left.

1.3 Pass the Huntington Ravine Trail on the right.

1.7 Pass the Huntington Ravine Fire Road on the right.

2.1 Pass the Raymond Path on the right.

2.3 Pass the Lion Head Trail on the right.

2.4 Reach Hermit Lake shelters, Hermit Lake, and buildings. Continue straight (west) on the Tuckerman Ravine Trail.

3.1 Reach the base of the headwall in Tuckerman Ravine.

3.4 Pass the Alpine Garden Trail on the right.

3.6 Reach Tuckerman Junction. Turn right (north) to continue on the Tuckerman Ravine Trail.

3.8 Pass the Lion Head Trail on the right.

Mount Washington

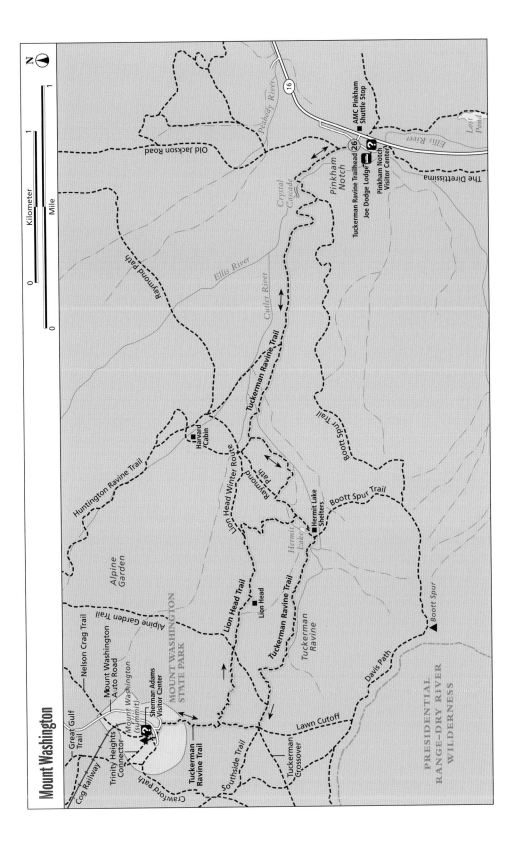

This panoramic view from Lion Head shows Tuckerman Ravine on the left, the Alpine Garden higher to the right, and the summit of Mount Washington straight ahead.

4.2 Cross the road, ascend wooden steps, and climb to the summit of Mount Washington. On your return, descend back down the Tuckerman Ravine Trail.

4.6 Turn left (east) on the Lion Head Trail.

5.1 Pass through the junction with the Alpine Garden Trail.

5.3 Reach Lion Head. Continue on the Lion Head Trail.

5.8 Follow the Lion Head Trail to the right (south) as you pass the Lion Head Winter Route on the left.

6.2 Turn left (northeast) onto the Tuckerman Ravine Trail. Follow this back to Pinkham Notch.

8.5 Arrive back at Pinkham Notch and the parking area.

Other Routes

There are many more options for the northern Presidential peaks, including long trips through the Great Gulf. Below are just a few reasonable options.

1. Mount Monroe and Mount Washington (hike 23)—distance: 10.5 miles; elevation gain: 4,450 feet

2. Tuckerman Ravine Trail to Huntington Ravine Trail to Nelson Crag Trail (summit) to Tuckerman Ravine Trail to Lion Head Trail to Tuckerman Ravine Trail—distance: 8.9 miles; elevation gain: 4,700 feet

3. Presidential Traverse (full) (hike 33)—distance: 22.9 miles; elevation gain: 10,050 feet

27 Mount Isolation

At first glance, it is easy to begrudge an almost 15-mile hike to a peak that tops out at just 3 feet over 4,000. But once you make the journey deep into the Presidential Range–Dry River Wilderness to the open summit with unparalleled views of the southern Presidentials and Boott Spur—surrounded by the impressive Dry River and Rocky Branch valleys on both sides and with few if any other hikers around—you are sure to feel a sense of privilege and awe at having the opportunity to experience the White Mountains in a way few people are lucky enough to share.

Distance: 14.6 miles out and back
Summit elevation: 4,003 feet
4,000-footers rank: 47 (tied)
Elevation gain: 3,900 feet
Difficulty: Difficult; long hike with many river crossings
Hiking time: About 8 hours
Trails used: Rocky Branch Trail, Isolation Trail, Davis Path, Mount Isolation Spur

Views: Excellent
Canine compatibility: Good in low water, but multiple river crossings can be dangerous for dogs in high water.
Special considerations: Numerous river crossings make this a hike that should be done well after spring melt-off and during dry periods.

Finding the trailhead: *From the junction of US 2 and NH 16 in Gorham (eastern junction),* follow NH 16 South for 14.6 miles to a paved road on the right with a small sign for the Rocky Branch Trail. Park in the lot at the end of the road in 0.1 mile. *From the junction of US 302 and NH 16 in Glen (just south of Storyland),* take NH 16 North for 7.7 miles to a paved road on the left with a small sign for the Rocky Branch Trail. This is just past a sign on the right that says, "Entering White Mountain National Forest." Park in the lot at the end of the road in 0.1 mile. **GPS:** N44 12.27' / W71 14.43'

The Hike

Deep within the Presidential Range–Dry River Wilderness, Mount Isolation sits just 3 feet above 4,000 yet garners one of the most exceptional views in the White Mountains. As a peak on the Montalban Ridge, flanked by the southern Presidentials on the west, Mount Washington to the north, and the much lower Rocky Branch Ridge to the east, Mount Isolation lives up to its name. Even on a busy summer weekend, you aren't likely to run across very many people.

Getting to Isolation is relatively straightforward and not very difficult, but multiple crossings of the Rocky Branch make this a hike you don't want to do after or during a big rain or during the spring melt-off, and the distance means you're in for a solid full-day adventure. The first part of the hike involves getting over Rocky Branch Ridge, and the climbing begins right from the outset.

You cross the Rocky Branch numerous times on your journey, so this is not a hike to do in wet weather.

Roughly following an old logging road, the trail climbs through a nice mixed forest as it switchbacks up the ridge, passing Avalanche Ski Trail at 0.5 and 0.7 mile, on the right and left, respectively. After climbing 1,700 feet in the first 1.8 miles, the trail levels and descends slightly for 0.5 mile on an old road after a sharp left (south) turn in the trail. At 2.3 miles the trail turns right (east) and begins to climb; at 2.4 miles you enter the Presidential Range–Dry River Wilderness.

After passing the height of land at just over 3,100 feet, the trail gradually begins to descend. It can be a bit wet here, as the trail sometimes merges with small streams as you follow the eroded path from rock to rock through mixed forest and sections lined with tall grasses. Eventually the trail curves back to the south followed shortly by your first crossing of the Rocky Branch, at 3.7 miles.

Although the river is not very wide, a lot of water comes through here, so be careful as you make your way across on the large boulders that hopefully will allow you to keep your feet dry. On the other side you meet up with the Isolation Trail.

Turn right (north) onto the Isolation Trail, which like many trails in the White Mountains, was heavily damaged during the intense flooding of Tropical Storm Irene in 2011. The climb along the Rocky Branch is gentle, but parts of the trail can be very wet and full of roots. Follow the west bank of the river up what used to be an old railroad bed before crossing the river again at 4.1 miles.

The trail climbs above the eastern bank of the river as it slowly curves toward the northwest, alternating between rugged rocky footing and an old logging road. You cross back over the river twice around 5.1 miles, where you will see a sign for tent camping. Keep your eye out for moose here, especially in late summer; they seem to like hanging out by the river. Cross the river one more time at 5.4 miles.

At times wet and rocky, the trail meets up with the Davis Path at 6.3 miles, just past a series of unofficial campsites. Turn left onto the Davis Path, make a short descent, and head south, past the site of the old Isolation Shelter, rolling up and down along the Montalban Ridge. At 6.9 miles make the final climb up the north side of Mount Isolation; at 7.2 miles turn right to take the short 0.1-mile Isolation Spur to the summit.

The broad summit has multiple flat rock ledges that provide amazing views north. Due north, the Montalban Ridge stretches up toward Boott Spur, the first high point above tree line, with Mount Washington just beyond. The dramatic Oakes Gulf drops down from Mount Washington as it drains a vast area into the Dry River watershed.

Clouds pour over the Presidential Range as seen from the summit of Mount Isolation.

Mount Isolation

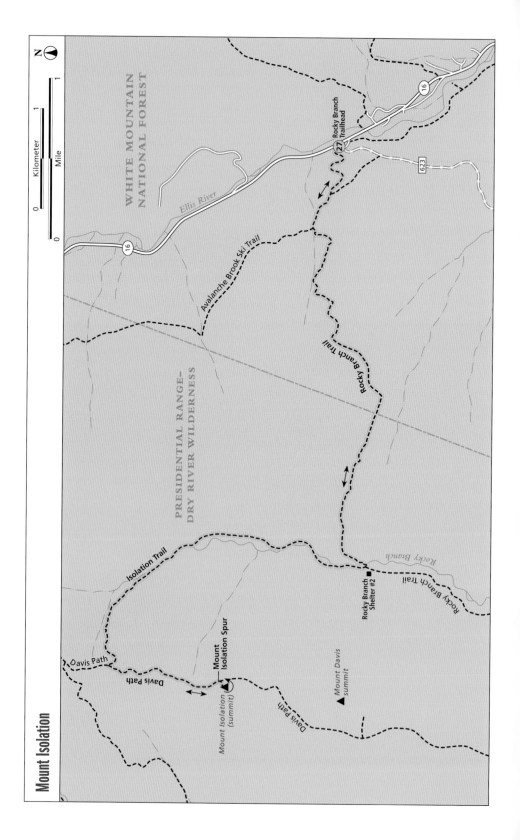

You get a perfect view of the east side of the entire southern Presidential Range, one few people get to see.

The sense of solitude is superb, and Mount Isolation is a prime example of the joys of peak-bagging where the goal of knocking off another 4,000-footer gets you to a unique peak deep in the Whites, one you may not have otherwise decided to visit. When you are ready to return, head back the same way you came, retracing your steps to the trailhead.

Miles and Directions

0.0 Start from the Rocky Branch Trailhead off NH 16.

0.5 Pass the junction with the Avalanche Ski Trail on the right.

0.7 Pass the junction with the Avalanche Ski Trail on the left.

1.8 The trail turns left onto an old road.

2.4 Enter the Presidential Range–Dry River Wilderness.

2.8 Reach the height of land on the Rocky Branch Ridge just after entering the wilderness.

3.7 Cross Rocky Branch for the first time then turn right at the intersection with the Isolation Trail.

4.1 Cross Rocky Branch for a second time.

5.1 Cross Rocky Branch two more times; pass a small sign for tent camping.

5.4 Cross Rocky Branch for the final time (on the ascent).

6.3 Turn left at the intersection onto the Davis Path.

7.2 Turn right onto a short steep spur up to the summit.

7.3 Reach the summit. The best view is from the open ledges; the high point is a cairn just beyond. Return the way you came.

14.6 Arrive back at the trailhead.

Other Routes

Glen Boulder Trail to Davis Path to Mount Isolation Spur out-and-back—distance: 12.2 miles; elevation gain: 5,300 feet

The Wildcat and Carter Ranges

Parts of the Wildcat Ridge Trail are so steep that wooden steps have been bolted onto the rocks.

28 Wildcat D and Wildcat Mountain (Wildcat A)

The near-vertical climb out of the Ellis River valley will leave you breathless, but the multiple views down the valley and across into Tuckerman and Huntington Ravines are ample reward. The ridge alternates between smooth walking and tough ups and downs, ending at Wildcat Mountain (Wildcat A) perched high above Carter Notch. Give yourself plenty of time for this hike—it will take longer than the typical 8.4 mile hike.

Distance: 8.4 miles out and back
Summit elevation: Wildcat D, 4,062 feet; Wildcat A, 4,422 feet
4,000-footers rank: Wildcat D, 37; Wildcat A, 20
Elevation gain: 4,000 feet
Difficulty: Very difficult
Hiking time: About 5.5 hours
Trails used: Wildcat Ridge Trail
Views: Excellent
Canine compatibility: Not very dog friendly due to the initial river crossing and extremely steep climb up to ridge, but doable for athletic dogs

Special considerations: At the very beginning of the hike you cross the Ellis River, which in high water can be very dangerous. You can start from Pinkham Notch and take the Lost Pond Trail down to the junction with the Wildcat Ridge Trail, bypassing the river crossing. This would add 1.6 miles (0.8 mile each way) to the length of the hike.

Finding the trailhead: *From the junction of US 2 and NH 16 in Gorham (eastern junction),* follow NH 16 South for 11.2 miles. Turn right onto a road at a sign for Glen Ellis Falls. Park in the lot and follow the trail under the road. *From the junction of US 302 and NH 16 in Glen (just south of Storyland),* take NH 16 North for 11 miles. Turn right onto a road at a sign for Glen Ellis Falls. Park in the lot and follow the trail under the road. **GPS:** N44 14.75' / W71 15.23'

The Hike

The Wildcats are a rugged set of peaks, and at almost no point during this journey will you be taking a relaxed stroll through the woods. The initial ascent from the Ellis River climbs 1,000 feet in just over 0.5 mile, and in the 4.2 miles out to Wildcat Mountain you climb almost 4,000 feet! Most of the route is contiguous with the Appalachian Trail, with white blazes leading the way. Wildcat Ridge summits are five peaks labeled Wildcat A, B, C, D, and E, but only peaks A and D are official 4,000-footers. Wildcat A is also called Wildcat Mountain.

From the parking area, take the trail under the road toward Glen Ellis Falls. The short trip to the falls is a worthwhile detour. To begin your climb, head over the embankment, cross the Ellis River, and in 0.1 mile reach the intersection with the Lost Pond Trail. Continue straight (west), climbing gradually for a few hundred yards before reaching the steeper part of the trail.

The climb up the Wildcat Ridge Trail is steep right from the outset.

At around 0.3 mile (2,350 feet), you get your first view; above this is a steep scramble over ledge and through a little notch. Continue to climb, making sure you have a good foothold before taking your next step as you pass a few more nice views. After another section of steep climbing, you reach another viewpoint. A steep push to 0.9 mile, at just over 3,000 feet, takes you to another dramatic view from a ledge.

The trail briefly moderates for a bit as you pass by a sign for water at just over 1.0 mile. After another bout of steep climbing, including a short section where wooden steps have been drilled into the rocks, you reach an open area at 1.5 miles, where across the valley you get amazing views into Mount Washington's eastern ravines of

Wildcat D & Wildcat Mountain (Wildcat A)

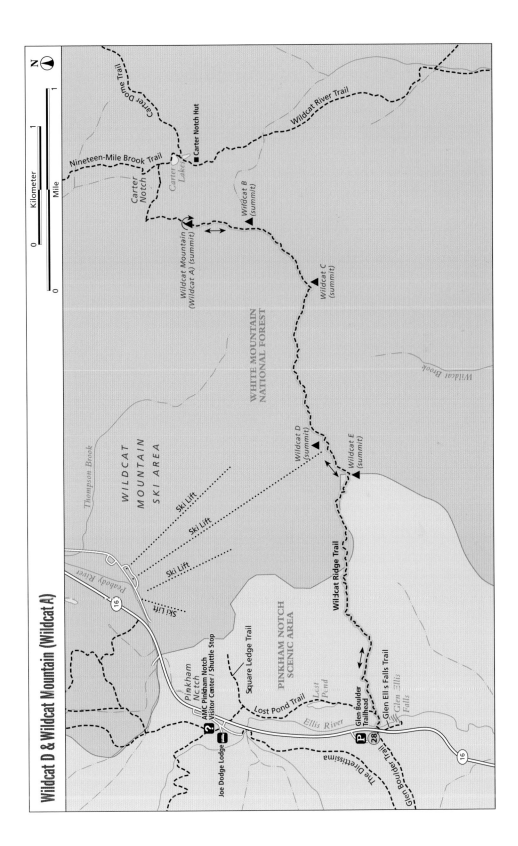

At the beginning of the hike, you cross the Ellis River not far above Glen Ellis Falls.

Gulf of Slides, Tuckerman Ravine, and Huntington Ravine. Finally, the trail begins to moderate as you pop over a small knob then summit Wildcat E at 1.9 miles. Originally on the 4,000-footer list, this was thought to be the higher peak, but it is now known that Wildcat D is the higher of the two.

A short descent takes you to the top of the gondola at Wildcat Mountain Ski Area. Just past this, at 2.2 miles, you reach the summit of Wildcat D, where a viewing platform provides excellent views. There is no rest for the weary, however, as the trail continues to the east, dropping 250 feet and reaching a col at 2.5 miles. The trail goes up and down a few more times before climbing in short bursts up to the summit of Wildcat C at 3.3 miles. As you climb, take the time to enjoy the occasional views back to the west.

The ridge is full of small wonders; the trail is lined by thick spruce, and many of the rocks are covered in a dense layer of green moss. Old man's beard hangs from the trees, while at times a forest of ferns blankets the ground. Head down again and up to Wildcat B at 3.8 miles; a final push takes you to Wildcat A (Wildcat Mountain) at 4.2 miles. Be sure to check out the short spur trail on the right for great views into Carter Notch before returning the way you came.

Miles and Directions

0.0 Start from the parking area for Glen Ellis Falls. Go under the road and head left at the embankment; go over the Ellis River and begin to head up the Wildcat Ridge Trail.

0.1 Stay on the Wildcat Ridge Trail at the junction with the Lost Pond Trail.

0.3 Reach the first view.

0.9 Reach a nice ledge with views to the south at just over 3,000 feet.

1.5 Reach a nice ledgy area with views out to the big ravines on Mount Washington.

1.9 Reach the summit of Wildcat E.

2.1 Reach the top of the gondola at Wildcat Mountain Ski Area.

2.2 Reach the summit of Wildcat D with an observation platform.

3.3 Reach the summit of Wildcat C.

3.8 Reach the summit of Wildcat B.

4.2 Reach the summit of Wildcat A. The summit is represented by a rock on the right, but the best views of Carter Notch and the Carter Range are from a ledge on a short spur to the right. Return the way you came.

8.4 Arrive back at the trailhead.

Other Routes

1. Wildcat Ridge Trail to Nineteen-Mile Brook Trail point-to-point—distance: 8.5 miles; elevation gain: 3,300 feet

2. Wildcat, Carters, and Moriah Traverse (hike 34)—distance: 18.8 miles; elevation gain: 7,500 feet

29 Carter Dome and South and Middle Carter Mountains

Start early on this long and challenging hike over three 4,000-footers. Although there are views off and on throughout, the most impressive views are from Mount Hight, a side peak of Carter Dome, where you get unobstructed line of sight to the entire northern Presidential Range. By cutting through Camp Dodge, this is a fun loop with just a short bit of road walking at the end.

Distance: 13.2-mile loop (includes loop over Mount Hight)
Summit elevation: Carter Dome, 4,832 feet; South Carter, 4,430 feet; Middle Carter, 4,610 feet
4,000-footers rank: Carter Dome, 9; South Carter, 19; Middle Carter, 15
Elevation gain: 4,950 feet (includes loop over Mount Hight)
Difficulty: Moderate to difficult

Hiking time: About 8 hours
Trails used: Nineteen-Mile Brook Trail, Carter Dome Trail, Carter-Moriah Trail, North Carter Trail, Imp Trail, Camp Dodge Cutoff, NH 16
Views: Excellent from Mount Hight; good views along ridge
Canine compatibility: Good; road walk at end
Special considerations: Bring plenty of water; you won't have much once you get near the ridge.

Finding the trailhead: *From the junction of US 2 and NH 16 in Gorham (eastern junction),* follow NH 16 South for 6.8 miles. Parking is in a dirt lot on the left side of the road. *From the junction of US 302 and NH 16 in Glen (just south of Storyland),* take NH 16 North for 15.5 miles. Parking is in a dirt lot on the right side of the road. **GPS:** N44 18.13' / W71 13.27'

The Hike

There are several ways to climb these peaks, but this route creates a nice loop with just a very short road walk at the end. Interestingly, the best views on this loop come from atop a peak that does not qualify as an official 4,000-footer, Mount Hight. **Option:** If you don't want to backtrack, you can also take Nineteen-Mile Brook Trail all the way to Carter Notch and then take the Carter-Moriah Trail up to Carter Dome from there. The mileage and vertical are very similar to the described route, but this alternate route climbs the extremely steep section of trail out of Carter Notch.

Nineteen-Mile Brook Trail begins on the left from the parking area; it follows the brook southeastward as it gradually ascends through a mixed forest and a nice section of hemlock trees on a relatively smooth trail. The brook is beautiful as it pours over large boulders on its way down to the Peabody River. Although occasionally veering away from the brook on short relocations, the trail mostly stays pretty close. Cross a small stream at around 0.5 mile, and at 1.1 miles reach a nice bridge that crosses a tributary coursing down off the ridge. The trail gets a little bit rougher as the valley begins to steepen, entering the mid-elevation birch forest. At 1.9 miles reach the intersection with the Carter Dome Trail.

You pass some beautiful cascades along Nineteen-Mile Brook.

Turn left (east) onto the Carter Dome Trail. Although slightly steeper, the route is still very moderate; the trail follows an old road that serviced a fire tower, which stood until 1947. You make a few stream crossings at 2.4 miles and another at 2.7 miles; as you gain elevation, switchbacks keep the grade moderate as the mountainside steepens. At Zeta Pass, 3.8 miles from the trailhead (around 3,900 feet), the Carter Dome Trail joins the Carter-Moriah Trail.

Head straight/right here, first east then south; at 4.0 miles the Carter-Moriah Trail heads left to climb Mount Hight. (You can choose to climb Mount Hight on the way out to Carter Dome, on the way back, or both if you are so inclined. This trail description includes an ascent of Mount Hight on the return trip from Carter Dome.) Stay straight (south) on the Carter Dome Trail as it gradually contours up to the south, passing the Carter-Moriah Trail again on the left as it merges once more with the Carter Dome Trail. Shortly after, you pass the Black Angel Trail on your left. This trail heads down into the Wild River Wilderness, which was designated a federal wilderness area in 2006. This beautiful, rugged basin encompasses 23,700 acres to the east of the Carter-Moriah ridgeline.

Continue south on the Carter Dome Trail. At 4.9 miles pass a short spur to an outlook and reach the summit at 5.0 miles. The remains of the old fire tower are visible here, and you can get a decent view from a spot on the northeast corner of the summit area. A huge fire in 1903 destroyed more than 12,000 acres, extending from the summit ridge down to the Wild River. The partial clearing on Carter Dome and the bigger clearing on Mount Hight are remnants of this fire.

Head back down the Carter Dome Trail to the north; as you descend, get a good look at South and Middle Carter ahead. This time, turn right at 5.4 miles onto the Carter-Moriah Trail to climb Mount Hight, where from the summit at 5.8 miles, you get a magnificent view across Pinkham Notch to the eastern side of the northern Presidential Range. You can see part of Tuckerman Ravine and Huntington Ravine to the north below the summit of Mount Washington, as well as a good portion of the winding auto road. Mounts Clay, Jefferson, Adams, and Madison are lined up from left to right.

Continue north on the Carter-Moriah Trail as you descend off Mount Hight. After a short steep section, the trail jogs to the left (west) before meeting up with the Carter Dome Trail again at 6.2 miles. Head right (north) to Zeta Pass at 6.4 miles; this time continue straight/right (north) on the Carter-Moriah Trail toward South Carter Mountain. The trail climbs fairly moderately at first, with a final steep ascent to the summit at 7.2 miles; the actual summit is a few yards left of the trail.

After a good descent of 0.4 mile with a few short steep sections to the col between Middle and South Carter, the trail climbs moderately, with one short steep ledge before reaching a nice view at 8.3 miles where you can see Middle Carter up ahead. At 8.5 miles you reach the wooded summit of Middle Carter. Over the next 0.6 mile the trail goes over a few knobs and ledges with some opportunities for fine views, reaching the junction with the North Carter Trail on the left in 9.1 miles.

Turn left (west) onto the North Carter Trail where it descends fairly steeply near the top, then moderately until reaching the Imp Trail at 10.3 miles. The Imp Trail comes in from both sides, so be sure to head left on the southern branch. The Imp Trail winds down an old logging road in a generally southwesterly heading before turning to the northwest around 2,000 feet in elevation.

At 2.1 miles from the junction with the North Carter Trail (12.4 miles total) keep your eye out as the trail crosses a newer logging road. (It is very helpful to have a GPS/smartphone with a map on it to know where this is.) This logging road, which looks like it has a hiking trail through it, is around 1,550 feet in elevation and cuts over to the AMC's Camp Dodge, which you hit in 0.2 mile. (If you find yourself going due north up a short climb on the Imp Trail, you have passed this junction.) From Camp Dodge, head downhill, veering left on the access road that meets up with NH 16 at 12.8 miles. Head left (south) on NH 16 and in 0.4 mile (13.2 total) arrive back at the Nineteen Mile Brook Trail parking area.

Miles and Directions

0.0 Start from the trailhead on the Nineteen Mile Brook Trail.

1.1 Cross a bridge over the brook.

1.9 Turn left onto the Carter Dome Trail (around 2,300 feet).

A family catches the view from an overlook on Carter Dome.

2.4 Cross the brook.

2.7 Cross the brook again.

3.8 Reach Zeta Pass and head straight/right (east to south) onto the combined Carter-Moriah Trail/Carter Dome Trail.

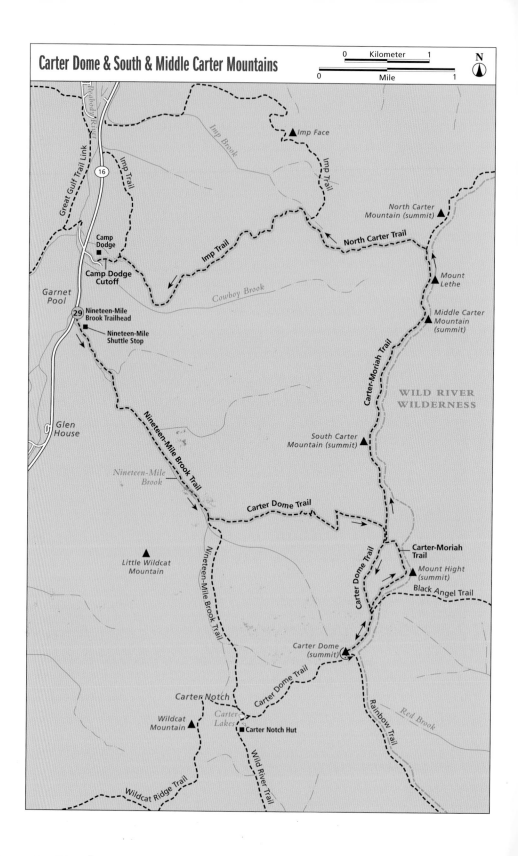

Carter Dome & South & Middle Carter Mountains

0   Kilometer   1

0   Mile   1

N

▲ Imp Face

Imp Brook

Imp Trail

Peabody River

Great Gulf Trail Link

16

Imp Trail

Camp Dodge ■

Camp Dodge
Cutoff

Garnet
Pool

29 Nineteen-Mile
Brook Trailhead ■

Nineteen-Mile
Shuttle Stop

Cowboy Brook

Imp Trail

North Carter Trail

North Carter
Mountain (summit) ▲

Mount ▲
Lethe

Middle Carter ▲
Mountain
(summit)

Carter-Moriah Trail

WILD RIVER
WILDERNESS

Glen
House

Nineteen-Mile
Brook

Nineteen-Mile Brook Trail

Carter Dome Trail

South Carter
Mountain (summit) ▲

▲
Little Wildcat
Mountain

Nineteen-Mile Brook Trail

Carter Dome Trail

Carter-Moriah
Trail

Mount Hight ▲
(summit)

Black Angel Trail

Carter Dome Trail

Carter Dome
(summit) ▲

Rainbow Trail

Red Brook

Carter Notch

Wildcat
Mountain ▲

Carter
Lakes

■ Carter Notch Hut

Wild River Trail

Wildcat Ridge Trail

4.0 At the junction where the Carter-Moriah Trail goes left to climb Mount Hight, stay straight/right (south) and follow the Carter Dome Trail toward Carter Dome.

4.6 The Carter-Moriah Trail comes in from the left, followed shortly by the Black Angel Trail on the left. Stay straight (south) at both intersections.

4.9 A short side path on the right leads to a nice view of the Presidential Range.

5.0 Reach the summit of Carter Dome. There is a nice viewpoint on the right, just before the summit as you enter the clearing. Turn around and head back down the trail.

5.4 Head right (northeast) at the split of the Carter Dome and Carter-Moriah Trails, continuing to follow the Carter-Moriah Trail to the summit of Mount Hight.

5.8 Reach the summit of Mount Hight. Continue straight (north) on the Carter-Moriah Trail.

6.2 Turn right (north) at the junction with the Carter Dome Trail.

6.4 Stay straight/right (north) on the Carter-Moriah Trail at Zeta Pass as the Carter Dome Trail heads back down to the left.

7.2 Reach the summit of South Carter Mountain.

8.5 Reach the summit of Middle Carter Mountain.

9.1 Turn left (west) onto the North Carter Trail.

10.3 At the junction with the Imp Trail, head straight/left (northwest to west) onto the south fork of the Imp Trail.

12.4 The south fork of the Imp Trail crosses a newer logging road at 1,550 feet in elevation. There is no sign, but turn left onto this logging road down to Camp Dodge.

12.6 Reach Camp Dodge. Follow the access road downhill and bear left at the junction.

12.8 Turn left (south) onto NH 16.

13.2 Arrive back at the trailhead.

Other Routes

1. Nineteen-Mile Brook Trail to Carter-Moriah Trail to North Carter Trail to Imp Trail to Camp Dodge Cutoff to NH 16 (road walk)—distance: 13.1 miles; elevation gain: 4,800 feet

2. Carter Dome only (with Mount Hight): Nineteen-Mile Brook Trail to Carter-Moriah Trail to Carter Dome Trail to Nineteen-Mile Brook Trail—distance: 10.2 miles; elevation gain: 3,800 feet

3. South Carter and Middle Carter only: Nineteen-Mile Brook Trail to Carter-Moriah Trail to North Carter Trail to Imp Trail to Camp Dodge Cutoff to NH 16 (road walk)—distance: 10.6 miles; elevation gain: 3,700 feet

4. Wildcat, Carters, and Moriah Traverse (hike 34)—distance: 18.8 miles; elevation gain: 7,500 feet

30 Mount Moriah

Although Mount Moriah is not a particularly tall mountain, the views from the last mile over multiple ledges are stunning, both across the valley to the northern Presidentials and toward the east side of the Carter Range. The route is never very steep, making this a reasonable day hike with plenty of time to enjoy the journey. Mount Moriah's summit, due to its location as the most eastern of the 4,000-footers, also provides good views into Maine and across to the rugged Mahoosuc Range.

Distance: 10.0 miles out and back
Summit elevation: 4,049 feet
4,000-footers rank: 41
Elevation gain: 3,400 feet
Difficulty: Moderate
Hiking time: About 6 hours

Trails used: Stony Brook Trail, Carter-Moriah Trail
Views: Excellent
Canine compatibility: Good; can be difficult in high water, and there is one steep ledge scramble near the summit.

Finding the trailhead: *From the junction of US 2 and NH 16 in Gorham (eastern junction),* follow NH 16 South for 1.8 miles. Turn left onto Stony Brook Road; parking will be in a lot on the left. The trailhead is a couple hundred feet up Stony Brook Road on the left. *From the junction of US 302 and NH 16 in Glen (just south of Storyland),* take NH 16 North for 20.6 miles. Turn right onto Stony Brook Road; parking will be in a lot on the left. The trailhead is a couple hundred feet up Stony Brook Road on the left. **Note:** Google maps calls Stony Brook Road Mount Carter Drive. **GPS:** N44 21.78' / W71 10.65'

The Hike

As the easternmost of New Hampshire's 4,000-footers, Mount Moriah provides a great view of the northern Presidential Range. The route up the mountain using the Stony Brook Trail, although 1.0 mile longer (round-trip) than the direct route up the Carter-Moriah Trail, has less overall vertical gain. More importantly, this route takes you on a gorgeous traverse over the stunning ledges on the south side of the Moriah summit ridge.

From the trailhead, the Stony Brook Trail heads into the woods, crossing the brook immediately, with another crossing on a bridge a few hundred yards later. The trail gains elevation gradually as it follows along the eastern side of the brook, passing through a nice hemlock forest.

At 1.0 mile the trail swings to the right, drops sharply, and crosses the brook one more time before turning left (south) again to follow the route of an old logging road. At 2.3 miles it crosses an upper branch of the brook. To this point the trail gains only 900 feet of elevation, but just after this crossing, it begins to gain elevation much more rapidly.

From the ledges on the Mount Moriah summit ridge, you get great views of the northern Presidential peaks.

Over the next 1.3 miles you gain almost 1,300 feet, with the last section up to the ridge the steepest and roughest. Once on the ridge, at 3.6 miles, turn left onto the Carter-Moriah Trail, passing the Moriah Brook Trail on the right, which leads down into the Wild River Wilderness, a rugged and remote area that was designated a federal wilderness in 2006.

Notice that the blazes have changed from blue to white, as you are now on the Appalachian Trail. During summer you may run into AT through-hikers, who, if they're northbound, will be just a few miles from entering Maine, the final state border they will cross on their journey from Georgia.

The trail climbs steeply at points, traversing big rock ledges with numerous outlooks. At 4.1 miles you get a fantastic view down into the Moriah Brook Valley to the south. Across the Wild River Wilderness, you can see the Meaders and Baldfaces, smaller but dramatic peaks that form the eastern boundary of the Wild River Valley. To the south is the Carter Range, and across the Peabody River Valley to the west, the northern Presidential peaks rise high above everything.

As you climb through the fir forest, the views become more expansive. Swinging around to the left (north), the trail goes over the open ledges on the south end of the summit ridge, where you can see the summit just ahead to the north. On the right you get good views into Maine, and after going through a wooded section near the top, you reach the junction with the Kenduskeag Trail at 5.0 miles.

Mount Madison provides a direct view over the valley to Mount Moriah, distinguished by its long sloping summit ridge.

Turn left at this junction to continue following the Carter-Moriah Trail. A short steep pitch up a rocky ledge will most likely require use of your hands. At the top, turn left to walk the short distance to the summit, which impresses with an expansive view. Another short spur on the right leads to another overlook.

From the summit ledge you get a great view of the northern Presidentials where (from right to left) Mount Madison, Mount Adams, Mount Jefferson, Mount Clay, Mount Washington, and Boott Spur form a massive wall to the west. Just to the left, much closer is the Carter Range with North, Middle, and South Carter Mountains and, beyond, Mount Hight and Carter Dome. Imp Mountain is the small promontory

Mount Moriah

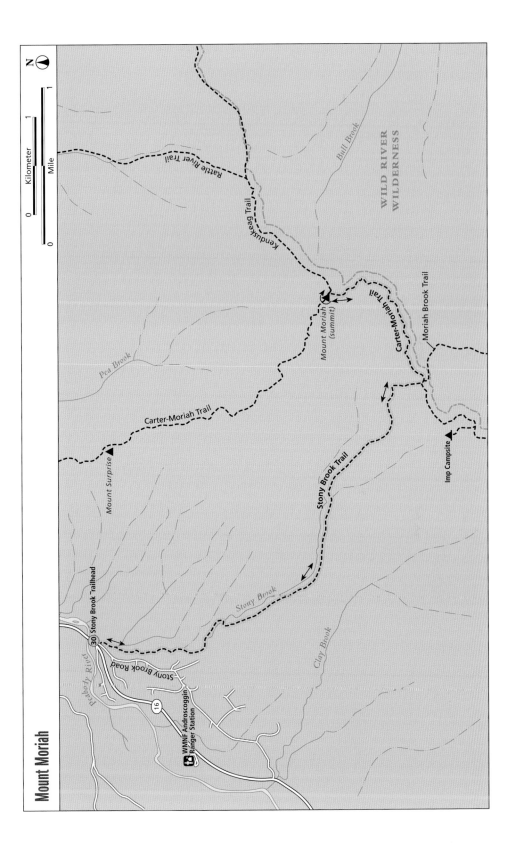

WILD RIVER
WILDERNESS

Rattle River Trail

Kenduskeag Trail

Bull Brook

Mount Moriah
(summit)

Pea Brook

Carter-Moriah Trail

Carter-Moriah Trail

Moriah Brook Trail

Mount Surprise

Stony Brook Trail

Imp Campsite

Stony Brook

Clay Brook

30 Stony Brook Trailhead

Peabody River

Stony Brook Road

WMNF Androscoggin
Ranger Station

16

N

Kilometer
0   1

Mile
0   1

You will stop to take pictures many times on your ascent of Mount Moriah.

between North Carter and Moriah; if you turn around and look to the northeast, the flat, ledgy summit of Shelburne Moriah Mountain dominates the view.

Retrace your steps, following the Carter–Moriah Trail to the south and then the Stony Brook Trail back to the trailhead.

Miles and Directions

0.0 Start from the Stony Brook Trailhead, immediately crossing the brook.

1.0 Cross Stony Brook.

2.3 Cross back over Stony Brook.

3.6 Reach the junction with the Carter-Moriah Trail. Turn left (northeast) and follow this past another junction on the right with the Moriah Brook Trail.

5.0 Reach the junction with the Kenduskeag Trail on the right. Head left up a short but steep ledge scramble on the Carter-Moriah Trail; at the top of the short scramble, go left to the open summit ledge. Follow the same route in reverse back to the trailhead.

10.0 Arrive back at the trailhead.

Other Routes

1. Carter-Moriah Trail out-and-back—distance: 9.0 miles; elevation gain: 3,600 feet

2. Wildcat, Carters, and Moriah Traverse (hike 34)—distance: 18.8 miles; elevation gain: 7,500 feet

The Northern Peaks

The ascent up Mount Cabot on the Bunnell Notch Trail makes for a nice winter hike, and you may run across snow-covered trees that look oddly like animals.

31 Mount Waumbek

This fairly easy and straightforward hike takes you up Mount Starr King first then along a short traverse over to Mount Waumbek. Although the views from the actual summit of Mount Waumbek are not amazing, an open area on Mount Starr King provides decent views to the Presidential Range, and a short journey past the summit of Mount Waumbek does get you to a nice overlook with views to the south and east.

Distance: 7.2 miles out and back
Summit elevation: 4,006 feet
4,000-footers rank: 46
Elevation gain: 2,900 feet
Difficulty: Easy to moderate

Hiking time: About 4 hours
Trails used: Starr King Trail
Views: Okay; restricted views off Starr King
Canine compatibility: Good

Finding the trailhead: *From I-93,* take exit 42. Turn (left if coming from the north, right if coming from the south) onto US 302 West and follow this for 1.5 miles to the junction with NH 116. Head east on NH 116 for 10.5 miles. In the town of Whitefield, NH 116 joins US 3 North for 500 feet. After making a right turn off US 3 back onto NH 116, head east for 8.8 miles. In the town of Jefferson, turn right onto US 2 East and in 0.6 mile turn left onto Starr King Road. Follow this road (which can be bumpy/rutted and veers left from Cottage Road) for 0.2 mile to the trailhead parking. *From the junction of US 2 and NH 16 in Gorham (western junction),* follow US 2 West for 16.2 miles. Turn right onto Starr King Road and follow this road (which can be bumpy/rutted and veers left from Cottage Road) for 0.2 mile to the trailhead parking. **GPS:** N44 25.12' / W71 28.03'

The Hike

Probably the least-strenuous hike in this book, the trip up Mount Waumbek is straightforward, without any real technical sections. This is one of those hikes where you appreciate the small things, such as the way light dances on the ferns and the magic of a moss-draped forest. Although the trail climbs at a rate that is never very steep, do not mistake easier for easy—you still climb 2,400 feet in the first 2.6 miles. Mount Waumbek does not get the same traffic as many other peaks in the White Mountains; on a weekday, you may have the trail to yourself for much of the hike.

Often lumped together with Mount Cabot as one of the two northern peaks, they are actually part of different ranges. Mount Waumbek and Mount Starr King, for which the trail is named, are part of the Pliny Range, whereas Mount Cabot is part of the Pilot Range. In fact, Mount Waumbek was formerly known as Pliny Major. The Pliny Range is a ring dike, which means it was formed by magma rising from a circular crack, usually by the collapsing of a caldera, that cools into hard, resistant rock.

Starting from the trailhead, the Starr King Trail begins ascending an old logging road before quickly joining another old logging road, briefly nearing a stream before

Mount Waumbek and the Pliny Range look small from high atop Mount Adams.

heading in a more easterly direction. You pass a moss-covered circular foundation of an old springhouse around 0.3 mile and then make a short jog to the right at around 0.7 mile. The mixed-hardwood forest surrounds you as you pass oak, birch, and maple trees.

Around 1.7 miles in, the trail levels out for a short bit as it traverses the west side of a knob to the south of Mount Starr King before heading up to the north. At 2.1 miles you pass a sign marking a spring on the left and continue to climb up through the forest, now mostly conifers, to the ridge. Just before reaching the summit of Mount Starr King, the trail makes a 180-degree turn to the south and then passes over a few open slabs to reach the summit at 2.6 miles. Just ahead is a small clearing that provides a decent stand-up view southeast toward the Presidential Range.

Here you reach an interesting site: the fireplace and chimney of an old shelter that was removed in 1980. You also get a somewhat obscured view of your destination, Mount Waumbek, ahead. The 1.0-mile traverse over to Mount Waumbek consists of a nice winding stroll through the fir forest. At times the trees come so close to the trail that you may find needles buried in your pockets and backpack, while at other times it is nice and open with partial views.

You drop just 150 feet in elevation before making a gradual 250-foot ascent to the final level traverse toward the summit. At 3.6 miles a rock cairn marks the summit; head another few hundred feet on the Kilkenny Ridge Trail to a short spur with a view over some blowdowns. From here you can see Mount Moriah and the Carter

Mount Waumbek

You pass the remains of an old springhouse on your way up the Starr King Trail.

Range to the east, with most of the Presidential Range spanning the horizon. When you have soaked up the views, return to the trailhead by retracing your steps back down the Starr King Trail.

Miles and Directions

0.0 Start on the Starr King Trail from the parking area.

2.1 Pass a spring (signed) on the left.

2.6 Reach the summit of Mount Starr King.

3.6 Reach the summit of Mount Waumbek. (Partial view is a few hundred feet past summit.) Return the way you came.

7.2 Arrive back at the trailhead.

Other Routes

Kilkenny Ridge Traverse (bonus hike 8)—distance: 24.8 miles; elevation gain: 8,550 feet

32 Mount Cabot

The most northern of New Hampshire's 4,000-footers, the actual summit of Mount Cabot is in the woods, but an old fire warden's cabin on the summit ridge provides a nice view and a chance to sit down. The journey up through Bunnell Notch and the view from Bunnell Rock provide a nice opportunity to enjoy the northern forest.

Distance: 9.6 miles out and back
Summit elevation: 4,170 feet
4,000-footers rank: 33
Elevation gain: 3,050 feet
Difficulty: Moderate
Hiking time: About 5 hours

Trails used: York Pond Trail, Bunnell Notch Trail, Kilkenny Ridge Trail
Views: Good from Bunnell Notch and near cabin; no views from summit
Canine compatibility: Good unless very high water

Finding the trailhead: *From I-93 (from the south),* take exit 41. Turn (left if coming from the north, right if coming from the south) onto Cottage Street and follow this for about 0.7 mile to the junction with NH 116. Turn right to head east on NH 116 for 10.5 miles. In the town of Whitefield, NH 116 joins US 3 North. Turn left to take this for 18.3 miles then turn right onto NH 110 East. In 17.6 miles, turn right onto York Pond Road and follow this for 7 miles. Around 5 miles in, you will see the sign for the fish hatchery. Trailhead parking is 2.1 miles past this sign, in a little lot on the left across from a tall fence guarding the fish raceway. *From I-91/I-93 (from the north),* take exit 1 off I-93 (in Vermont) and turn left onto VT 18. Follow this for 0.6 mile then turn right onto US 2 East. In 23.9 miles, continue straight onto VT 102 North and go another 7.4 miles before making a left turn onto US 3 North. Follow US 3 North for 3.2 miles; turn right onto NH 110 East and go another 17.6 miles. Turn right onto York Pond Road and follow this for 7 miles. Around 5 miles in, you will see the sign for the fish hatchery. The trailhead is 2.1 miles past this sign, in a little lot on the left across from a tall fence guarding the fish raceway. *From the west/north junction of US 2 and NH 16 in Gorham,* take NH 16 North for 5 miles; veer left onto Green Street where NH 16 heads right. From the traffic light at Green and Pleasant, continue straight on NH 110 for another 7.2 miles. Turn left onto York Pond Road and follow this for 7 miles. Around 5 miles in, you will see the sign for the fish hatchery. The trailhead is 2.1 miles past this sign, in a little lot on the left across from a tall fence guarding the fish raceway. **GPS:** N44 29.80' / W71 21.53'

The Hike

Mount Cabot is the northernmost of the New Hampshire 4,000-footers and is the highest mountain of the Pilot Range, located in a region called the Kilkenny, after the name of the unpopulated township in which the mountain exists. Named for Sebastian Cabot, an English sea captain who explored the New England coast, this peak feels very remote; even on a nice weekday in summer, it's unlikely you will meet many other hikers. If you do, they most likely are there to complete their

Bunnell Rock is a great viewpoint near the summit of Mount Cabot.

4,000-footers as well. A cabin with nice views is situated on the summit; it's a good place for a break, as the summit itself is completely wooded.

From the parking area, take the York Pond Trail along a flat logging road for 0.2 mile then turn right (west) onto the Bunnell Notch Trail. This route is also an old logging road in the beginning, and it stays pretty flat as it gently rolls in an easterly direction. Following the trail, stay straight at 0.5 mile as another logging road joins from the left. You can catch decent views of Mount Cabot straight ahead before making a short descent to cross a few streams, including the main stream coming off Bunnell Notch at 0.7 mile. Soon the trail turns off the old logging road and slowly begins to climb. After a sharp turn to the right at around 1.2 miles, the trail rejoins the stream and follows it up the valley.

Over the next 1.7 miles, the trail climbs steadily but gently, gaining 1,100 feet. After a shorter steep section around mile 2.6, the trail makes a slight right turn to climb gently to Bunnell Notch at 2.9 miles. Along the way the trail transitions from mixed hardwoods to a mix of birch and conifers. A short descent leads to the junction with the Kilkenny Ridge Trail at 3.0 miles.

Continue right/straight (west) on the Kilkenny Ridge Trail as it continues to descend for the next 0.2 mile before beginning to climb again. The trail swings to the right (north) at around 3.4 miles in and begins to climb in earnest, making another sharp right (east) at around 3.8 miles. By this point, the forest is mostly fir.

At 3.9 miles, reach a short spur to Bunnell Rock, where you get a nice view to the south. The closest mountain across Bunnell Notch is the north peak of Terrace

DID YOU KNOW? Both Mount Waumbek and Mount Cabot are on the Cohos Trail, a 170-plus-mile hiking trail that travels from Crawford Notch to the border of Canada, all the way through Coos County, the most northern county in New Hampshire. Much of the trail is very remote and travels through some beautiful country. It traverses the incredible Rogers Ledges and the rounded Percy Peaks; passes the Connecticut Lakes, the headwaters of the Connecticut River; and even travels over the Presidential Range and along the Davis Path. For a truly stunning journey, through-hike it in the fall and experience the peak of northern New England foliage. You can find out more at cohostrail.org.

Mountain, the next peak south on the Kilkenny Ridge Trail.

Over the next 0.5 mile, a series of switchbacks takes you to an old fire warden's cabin at 4.4 miles, just to the northwest of the southern peak of Mount Cabot. Although the fire tower was removed in 1965, the cabin is still maintained by local Boy Scouts and the USDA Forest Service and is an option if you want to spend the night high on a mountain. Just beyond the cabin is the site of the old tower, with decent views.

To reach the summit, continue along the trail, heading northwest with a short descent then a gentle climb through dense balsam fir. A short path just beyond the summit sign leads to a slightly higher point, the true summit.

Follow your route in reverse to return to the trailhead. **Option:** For a bigger

The sky glows behind Mount Cabot and the Pilot Range.

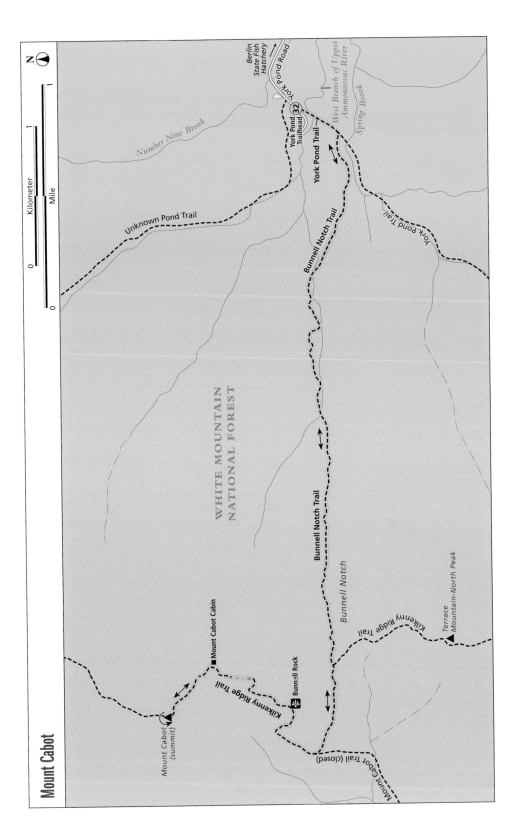

Terrace Mountain rises across Bunnell Notch, as seen from Bunnell Rock.

adventure on an 11.4-mile loop, you can continue north on the Kilkenny Ridge Trail past the summit of Mount Cabot to the Horn, which has a great view back toward Mount Cabot, then past Unknown Pond to the Unknown Pond Trail, which will take you back to the parking area.

Miles and Directions

0.0 Start from the parking area and follow the York Pond Trail southwest.

0.2 Turn right (west) onto the Bunnell Notch Trail.

0.7 Cross the main stream from Bunnell Notch.

2.9 Reach Bunnell Notch.

3.0 Stay straight (west) now on the Kilkenny Ridge Trail as it joins from the left (south).

3.4 Turn right/straight (north) continuing on the Kilkenny Ridge Trail as the unmaintained Mount Cabot Trail joins from the left.

3.9 Reach Bunnell Rock.

4.4 Reach the forester's cabin and, just beyond, the old fire tower clearing.

4.8 Reach the summit of Mount Cabot. (The actual summit is just beyond the sign.) Return by the same route.

9.6 Arrive back at the trailhead.

Other Routes

1. York Pond Trail to Bunnell Notch Trail to Kilkenny Ridge Trail to Horn Spur (summit The Horn) to Kilkenny Ridge Trail to Unknown Pond Trail—distance: 11.4 miles; elevation gain: 3,600 feet

2. Kilkenny Ridge Traverse (bonus hike 8)—distance: 24.8 miles; elevation gain: 8,550 feet

Overnights and Traverses

The Franconia Ridge traverse between Mounts Lafayette and Lincoln provides some of the best hiking in the White Mountains.

A traverse over the entire Presidential Range is one of the most challenging, and rewarding, hikes in the White Mountains. With views for most of the journey, you will feel like you are on top of the world. This traverse can be done in one, two, or three days, but overnights will take some planning and will most likely include staying at a hut, which requires reservations. You will summit eight 4,000-footers along the route: Mounts Madison, Adams, Jefferson, Washington, Monroe, Eisenhower, Pierce, and Jackson. Although the basic traverse does not include Mount Jackson, this hike description includes the journey from Mount Madison all the way over Jackson and Webster.

Distance: 22.9 miles point to point (19.5 miles for basic traverse without Jackson or Webster)
Summit elevation: Mount Madison, 5,366 feet; Mount Adams, 5,799 feet; Mount Jefferson, 5,716 feet; Mount Washington, 6,288 feet; Mount Monroe, 5,372 feet; Mount Eisenhower, 4,760 feet; Mount Pierce, 4,312 feet; Mount Jackson, 4,052 feet
4,000-footers rank: Mount Madison, 5; Mount Adams, 2; Mount Jefferson, 3; Mount Washington, 1; Mount Monroe, 4; Mount Eisenhower, 12; Mount Pierce, 27; Mount Jackson, 39
Elevation gain: 10,050 feet
Difficulty: Very difficult
Hiking time: 14 hours to 3 days, depending on hiking speed

Trails used: Valley Way, The Brookside, Watson Path, Osgood Trail, Star Lake Trail, Lowe's Path, Gulfside Trail, Mount Jefferson Loop, Mount Clay Loop, Trinity Heights Connector, Crawford Path, Mount Monroe Loop, Webster Cliff Trail, Webster-Jackson Trail
Views: Excellent
Canine compatibility: Tough for dogs
Special considerations: Once you're on the ridge, there are few places to get water. Use the huts and the summit of Mount Washington to get water. Over the course of the hike, you will pass the Madison Spring Hut, Mount Washington's Sherman Adams Building, the Lakes of the Clouds Hut, and the Mizpah Hut.

Finding the trailhead: You can park your car at the AMC Highland Center and take the AMC Hikers Shuttle from the center to the Appalachia Trailhead parking on US 2. Otherwise you will need to drop a car off at the parking area just south of Saco Lake on US 302.

  Vehicle drop-off (Webster-Jackson Trail parking): From the junction of US 302 and US 3 in Twin Mountain/Carroll, follow US 302 East for 8.7 miles. Parking is on the right just past Saco Lake and right before the sign for Crawford Notch State Park. The trailhead is across the road. *From the junction of US 302 and NH 16 in Glen,* follow US 302 West for 20.3 miles. Parking is on the left just after you pop out of the notch at the top of the hill. If you pass Saco Lake on the right, you have gone too far. The trailhead is across from the parking area. **GPS: N44 12.90' / W71 24.50'**

  Starting trailhead (Appalachia Trailhead): From the junction of US 2 and NH 16 in Gorham (western junction), follow US 2 West for 5.4 miles. Parking for the Appalachia Trailhead will be on the left. *From I-93,* take exit 40 and head right on US 302 East for 11.1 miles. Turn left onto US 3 North and then turn right onto NH 115 North in 2.0 miles. Continue for 9.7 miles to the intersection with US 2. Turn right and on US 2 East and go 7.1 miles. Parking for the Appalachia Trailhead will be on the right. **GPS: N44 22.28' / W71 17.37'**

The Hike

Important note: This is the author's general guide to completing the traverse. Mileage is approximate, and depending on the exact route and small variations, as well as differing distances on GPS and maps, your actual hiking distance may be slightly higher or lower than listed. As there are multiple variations and this is a big hike, those attempting the traverse should plan out their route using maps and available resources. Directions here are less specific than earlier hikes in this book and are to be used as guidelines for a Presidential ("Presi") Traverse. This route also includes a few trails that aren't typically part of the traverse, including Brookside Trail, Watson Path, and Star Lake Trail.

In its simplest form, a Presi Traverse requires hiking over all the major peaks in the Presidential Range that are named for actual presidents in one contiguous hike. Usually hiked from north to south, at minimum a Presi Traverse entails climbing over Mounts Madison, Adams, Jefferson, Washington, Monroe, Eisenhower, and Pierce. Many people include Mounts Clay and Franklin (not official 4,000-footers), and by

The Gulfside Trail heads toward Mount Clay.

Much of the first half of the Presi Traverse follows the Gulfside Trail.

adding Jackson (not named for the president), all eight 4,000-footers are summited. For a full traverse of the range, Mount Webster can also be added as it is here.

Exact mileage and elevation gain can be a bit difficult to figure out, but the minimum Presi Traverse covers about 19.5 miles with 8,500 feet of elevation gain; the version that includes Clay, Franklin, Jackson, and Webster (described here) is closer to 23 miles with about 10,000 feet of elevation gain.

By starting in the north and summiting Mount Madison at the start of the traverse, hikers do the majority of climbing and cover the most difficult terrain first. After summiting Mount Washington, the Crawford Path provides a much faster, less technical, mostly descending route for the second half of the hike.

Many fit hikers attempt to complete the traverse in a day. There are numerous bailout points, and by making it a single-day excursion, you can keep the pack weight to a minimum. Otherwise, hikers need to figure out logistics as to where to stay overnight, with many making reservations for the first night at the Madison Hut and a second night at the Lakes of the Clouds Hut. There is no camping in the alpine zone, so to camp along the route, hikers must descend below tree line to camp, possibly using one of the Randolph Mountain Club camps.

Once on the ridge, the route is pretty straightforward, although there are a few options. The biggest choices are which trail to climb up Mount Madison and where you want to end the traverse. Most people choose to start from the Appalachia Trailhead in Randolph on US 2, and the most popular route up is the Valley Way. Since the Valley Way requires an out-and-back to the summit of Mount Madison from the Madison Spring Hut, the author suggests taking the Watson Path from The Brookside to have a true traverse without repeating any section.

The description of the Presi Traverse here includes this route to Mount Madison and includes summiting all the major trail-accessible peaks, including Mounts Clay, Franklin, Jackson, and Webster, and does not include camping suggestions.

From the Appalachia Trailhead, follow signs for the Valley Way. At 0.8 mile get onto The Brookside, and at 2.4 miles reach the junction with the Watson Path. Turn left onto the Watson Path then cross Snyder Brook at Duck Fall. Immediately after crossing the brook, the trail begins its very steep climb up to Mount Madison along Gordon Ridge. From the Valley Way, crossing to the summit, the Watson Path climbs 2,200 feet in just 1.5 miles. At 3.2 miles it emerges in the rocky alpine terrain and continues to climb steeply to Mount Madison's summit at 3.9 miles.

From the summit, follow the Osgood Trail down to the Madison Spring Hut at 4.4 miles. Although the most common route is to follow the Gulfside Trail to Air Line to climb Mount Adams, a more interesting option is to climb the Star Lake Trail. At the hut, head left (south) on the Star Lake Trail, passing the small but beautiful Star Lake and then the junction with the Buttress Trail on the left at 4.7 miles. The Star Lake Trail climbs steeply below a subpeak called John Quincy Adams and has some difficult talus hopping and ledge scrambling near the top. Off to your left as you climb, you get a terrific view into the Great Gulf Wilderness. Reach the summit of Mount Adams at 5.4 miles.

From the summit of Mount Adams, take Lowe's Path west until you reach Thunderstorm Junction at 5.7 miles. Just before Thunderstorm Junction, there is a shortcut using Israel Ridge Path west over to the Gulfside Trail, but if that's not clear, just reach Thunderstorm Junction where the Gulfside Trail, Lowe's Path, and the Great Gully Trail all converge. Follow the Gulfside Trail left (southwest) toward Mount Jefferson.

The ridge provides a great chance to experience this unique alpine environment. The Gulfside Trail continues heading down, with a slight rise before the junction with the Israel Ridge Path, then descends southwest on the dramatic ridge that separates Jefferson Ravine on the left (south) and Castle Ravine on the right (north). You reach Edmonds Col, the low point between Mount Adams and Mount Jefferson at 7.0 miles, at just under 5,000 feet in elevation.

Continue on the Gulfside Trail for another 0.2 mile; at 7.2 miles, just after the Gulfside Trail turns to the south, turn right (southwest) onto the Mount Jefferson Loop. A 500-foot climb in 0.4 mile takes you to the summit of Mount Jefferson at 7.6 miles. The trail junction is just a few dozen yards below the actual summit, so a quick hop up to the summit is in order from the summit junction.

Head left (south) to follow the second part of the Mount Jefferson Loop to the junction with the Gulfside Trail again at 7.9 miles. Continue south, past the Sphinx Trail on the left, over the Sphinx Col (low point) to the Mount Clay Loop at 8.6 miles. Climb 500 feet and 0.5 mile to the summit of Mount Clay at 9.1 miles. (Mount Clay does not count as an official 4,000-footer, as it does not have 200 feet of prominence.) Continue straight and rejoin the Gulfside Trail at 9.8 miles.

Here you are treated to a fantastic view down into the Great Gulf. As you continue toward Mount Washington on the Gulfside Trail, you walk around the upper rim of the ravine. Pass the Westside Trail (which bypasses the Mount Washington summit to join the Crawford Path) and continue curving around to the east until you reach the junction with the Great Gulf Trail at 10.4 miles. Turn right, cross the cog railway tracks, and at 10.6 miles turn left onto the Trinity Heights Connector, which will take you to the summit of Mount Washington.

Leaving the summit, follow signs for the Crawford Path, which is on the west side of the cog railway tracks and head southwest between the Yankee Building on the right and the Stage Office on the left. Turn right (northwest) at a cairn and sign for the Crawford Path and follow this for 0.2 mile to the junction with the Gulfside Trail. Turn left at the junction to continue on the Crawford Path past numerous trail junctions to the Lakes of the Clouds Hut at 12.3 miles. The Crawford Path is still pretty rocky, with a decent drop up to the hut, but as you progress farther south, the trail becomes much easier, both in vertical elevation change and quality of footing.

Leaving the hut, follow the Crawford Path for 0.1 mile to the south before turning right (southwest) onto the Mount Monroe Loop, reaching the summit at 12.7 miles. The Mount Monroe Loop heads over the west peak then descends to the south, reaching the Crawford Path at 13.1 miles. Turn right (southwest) onto the Crawford Path and in 0.4 mile, just around 4,900 feet in elevation, take the short side loop over Mount Franklin on the left, rejoining the Crawford Path in 0.1 mile, at 13.6 miles.

At 14.5 miles the Crawford Path heads left (southwest) as the Mount Eisenhower Loop heads straight/right (west). Take the Mount Eisenhower Loop, passing Edmands Path on the right, and wind your way up to the broad rounded dome of Mount Eisenhower, reaching the summit at 14.9 miles. This is the last peak along the range where the summit is truly in the alpine zone, although there still are plenty of views ahead.

Continue straight ahead, reaching the Crawford Path again at 15.3 miles. Continue heading southwest, through scrub, krummholz, short woods, and open ledges,

Three hikers walk along the Crawford Path.

until you reach the junction with the Webster Cliff Trail at 16.5 miles. From here the Crawford Path heads down to the road, not far from the AMC Highland Center. Head straight/left (southwest) on the Webster Cliff Trail to the summit of Mount Pierce at 16.6 miles.

If you are doing the basic traverse, head back to the junction and go down the Crawford Path for a total of about 19.5 miles. Mount Pierce is the most southern peak on the range that is named for a US president.

To complete the full traverse, continue past the summit of Mount Pierce down a winding path through the woods to the Mizpah Spring Hut at 17.4 miles. Continue on the Webster Cliff Trail, first descending then rolling up to Mount Jackson at 19.1 miles. The summit of Mount Jackson has incredible views up the ridge as well as into the Presidential Range–Dry River Wilderness and down to the south.

Pass the Webster-Jackson Trail on the right, heading south of the summit, descending down a short steep section and across to the final peak, Mount Webster. At 20.4 miles, at the junction with the second Webster-Jackson branch, turn left and head up to the summit at 20.5 miles. You can stand at the edge of the cliff, enjoying the view to Mount Field and reveling in your accomplishment—it's all downhill from here!

Head back to the junction at 20.6 miles and turn left (northwest) down the Webster-Jackson Trail. The top part is steep and rocky and can be slow going, but once you get past the waterfall and join the other branch, the footing gets better. Reach the parking area on US 302 at 22.9 miles.

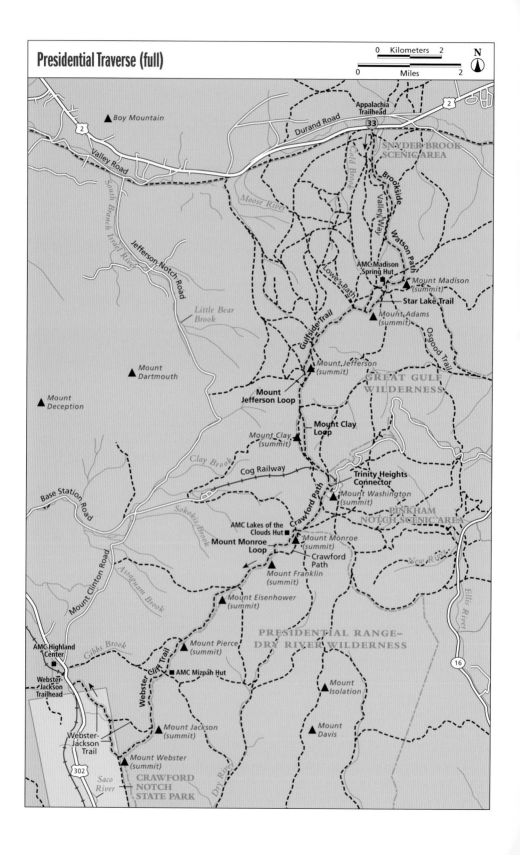

Presidential Traverse (full)

Boy Mountain

Appalachia Trailhead

Durand Road

SNYDER BROOK SCENIC AREA

Valley Road

Moose River

Brookside

Cold Brook

Valley Way

Watson Path

Jefferson-Notch Road

AMC Madison Spring Hut

Mount Madison (summit)

Lowe's Path

Star Lake Trail

Little Bear Brook

Gulfside Trail

Mount Adams (summit)

Osgood Trail

Mount Dartmouth

Mount Jefferson (summit)

GREAT GULF WILDERNESS

Mount Deception

Mount Jefferson Loop

Mount Clay Loop

Mount Clay (summit)

Clay Brook

Cog Railway

Trinity Heights Connector

Base Station Road

Crawford Path

Mount Washington (summit)

PINKHAM NOTCH SCENIC AREA

Sokokis Brook

AMC Lakes of the Clouds Hut

Mount Monroe (summit)

New River

Mount Monroe Loop

Crawford Path

Mount Clinton Road

Assaquam Brook

Mount Franklin (summit)

Mount Eisenhower (summit)

Ellis River

PRESIDENTIAL RANGE- DRY RIVER WILDERNESS

AMC Highland Center

Gibbs Brook

Mount Pierce (summit)

16

Webster- Jackson Trailhead

Webster Cliff Trail

AMC Mizpah Hut

Mount Isolation

Webster- Jackson Trail

Mount Jackson (summit)

Mount Davis

302

Saco River

Mount Webster (summit)

Dry River

CRAWFORD NOTCH STATE PARK

Miles and Directions

0.0 Start up the Valley Way from the Appalachia Trailhead.

0.8 Turn left/straight onto The Brookside.

2.4 Turn left onto the Watson Path.

3.9 Reach the summit of Mount Madison. Turn right (west) to follow the Osgood Trail.

4.4 Reach the Madison Spring Hut. Head left (south) onto the Star Lake Trail.

5.4 Reach the summit of Mount Adams. Continue straight (west) onto Lowe's Path toward Thunderstorm Junction.

5.7 At Thunderstorm Junction, head left (southwest) to follow the Gulfside Trail.

7.2 Turn right (southwest) onto the Mount Jefferson Loop.

7.6 Reach the summit of Mount Jefferson. Continue on the Mount Jefferson Loop.

7.9 Turn right, back onto the Gulfside Trail.

8.6 Turn left (southeast) onto the Mount Clay Loop.

9.1 Reach the summit of Mount Clay. Continue south on the Mount Clay Loop.

9.8 Rejoin the Gulfside Trail.

10.4 At the junction with the Great Gulf Trail on the left, turn right (south) to continue following the Gulfside Trail. Cross over the cog railway tracks.

10.6 Turn left onto the Trinity Heights Connector.

10.8 Reach the summit of Mount Washington. Head southwest from the summit, between buildings, to the Crawford Path.

11.0 Turn left (southwest) at the junction with the Gulfside Trail to continue on the Crawford Path.

12.3 Reach the Lakes of the Clouds Hut. Continue on the Crawford Path.

12.4 Turn right onto the Mount Monroe Loop.

12.7 Reach the summit of Mount Monroe.

13.1 Rejoin the Crawford Path and head right (southwest).

13.5 Head left on the unofficial loop trail over the summit of Mount Franklin.

13.6 Rejoin the Crawford Path.

14.5 Head straight onto the Mount Eisenhower Loop.

14.9 Reach the summit of Mount Eisenhower.

15.3 Rejoin the Crawford Path.

16.5 Head straight/left (southwest) onto the Webster Cliff Trail.

16.6 Reach the summit of Mount Pierce. Continue ahead on the Webster Cliff Trail. (**Option:** If doing the minimal traverse, head back down the trail to the last junction and take the Crawford Path down to the valley.)

17.4 Reach the Mizpah Spring Hut. Continue on the Webster Cliff Trail.

19.1 Reach the summit of Mount Jackson. Continue ahead on the Webster Cliff Trail.

20.4 At the junction with the Webster-Jackson Trail (Webster Branch), continue straight/left to the summit of Mount Webster.

20.5 Reach the summit of Mount Webster then return to the previous junction.

20.6 Turn left (west) onto the Webster Jackson Trail.

22.9 Arrive at the parking area on US 302.

FASTEST KNOWN TIMES

For some, simply hiking the 4,000-footers isn't enough. A growing movement that has merged the hiking and ultra-running communities is the pursuit of FKTs, or Fastest Known Times. Going for speed records in the White Mountains is an age-old tradition, but in recent years a more formalized accounting has begun, and competition has become fierce.

For example, the women's record as of early 2018 for the Presidential Traverse (not the extended version previously described) is 5 hours and 32 minutes by Kristina Folcik; the men's record is 4 hours, 9 minutes, and 35 seconds by Ryan Atkins in 2018.

What's the record for the 4,000-footers? Brianna Tidd set a women's FKT in 2014 of 4 days, 19 hours, and 40 minutes; also that year, Andrew Thompson (who at one point also held the Appalachian Trail speed record) climbed all forty-eight peaks in 3 days, 14 hours, and 59 minutes! They both had support, meaning friends/family helped with transportation and pacing, as well as helped provide food and water.

Then of course there is the "direttissima," a term used in climbing context as a direct climb to a summit up the fall line. The White Mountain Direttissima is a challenge to hike all forty-eight peaks in a direct route without any outside support. Very few people have completed this, but in July 2016, Andrew Drummond did it in 5 days, 23 hours, and 58 minutes for the FKT. He carried all his food and gear, slept very little, climbed around 80,000 vertical feet, and traveled 240 miles. And those are White Mountain miles, so they're worth double!

Mount Adams looms ahead as the second peak on the Presi Traverse.

34 Wildcat, Carters, and Moriah Traverse

A full traverse of the most eastern range of the 4,000-foot peaks is not long, but it is challenging. Steep climbs up to Wildcat Ridge and out of Carter Notch will take you up along some fantastic ridgeline walking, and even though most of the summits are not technically above tree line, there are many views along the way. This journey includes the short trip over Mount Hight too, which has the best views on the ridge. If making this a multiday journey, options for overnight include the Carter Notch Hut and Imp Campsite.

Distance: 18.8 miles point to point
Summit elevation: Wildcat D, 4,062 feet; Wildcat Mountain (A), 4,422 feet; Carter Dome, 4,832 feet; South Carter Mountain, 4,430 feet; Middle Carter Mountain, 4,610 feet; Mount Moriah, 4,049 feet
4,000-footers rank: Wildcat D, 37; Wildcat Mountain (A), 20; Carter Dome, 9; South Carter Mountain, 19; Middle Carter Mountain, 15; Mount Moriah, 41

Elevation gain: 7,500 feet
Difficulty: Very difficult
Hiking time: About 13 hours
Trails used: Wildcat Ridge Trail, Nineteen-Mile Brook Trail, Carter-Moriah Trail
Views: Great, especially from Mount Hight and the ledges on Mount Moriah
Canine compatibility: Not dog friendly due to the length and the extremely steep climb up the Wildcat Ridge Trail

Finding the trailhead: *Starting trailhead (Glen Ellis Falls): From the junction of US 2 and NH 16 in Gorham (eastern junction),* follow NH 16 South for 11.2 miles. Turn right onto a road at a sign for Glen Ellis Falls. Park in the lot and follow the trail under the road. *From the junction of US 302 and NH 16 in Glen (just south of Storyland),* take NH 16 North for 11 miles. Turn right onto a road at a sign for Glen Ellis Falls. Park in the lot and follow the trail under the road. **GPS:** N44 14.75' / W71 15.23'

Ending trailhead (Carter-Moriah Trailhead): From the eastern junction of US 2 and NH 16 in Gorham, follow US 2 East for 0.5 mile. Turn right onto Bangor Street and go 0.5 mile to the parking area. **GPS:** N44 22.92' / W71 10.14'

The Hike

Not all miles are equal, and over the approximately 19 miles of this traverse, you will definitely get your money's worth. This traverse over the easternmost range that includes New Hampshire 4,000-footers, you will get great views, exciting ledge scrambles, and a true sampling of what makes hiking in the White Mountains so challenging—and so interesting. Most of the route follows the Appalachian Trail as well.

For a very fit hiker, this traverse is definitely doable in a day. Unlike the Presidential Traverse (hike 33), you are not above tree line for most of the hike, although there is still a significant amount of exposure to the elements. Due to the steep rocky

The Imp Campsite is a good place to stay if you are doing the Wildcat, Carters, and Moriah Traverse as a multiday adventure.

sections that can be dangerous when wet, do this traverse only when you know you will have good weather.

If you plan on spreading this hike out over multiple days, the most obvious places to stay are at the Carter Notch Hut and the Imp Campsite. This makes the trip much more relaxed but also means you will need to carry a heavier backpack with food and camping/sleeping gear. One important factor is water; there are not a lot of spots along the route where water is guaranteed. Definitely pick up water at the Carter Notch Hut.

As it is much easier to climb up the Wildcat Ridge Trail from NH 16 than go down it, and it is also best to get the biggest climb over with at the beginning of the hike, this route is described from south to north. By going this way, you also do less climbing than you would by going north to south, since the southern trailhead is more than 1,000 feet higher than the northern trailhead.

From the parking area for Glen Ellis Falls, you cross under NH 16, cross over the Ellis River, and climb the Wildcat Ridge Trail, which is very steep and only safe when dry. You will pass numerous spots with wonderful views, including ledges at 0.9 miles 1.5 miles and even a section with wooden steps built into the rocks. Eventually you top out on Wildcat E before continuing up past the top of the Wildcat Mountain Ski Area gondola to the summit of the official 4,000-footer, Wildcat D, at 2.2 miles which has a nice viewing platform.

You continue along the ridge, with a fair amount of up and down, passing over Wildcat C at 3.3 miles, and Wildcat B at 3.8 miles, to the summit of Wildcat Mountain (aka Wildcat A) at 4.2 miles. Make sure to check out the view into Carter Notch from the spur trail on the right near the summit. Continue heading north on the

Wildcat Ridge Trail. The trail heads down along switchbacks then makes a sharp turn to the southeast, crossing an old landslide (with a view north) and reaching Nineteen-Mile Brook Trail at 4.9 miles.

Turn right (south) on the Nineteen-Mile Brook Trail and drop down a short steep pitch to the larger Carter Lake; reach the junction with the Carter-Moriah Trail at 5.0 miles. **Note:** To go to the hut, continue south on the Nineteen-Mile Brook Trail between the two lakes for less than 0.1 mile. You can pick up some water, purchase a baked snack if the hut is open, and rest up for a few minutes before the next big climb.

At the junction of the Nineteen-Mile Brook and Carter-Moriah Trails, turn left (west) (or right if you are coming from the hut) to begin the climb up to Carter Dome on the Carter-Moriah Trail. The next section of trail is extremely steep. In 0.3 mile, or 5.3 miles from the trailhead, a short side trail on the right leads to a great view into Carter Notch and the boulder field called The Ramparts. The trail continues to climb, but soon the grade lessons. At 5.7 miles a path on the left leads to a spring, a good place to get water if you didn't pick up any in the notch. At 6.2 miles you reach the summit clearing of Carter Dome.

The boulder field called The Ramparts is seen from the Carter-Moriah Trail above Carter Notch.

A hiker admires the view from Mount Hight.

From the summit, the best view is at the northeast end of the clearing on the left. Continue straight (northeast) on the Carter-Moriah Trail, passing a nice overlook not far from the summit on the left. Just after passing the Black Angel Trail on your right, at the junction with the Carter Dome Trail, head right (northeast) at 6.6 miles as you continue to follow the Carter-Moriah Trail to the summit of Mount Hight at 7.0 miles.

Mount Hight, although not an official 4,000-footer, provides a fantastic view in all directions and affords the premier view on the ridge. To the west, the northern Presidential peaks rise up out of the valley, and over to the left (southwest) you can see the rounded shape of the peak you just summited, Carter Dome. Over to the right (north) you can see the Carter-Moriah ridgeline heading north, giving you a sense of what lies ahead on your journey.

Head northwest off the summit, which is fairly steep for a short section, reaching the junction with the Carter Dome Trail at 7.4 miles. (The next few miles are the same as the middle section of hike 29.) Turn right (north) and continue to follow the Carter-Moriah Trail (also the Carter Dome Trail), descending to Zeta Pass at 7.6 miles. The Carter Dome Trail heads off to the left; continue forward (north) on the Carter-Moriah Trail, with a final short steep climb to the summit of South Carter at 8.4 miles. At the height of land, the actual summit is just off to the left on a short side trail.

Head north, reaching the col between South Carter and Middle Carter at 8.8 miles. The climb is fairly gentle, and after a short dip, you climb to the mostly level ridge, reaching a nice view to the west at 9.5 miles. Just up the ridge, at 9.7 miles, you reach the summit of Middle Carter.

Just past the summit is another nice view. You will be treated to a few more restricted views as you traverse the rolling ridge to the north, descending to the junction with the North Carter Trail on the left at 10.3 miles. Continue north on the Carter-Moriah Trail, passing a nice view into the Wild River Wilderness to the east on your right and reaching the summit of North Carter (not an official 4,000-footer) at 10.6 miles.

From the summit of North Carter, the trail begins with a gentle descent but shortly after turns right (northeast) and makes a very steep descent on a series of rock ledges. Take your time, and enjoy the views to the north. The trail eases for a bit then makes another short but steep descent before the grade eases about 0.7 mile north of the summit. The trail continues north along the ridge, mostly at a gentle grade with occasional short climbs, and passes through a wet area, crossing a small brook and reaching the junction with the 0.2-mile spur trail to the Imp Campsite at 12.2 miles, where you can refill your water if you are running low.

Continue on the Carter-Moriah Trail as it ascends to an area of ledges with a view, turns left (northwest) and descends, then turns right (northeast) and continues through a series of short ups and downs before reaching the junction with the Stony Brook Trail on the left at 12.9 miles. Turn right, pass the junction with the Moriah Brook Trail in a few dozen yards, then continue up toward Mount Moriah. You pass a series of open ledges with fantastic views, heading mainly in a northeasterly direction before curving around to the north on the summit ridge.

Continue up and down along the ridge, heading through forest, reaching the junction with the Kenduskeag Trail at 14.3 miles. Turn left here, scrambling up a very steep section of ledge where you will need to use your hands, and reach the junction with a short spur on your left that leads in a few dozen yards to the summit of Mount Moriah.

Nearby to the northeast, Middle Moriah and Shelburne Moriah Mountains rise along the ridge; due north across the valley, the ridges of the Mahoosuc Range are visible. To the west you get a great view of the northern Presidentials, and to the left of that, looking southwest, you can see the ridge you just traversed. South Carter is hidden, but you can see North and Middle Carter Mountains nearby and Mount Hight and Carter Dome farther off to the left.

Head off the spur and then go left (northwest) to continue following the Carter-Moriah Trail down the northwest ridge. The initial descent is steep, but then the grade lessons and the trail makes a few ups and downs, continues more steeply to the north, and passes over a series of ledges with nice views. Head over the small Mount Surprise and continue to descend, leaving the White Mountain National Forest at 17.7 miles. Reach the Carter-Moriah Trailhead at 18.8 miles.

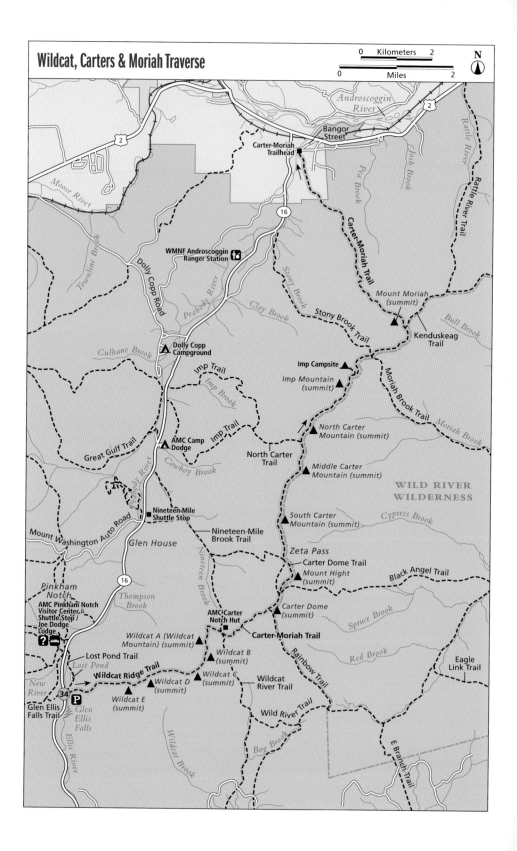

0   Kilometers   2

0   Miles   2

N

Androscoggin River

Rattle River

2

Bangor Street

Moose River

2

Carter-Moriah Trailhead

Josh Brook

Pea Brook

Rattle River Trail

Dolly Copp Road

Townline Brook

WMNF Androscoggin Ranger Station

16

Carter-Moriah Trail

Peabody River

Stony Brook

Clay Brook

Mount Moriah (summit)

Bull Brook

Stony Brook Trail

Kenduskeag Trail

Culhane Brook

Dolly Copp Campground

Imp Trail

Imp Brook

Imp Campsite

Imp Mountain (summit)

Moriah Brook Trail

Moriah Brook

Great Gulf Trail

AMC Camp Dodge

Imp Trail

Cowboy Brook

North Carter Mountain (summit)

North Carter Trail

Middle Carter Mountain (summit)

WILD RIVER WILDERNESS

Peabody River

Nineteen-Mile Shuttle Stop

South Carter Mountain (summit)

Cypress Brook

Mount Washington Auto Road

Glen House

Nineteen-Mile Brook Trail

Nineteen Brook

Zeta Pass

Carter Dome Trail

Mount Hight (summit)

Black Angel Trail

Pinkham Notch

AMC Pinkham Notch Visitor Center / Shuttle Stop / Joe Dodge Lodge

Thompson Brook

16

AMC Carter Notch Hut

Carter Dome (summit)

Carter-Moriah Trail

Spruce Brook

Red Brook

Lost Pond Trail

Lost Pond

Wildcat A (Wildcat Mountain) (summit)

Wildcat B (summit)

Wildcat Ridge Trail

Wildcat C (summit)

Rainbow Trail

Eagle Link Trail

New River

34

P

Wildcat D (summit)

Wildcat E (summit)

Wildcat River Trail

Glen Ellis Falls Trail

Glen Ellis Falls

Ellis River

Wildcat Brook

Bog Brook

Wild River Trail

E Branch Trail

Miles and Directions

0.0   Start from the parking area for Glen Ellis Falls. Go under road, head left at the embankment, go over the Ellis River, and begin to head up the Wildcat Ridge Trail.

0.1   Stay on the Wildcat Ridge Trail at the junction with the Lost Pond Trail.

1.9   Reach the summit of Wildcat E.

2.1   Reach top of the gondola at Wildcat Mountain Ski Area.

2.2   Reach the summit of Wildcat D with an observation platform.

3.3   Reach the summit of Wildcat C.

3.8   Reach the summit of Wildcat B.

4.2   Reach the summit of Wildcat A (aka Wildcat Mountain). Enjoy a great view into notch from the spur trail on right.

4.9   Turn right (south) onto Nineteen-Mile Brook Trail.

5.0   Turn left (west) onto the Carter-Moriah Trail. (**Option:** Continue past two lakes on Nineteen-Mile Brook Trail for a few hundred yards to reach the Carter Notch Hut.)

5.3   Reach the short spur to a nice view into the notch.

5.7   Reach the path to the spring.

6.2   Arrive at the summit of Carter Dome. Continue straight (northeast) on the combined Carter Dome Trail/Carter-Moriah Trail.

6.6   Pass Black Angel Trail on right then head right, following the Carter-Moriah Trail to the summit of Mount Hight.

7.0   Reach the summit of Mount Hight. Continue northwest on the Carter-Moriah Trail.

7.4   Turn right (north) at the junction of the Carter-Moriah and Carter Dome Trails.

7.6   At Zeta Pass, turn right (north) to continue on the Carter-Moriah Trail as the Carter Dome Trail heads down to the west off the ridge.

8.4   Reach the summit of South Carter Mountain.

9.7   Reach the summit of Middle Carter Mountain.

10.3 Pass the North Carter Trail on the left.

10.6 Reach the summit of North Carter Mountain.

12.2 Reach the spur trail to the Imp Campsite.

12.9 Pass Stony Brook Trail on the left and, shortly after, Moriah Brook Trail on the right. Continue on the Carter-Moriah Trail.

14.3 At the junction with the Kenduskeag Trail, turn left (west), following the Carter-Moriah Trail up a steep ledgy section to the summit cone; a short spur on the left then leads to the summit of Mount Moriah. From the spur, head left (northwest) down the Carter-Moriah Trail.

18.8 Arrive at the Carter-Moriah Trailhead.

35 Bonds, Zealand, and Twins Traverse

The hike over Bondcliff, Mount Bond, and West Bond takes you deep within the heart of the Pemigewasset Wilderness. The clifftop views from Bondcliff and the walk along the ridge to Mount Bond are breathtaking. This route takes you over Mount Guyot to a quick out-and-back to Zealand Mountain and then over South and North Twin Mountains, with South Twin providing some of the best views in the White Mountains. This can be done as a long day hike or an overnight by staying at Guyot Campsite.

Distance: 23.1 miles point to point
Summit elevation: Bondcliff, 4,265 feet; Mount Bond, 4,698 feet; West Bond, 4,540 feet; Zealand Mountain, 4,260 feet; South Twin, 4,902 feet; North Twin, 4,761 feet
4,000-footers rank: Bondcliff, 30; Mount Bond, 14; West Bond, 16; Zealand Mountain, 31; South Twin, 8; North Twin, 11
Elevation gain: 6,800 feet
Difficulty: Very difficult
Hiking time: About 13 hours

Trails used: Lincoln Woods Trail, Bondcliff Trail, West Bond Spur, Twinway, Zealand Mountain Spur, North Twin Spur, North Twin Trail
Views: Excellent
Canine compatibility: Not very dog friendly due to a few steep pitches, length, and multiple river crossings
Special considerations: On the last section of the hike, you cross the Little River numerous times; during high water, these crossings can be very dangerous. Haystack Road is not plowed in winter, adding an extra 2.5 miles at the end of the hike.

Finding the trailhead: *Starting trailhead (Lincoln Woods):* The hike begins from Lincoln Woods Trailhead. *From I-93 (from the south),* take exit 32 for NH 112 (Kancamagus Highway). Turn left onto NH 112 East, and in 5.1 miles turn left into the parking area for the Lincoln Woods Trail. *From I-93 (from the north),* take exit 32 for NH 112 (Kancamagus Highway). Turn left onto NH 112 East, and in 5.5 miles turn left into the parking area for the Lincoln Woods Trail. *From the junction of NH 16 and NH 112 in Conway,* take NH 112 West for 30 miles; turn right into the parking area for the Lincoln Woods Trail. **GPS:** N44 03.83' / W71 35.27'

Ending Trailhead (North Twin Trailhead): From I-93 (from the south), take exit 35 and continue onto US 3 North. Follow US 3 North for 7.8 miles. Turn right onto Haystack Road; the trailhead is at the end of the road in 2.5 miles. *From I-93 (from the north),* take exit 36 and turn left onto NH 141 East toward US 3 North. In 0.8 mile, join US 3 North for 7 miles. Turn right onto Haystack Road; the trailhead is at the end of the road in 2.5 miles. *From the junction of US 302 and US 3 in Twin Mountain/Carroll,* head south on US 3 for 2.5 miles. Turn left onto Haystack Road; the trailhead is at the end of the road in 2.5 miles. **GPS:** N44 14.28' / W71 32.85'

The Hike

Logistics for this point-to-point hike are difficult if you do not have a second vehicle.

From the Lincoln Woods Trailhead, cross over the river on the suspension bridge, turn right, and head north on the Lincoln Woods Trail. Follow this flat trail for 2.9 miles; after crossing a bridge over Franconia Brook, continue straight (northeast) on the Bondcliff Trail.

The Bondcliff Trail turns left (north) away from the river at 4.7 miles; you follow this for the next 4.4 miles to the summit of Bondcliff, at 9.1 miles. It's a long climb with some scrambling near the top of Bondcliff, however the dramatic view from the edge of the cliffs is just reward for your hard work. When you have soaked it all in, continue on the Bondcliff Trail to Mount Bond at 10.3 miles, with a short descent and then a good climb in and out of the trees to the top. At 10.8 miles turn left onto the West Bond Spur Trail, reaching the summit of West Bond at 11.3 miles. Head back to the junction with the Bondcliff Trail at 11.8 miles.

Signs atop South Twin Mountain remind the hiker that the Twinway is also the Appalachian Trail.

Hikers climb up toward Mount Guyot.

Turn left back onto the Bondcliff Trail, reaching the junction with the spur trail to the Guyot Campsite at 12.0 miles. It is a short steep trail down to the campsite, but it is the only decent water source for much of the remainder of the hike; if you are running low, definitely fill up. Continue north on the Bondcliff Trail to the junction with the Twinway at 12.6 miles.

If you are going to make the trip out to Zealand Mountain, turn right (east) on the Twinway. You will make a short climb over the open, rounded summit of Mount Guyot. You quickly enter the woods and begin descending. Although the trail is not very steep, there are some places with difficult footing. Note that the blazes are white here, as you are on the Appalachian Trail.

After curving to the north, the trail makes a sharp right turn to the east then gently curves back to the north, reaching the low point at 13.6 miles. A short steep climb takes you to the junction with the Zealand Mountain Spur Trail on the left at 13.9 miles. Follow this for 0.1 mile, reaching the wooded summit of Zealand Mountain at 14.0 miles. Retrace your steps to follow the Twinway back over Mount Guyot to the junction with the Bondcliff Trail at 15.4 miles; turn right (north) to continue following the Twinway.

The trail is pretty rocky near Mount Guyot, but it soon becomes easier as you head northwest along the ridge between Mount Guyot and South Twin Mountain. You gain elevation slowly as you go up and down along the broad ridge, which offers only a few restricted views. A final steep climb takes you to the summit of South Twin at 17.5 miles. The summit of South Twin affords incredible views in all directions.

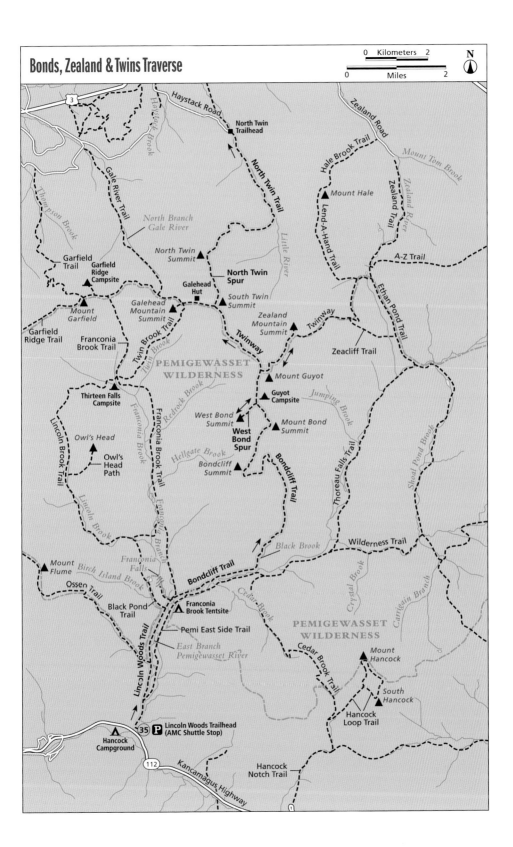

Bonds, Zealand & Twins Traverse

0 Kilometers 2

0 Miles 2

N

Haystack Road

Zealand Road

Mount Tom Brook

3

North Twin Trailhead

Hale Brook Trail

Haystack Brook

Gale River Trail

North Branch Gale River

North Twin Trail

Little River

Mount Hale

Zealand River

Zealand Trail

Lend-A-Hand Trail

Thompson Brook

Garfield Trail

Garfield Ridge Campsite

North Twin Summit

North Twin Spur

A-Z Trail

Galehead Hut

South Twin Summit

Ethan Pond Trail

Mount Garfield

Galehead Mountain Summit

Twin Brook Trail

Zealand Mountain Summit

Twinway

Garfield Ridge Trail

Franconia Brook Trail

Twinway

Zeacliff Trail

Twin Brook

PEMIGEWASSET WILDERNESS

Redrock Brook

Mount Guyot

Jumping Brook

Thirteen Falls Campsite

Guyot Campsite

Franconia Brook

Franconia Brook Trail

West Bond Summit

Mount Bond Summit

Lincoln Brook Trail

Owl's Head

Owl's Head Path

West Bond Spur

Hellgate Brook

Bondcliff Summit

Bondcliff Trail

Thoreau Falls Trail

Shoal Pond Brook

Lincoln Brook

Mount Flume

Franconia Falls

Franconia Branch

Black Brook

Wilderness Trail

Osseo Trail

Birch Island Brook

Bondcliff Trail

Crystal Brook

Carrigain Branch

Black Pond Trail

Cedar Brook

Franconia Brook Tentsite

PEMIGEWASSET WILDERNESS

Lincoln Woods Trail

Pemi East Side Trail

East Branch Pemigewasset River

Cedar Brook Trail

Mount Hancock

South Hancock

Hancock Loop Trail

35

P

Lincoln Woods Trailhead (AMC Shuttle Stop)

Hancock Campground

Hancock Notch Trail

112

Kancamagus Highway

The Twinway (also the Appalachian Trail) continues steeply down to the east to the Galehead Hut. Instead, head north on the North Twin Spur over the north knob of South Twin, down off the shoulder and into a mix of woods and more open areas often filled with ferns, to the col between North and South Twin Mountains; then ascend to the summit of North Twin at 18.8 miles.

Although there are no views from the summit of North Twin, a short spur to the left (west) takes you to an open ledge with great views. From the summit of North Twin, follow the North Twin Trail north, at first gently then steeply down to the Little River. The trail becomes much less steep as you head northwest to the trailhead along the river, crossing it numerous times. Reach the North Twin Trailhead at 23.1 miles.

Miles and Directions

0.0 Start at the ranger station and head left. Cross the bridge over the East Branch of the Pemigewasset River and turn right onto the Lincoln Woods Trail.

1.4 Pass the junction with the Osseo Trail on the left.

2.6 Pass the junction with Black Pond Trail on the left.

2.9 Pass the junction with the Franconia Falls Trail on left; cross the bridge and head straight/right (northeast) onto the Bondcliff Trail.

4.7 The Bondcliff Trail turns left, away from the river.

6.1 Cross Black Brook.

6.6 Cross Black Brook again, often the last place for guaranteed water.

7.2 Cross Black Brook again (often dry). Shortly after, get the hike's first good view.

9.1 Reach the summit of Bondcliff.

10.3 Reach the summit of Mount Bond.

10.8 Turn left onto the West Bond Spur Trail.

11.3 Reach the summit of West Bond. Turn around and head back to the Bondcliff Trail.

11.8 Turn left (north) onto the Bondcliff Trail.

12.0 Pass the spur to Guyot Campsite on the right. (**Option:** Head down 0.2 mile to reach the spring for water, shelter, and tent platforms.)

12.6 Turn right (east) onto Twinway.

13.9 Turn left (north) at the Zealand Mountain Spur Trail.

14.0 Arrive at the Zealand Mountain summit. Return along Twinway to Guyot.

15.4 At the junction with the Bondcliff Trail, continue right (north) on Twinway.

17.5 Reach the summit of South Twin Mountain. Head right (north) onto North Twin Spur.

18.8 Reach the summit of North Twin Mountain. A short path on the left leads to a ledge with views. Continue to the north on the North Twin Trail.

21.2 Cross Little River.

21.8 Cross Little River.

22.3 Cross Little River.

23.1 Arrive at the North Twin Trailhead.

36 Pemigewasset Extended Loop (counterclockwise)

This hike, which happens to be the author's favorite hike in the White Mountains, makes a big loop through the Pemigewasset Wilderness. The basic loop is shorter, but with a few extra out-and-backs, described below, you will summit twelve 4,000-footers: Bondcliff, Mount Bond, West Bond, Zealand Mountain, South and North Twin Mountains, Galehead Mountain, Mount Garfield, and Mounts Lafayette, Lincoln, Liberty, and Flume. Along the way you traverse the beautiful Bond Range and the stunning and dramatic Franconia Ridge. This loop can be completed in one, two, three, or even four days if taking your time.

Distance: 38.5-mile lollipop loop with spurs (31.5-mile basic loop without West Bond, Zealand, North Twin, and Galehead Mountains)
Summit elevation: Bondcliff, 4,265 feet; Mount Bond, 4,698 feet; West Bond, 4,540 feet; Zealand Mountain, 4,260 feet; South Twin Mountain, 4,902 feet; North Twin Mountain, 4,761 feet; Galehead Mountain, 4,024 feet; Mount Garfield, 4,500 feet; Mount Lafayette, 5,260 feet; Mount Lincoln, 5,089 feet; Mount Liberty, 4,459 feet; Mount Flume, 4,328 feet
4,000-footers rank: Bondcliff, 30; Mount Bond, 14; West Bond, 16; Zealand Mountain, 31; South Twin Mountain, 8; North Twin Mountain, 11; Galehead Mountain, 44; Mount Garfield, 17; Mount Lafayette, 6; Mount Lincoln, 7; Mount Liberty, 18; Mount Flume, 25
Elevation gain: 12,500 feet (basic loop: 10,000 feet)
Difficulty: Very difficult

Hiking time: 15 hours to 3 days
Trails used: Lincoln Woods Trail, Bondcliff Trail, West Bond Spur, Twinway, Zealand Spur, North Twin Spur, Frost Trail, Garfield Ridge Trail, Franconia Ridge Trail, Osseo Trail
Views: Excellent
Canine compatibility: Very difficult for dogs due to distance, distance between water sources, and steep ledge scrambles
Special considerations: During busy periods, the official campsites along the route (Guyot Campsite, Garfield Ridge Campsite, Liberty Spring Tentsite) can fill up and they are first come, first served. There are not many other options along the route, and the Galehead Hut requires reservations. There are long sections at times between water sources, so prepare accordingly. You can basically assume that when you are along a ridgeline you are unlikely to find reliable water.

Finding the trailhead: From I-93 (from the south), take exit 32 for NH 112 (Kancamagus Highway). Turn left onto NH 112 East, and in 5.1 miles turn left into the parking area for the Lincoln Woods Trail. From I-93 (from the north), take exit 32 for NH 112 (Kancamagus Highway). Turn left onto NH 112 East, and in 5.5 miles turn left into the parking area for the Lincoln Woods Trail. From the junction of NH 16 and NH 112 in Conway, take NH 112 West for 30 miles; turn right into the parking area for the Lincoln Woods Trail. **GPS:** N44 03.83' / W71 35.27'

The Hike

The Pemigewasset Loop, or "Pemi Loop" as it's most often called, is a classic and premier hike in the White Mountains. Either within or on the border of the Pemigewasset Wilderness for most of the loop, you are treated to incredible views as you traverse some of the most beautiful ridgelines in New England.

The version described here includes peaks that are nearby but not actually on the basic version of the loop, including West Bond, Zealand Mountain, North Twin Mountain, Galehead Mountain, and Mount Garfield. Most people who do the standard Pemi Loop still include Mount Garfield, as it is just a few hundred yards out on a spur, but by including these extra peaks, you get a total of twelve official 4,000-footers on one hike! Once you are up on the ridge, it makes sense to bag these peaks while you are so close.

For most backpackers, this is a very doable three-day trip, while those who are fit should have no trouble doing it in two days. Completing the regular loop, and especially the extended loop, in a day is a big challenge and one that any hiker should be proud of. If the weather changes or you are slowed down due to injury or anything else, there are multiple bailout points along the way, although those would require finding a ride back to the trailhead.

By going counterclockwise, as described here, you do most of the flat walking along the Lincoln Woods and Bondcliff Trails at the beginning of the hike, leaving Franconia Ridge as the culminating traverse before heading back down. Going clockwise, you would get the biggest climb done early but spend more time at the end of the hike below tree line.

There are not a lot of guaranteed water sources along the route, so it is vitally important to fill up and drink when you have the opportunity. Keep in mind that once above tree line, the likelihood of finding water is low.

From the Lincoln Woods Trailhead, cross over the river on the suspension bridge, turn right, and head north on the Lincoln Woods Trail. Follow this flat trail for 2.9 miles; after crossing a bridge over Franconia Brook, continue straight (northeast) on the Bondcliff Trail.

The Bondcliff Trail turns left (north) away from the river at 4.7 miles; you follow this for the next 4.4 miles to the summit of Bondcliff, at 9.1 miles. It's a long climb with some scrambling near the top of Bondcliff, however the dramatic view from the edge of the cliffs is just reward for your hard work. When you have soaked it all in, continue on the Bondcliff Trail to Mount Bond at 10.3 miles, with a short descent and then a good climb in and out of the trees to the top. At 10.8 miles turn left onto the West Bond Spur Trail, reaching the summit of West Bond at 11.3 miles. Head back to the junction with the Bondcliff Trail at 11.8 miles.

Turn left (north) back onto the Bondcliff Trail, reaching the spur for the Guyot Campsite at 12.0 miles. If you are doing this as a three-day adventure, Guyot Campsite is a logical place to spend the first night. It is 0.2 mile down a fairly steep trail to

Mounts Liberty and Flume poke above the clouds.

the shelter and tent platforms. It is also the only place where you are likely to find water until you reach Galehead Hut, so if you are running low, it's worth leaving your bag at the junction and heading down to the spring to get some water, even if you are not planning on spending the night.

From the junction with the spur trail, continue north on the Bondcliff Trail to the junction with the Twinway, just below Mount Guyot at 12.6 miles. From here, most of your route until reaching Liberty Spring Trail just north of Mount Liberty on Franconia Ridge, will be following the Appalachian Trail, marked with white blazes on rocks and trees.

Turn right (east) and follow the Twinway to the Zealand Spur, turning left on the spur and reaching Zealand Mountain at 14.0 miles. Return along the Twinway, and at the junction with the Bondcliff Trail, head right (north) on the Twinway, following the ridge to the summit of South Twin Mountain at 17.5 miles. Head out on the North Twin Spur to North Twin Mountain at 18.8 miles, with a nice view off a short spur trail to the left.

Head back along the North Twin Spur to the summit of South Twin at 20.1 miles. As you look west down the Twinway, you can make out Galehead Hut far below. This is a very steep section, down big rocks, so take your time. You drop more than 1,100 vertical feet in just 0.8 mile, reaching the hut at 20.9 miles.

Get water, purchase a baked snack at the hut (during operating months), and enjoy the nice view to the south from the opening. To summit Galehead Mountain,

The light of the setting sun reaches the cliffs near the summit of Mount Liberty.

follow signs for the Frost Trail, heading past the Twin Brook Trail and up a short steep section. An outlook is just to the left at the top of the short pitch, where you get a nice view of the hut and North and South Twin Mountains behind it. A winding path ahead takes you to the summit at 21.4 miles. Return to the hut at 21.9 miles.

If you are doing the loop in two days, Galehead Hut is a logical place to stay for the night. If you don't want to stay at the hut, or could not get a reservation, continue on the loop to the Garfield Ridge Campsite. From the hut, follow signs for the Garfield Ridge Trail. You descend a short steep pitch and traverse over some big rocks, first heading north then west until you reach the junction with the Gale River Trail on the right at 22.5 miles.

This next section of trail is very difficult. With odd foot angles, lots of little ups and downs, roots, rocks, and some wet sections, do not be surprised if the traverse over to Mount Garfield takes longer than you thought it would. Continue heading west, passing the Franconia Brook Trail on your left at 24.1 miles. A short climb, then a level section, takes you to the steepest section of the loop.

Unless it is during an extremely dry period, this section may seem more like a steep waterfall than an actual trail. Take your time, and make sure to use your hands and secure your footing before taking your next step. At 24.6 miles you reach the spur trail to the Garfield Ridge Campsite. A spring at the junction provides good water. This campsite is a nice spot for a first night if you are really moving, or a second night if you are taking your time.

Continue climbing the steep rocky trail, passing the Garfield Trail on your right at 24.8 miles and reaching the short spur to the summit of Mount Garfield at 25.0 miles. Head left and up along the rocks to the summit of Mount Garfield. The concrete base walls of an old fire tower can provide some relief it it's windy. The views are marvelous, with the Pemigewasset Wilderness spreading out in front of you to the south and Franconia Ridge rising high up to the west. You get one of the best views of remote Owl's Head Mountain to the south and over to the east you see Galehead Mountain and the Twins rising above.

Continue on the Garfield Ridge Trail to the west. As you descend off the summit, you might notice Garfield Pond, with an informal trail to the shore on the right about 0.5 mile and about 600 vertical feet below the summit. As you continue, the trail is rough at times, first descending gradually then climbing over a few knobs before reaching the low point at 26.6 miles.

Begin the climb up toward Mount Lafayette, steeply at times, as the forest shrinks and recedes while you gain elevation along the northeast shoulder. At 27.5 miles the Skookumchuck Trail enters from the right (west); soon you reach the north knob of Mount Lafayette, followed by the summit at 28.3 miles.

A lone cloud hovers over Mount Lincoln.

The descent from South Twin to the Galehead Hut is short but steep.

The highest point on the loop, Mount Lafayette provides an unparalleled view of the region. Across Franconia Notch is Cannon Mountain and the Kinsman Range to the south. You are high enough now that to the east you can see the Presidential Range. In fact, from the summit of Mount Lafayette, you can see thirty-eight 4,000-footers.

If you are doing the loop on a nice weekend in summer, you will probably see a lot of people over the next few miles, as the hike along Franconia Ridge is one of the most popular hikes in the White Mountains. Rightfully so, as the prominent and narrow ridge makes for a stunning traverse, and even the most experienced hikers enjoy the unique thrill of walking along a ridge with steep drops on both sides and incredible views the entire way.

As you've reached the highest point on the loop, it's all downhill from here! Well, not really, but that is actually not far from the truth. Savor the ridge. You put in a lot of hard work to get here, and over the next 2.0 miles you get to enjoy some of the best alpine ridge walking in New England.

Head south on the Franconia Ridge Trail, going over a little hump and climbing to Mount Lincoln at 29.3 miles. Continue straight, reaching Little Haystack and the junction with the Falling Waters trail at 30.0 miles. From here you are mostly within scrub and forest as you follow the ridge down to a low point of around 4,100 feet then gently up to the junction with the Liberty Spring Trail at 31.8 miles.

This is where your journey with the Appalachian Trail ends as the white blazes descend the Liberty Spring Trail. If you need some water desperately, or are planning an additional night out, the Liberty Spring Tentsite is 0.3 mile down the trail.

Continue south on the Franconia Ridge Trail, popping out near a cool rock formation of giant boulders and onto the rocky cone that defines the summit of Mount Liberty at 32.1 miles. You get a great 360-degree view from the flat area on the summit. To the southwest you can see the slides coming off the next peak along the ridge, Mount Flume, your last peak and final 4,000-footer on this journey.

The trail continues left (west) from the peak and descends rather steeply then moderates as it climbs Mount Flume, reaching the summit at 32.9 miles. The cliffs drop away and the rockslides fall deep into the valley on the right (west) side of the ridge. One fin juts out over the valley in line with Mount Moosilauke to the southwest. Head along the cliffs and then left down to the junction with the Flume Slide Trail at 33.0 miles.

Continue south on the Osseo Trail, first down a ridge to the south then a curve to the west. Head down a sustained series of winding switchbacks and steep wooden staircases, eventually off the ridge and down along a fairly straight trail following a path paralleling Osseo Brook below. The trail levels out and reaches the Lincoln Woods Trail at 37.1 miles. Head right (south) down the Lincoln Woods Trail, the flat walking giving you a chance to absorb the incredible journey you just had before reaching the bridge and parking area at 38.5 miles.

Miles and Directions

0.0 Start at the ranger station and head left. Cross the bridge over the East Branch of the Pemigewasset River and turn right onto the Lincoln Woods Trail.

1.4 Pass the junction with the Osseo Trail on the left.

2.6 Pass the junction with Black Pond Trail on the left.

2.9 Pass the junction with the Franconia Falls Trail on the left, cross the bridge, and head straight/right (northeast) onto the Bondcliff Trail.

4.7 The Bondcliff Trail turns left, away from the river.

6.1 Cross Black Brook.

6.6 Cross Black Brook again, often the last place for guaranteed water.

7.2 Cross Black Brook again (often dry). Shortly after, get the first good view on the hike.

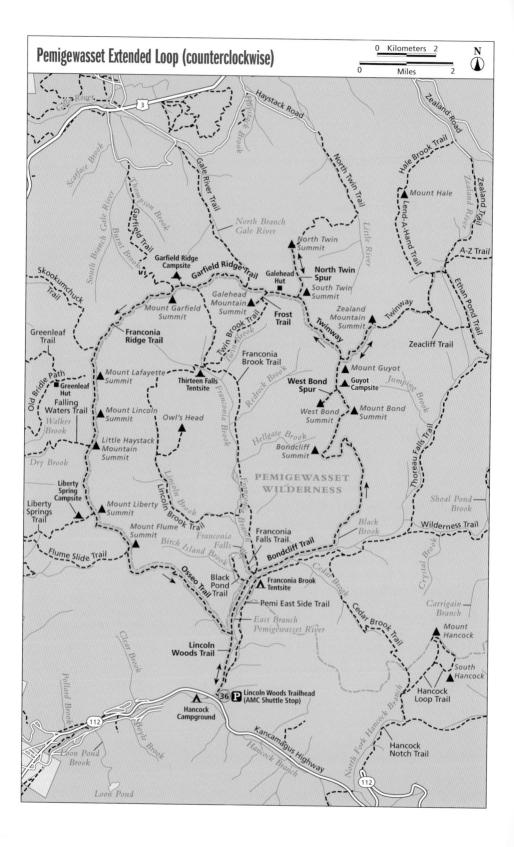

Pemigewasset Extended Loop (counterclockwise)

0 Kilometers 2
0 Miles 2

N

Gale River
3
Haystack Road
Zealand Road

Scarface Brook
Haystack Brook
Hale Brook Trail
Zealand Trail

Thompson Brook
Mount Hale
Zealand River
Lend-A-Hand Trail
A-Z Trail

South Branch Gale River
Gale River Trail
North Branch Gale River
North Twin Trail
Little River

Burnt Brook
Garfield Trail
North Twin Summit
Ethan Pond Trail

Skookumchuck Trail
Garfield Ridge Campsite
Garfield Ridge Trail
Galehead Hut
North Twin Spur
South Twin Summit

Greenleaf Trail
Mount Garfield Summit
Galehead Mountain Summit
Frost Trail
Zealand Mountain Summit
Twinway
Twinway
Zeacliff Trail

Franconia Ridge Trail
Twin Brook Trail
Twin Brook
Franconia Brook Trail

Old Bridle Path
Mount Lafayette Summit
Thirteen Falls Tentsite
Redrock Brook
Mount Guyot
Guyot Campsite
Jumping Brook

Greenleaf Hut
Falling Waters Trail
Mount Lincoln Summit
Owl's Head
Franconia Brook
West Bond Spur
West Bond Summit
Mount Bond Summit

Walker Brook
Little Haystack Mountain Summit
Hellgate Brook
Bondcliff Summit
Thoreau Falls Trail

Dry Brook
PEMIGEWASSET WILDERNESS
Shoal Pond Brook

Liberty Spring Campsite
Lincoln Brook Trail
Black Brook
Wilderness Trail

Liberty Springs Trail
Mount Liberty Summit
Lincoln Brook Trail
Franconia Falls Trail
Crystal Brook

Mount Flume Summit
Franconia Falls
Franconia Falls Trail
Bondcliff Trail
Carrigain Branch

Flume Slide Trail
Birch Island Brook
Cedar Brook
Mount Hancock

Osseo Trail
Black Pond Trail
Franconia Brook Tentsite
Cedar Brook Trail
South Hancock

Pemi East Side Trail
East Branch Pemigewasset River
Hancock Loop Trail

Clear Brook
Lincoln Woods Trail

Pollard Brook
36
Lincoln Woods Trailhead (AMC Shuttle Stop)
North Fork Hancock Branch

112
Hancock Campground
Hancock Notch Trail

Boyle Brook
Kancamagus Highway

Loon Pond Brook
Hancock Branch
112

Loon Pond

9.1 Reach the summit of Bondcliff.

10.3 Reach the summit of Mount Bond.

10.8 Turn left onto the West Bond Spur.

11.3 Reach the summit of West Bond. Turn around and head back to the Bondcliff Trail.

11.8 Turn left (north) onto the Bondcliff Trail.

12.0 Pass the spur to the Guyot Campsite on the right. (**Option:** Head down 0.2 mile to reach spring for water, shelter, and tent platforms.)

12.6 Turn right onto Twinway to get to Zealand Mountain.

13.9 Turn left (north) at the Zealand Mountain Spur.

14.0 Arrive at the Zealand Mountain summit. Return along Twinway to Guyot.

15.4 At the junction with the Bondcliff Trail, continue right (north) on Twinway.

17.5 Reach the summit of South Twin Mountain. Head right (north) on the North Twin Spur.

18.8 Reach the summit of North Twin Mountain. The short path on the left leads to a ledge with views. Turn around and head back south on the North Twin Spur.

20.1 Back at the South Twin Mountain summit, turn right (west) down Twinway.

20.9 Arrive at the Galehead Hut. Follow signs for the Frost Trail.

21.0 Pass the Twin Brook Trail on left.

21.2 Reach a view on the left.

21.4 Reach the summit of Galehead Mountain. Head back to the Galehead Hut.

21.9 Arrive back at the Galehead Hut. Follow signs to the Garfield Ridge Trail.

22.5 Pass the Gale River Trail on the right.

24.1 Pass the Franconia Brook Trail on the left.

24.6 Reach the spur trail to the Garfield Ridge Campsite with shelter and tentsites. There's a good spring right at the junction.

24.8 Pass the Garfield Trail on the right.

25.0 Reach a short spur on the left up to Mount Garfield's summit. From the summit, head back down to the Garfield Ridge Trail, following it down to the west.

27.5 Pass the Skookumchuck Trail on the right. Continue up toward Mount Lafayette.

28.3 Reach the summit of Mount Lafayette. Continue south on the Franconia Ridge Trail.

29.3 Reach the summit of Mount Lincoln. Continue south on the Franconia Ridge Trail.

30.0 Pass the Falling Waters Trail on the right.

31.8 Reach the junction with the Liberty Spring Trail. Continue straight. (**Option:** For water or camping, head west 0.3 miles down the Liberty Spring Trail to the Liberty Spring Tentsite.)

32.1 Reach the summit of Mount Liberty. Head left (east) off the summit to continue following the Franconia Ridge Trail.

32.9 Reach the summit of Mount Flume. Head down along ledges then left off the ridge.

33.0 Reach junction of the Osseo and Flume Slide Trails. Continue straight (south) on the Osseo Trail.

37.1 Turn right (south) onto the Lincoln Woods Trail.

38.5 Cross the bridge and arrive back at the Lincoln Woods Trailhead.

OTHER PEAK-BAGGING LISTS

Below are some other peak-bagging lists you may find interesting:

- New England 50 Finest
- New England 4,000-footers
- New England 100 Highest
- Northeast 111 Club
- Terrifying 25
- 52 with a View

The water glows in the morning at the Lakes of the Clouds.

Bonus Hikes at a Glance

The traverse across Franconia Ridge is one of the most stunning hikes in the White Mountains.

1 Kinsman Ridge Traverse (point-to-point)

Description: A traverse of Kinsman Ridge is a tough, classic White Mountain hike that takes you along the western side of Franconia Notch over three 4,000-foot peaks and numerous smaller peaks. The ridge runs from south to north and can be hiked in either direction. The southern portion of the route is also the Appalachian Trail. Although this can be done in a day by fit hikers, Eliza Brook Shelter and Campsite is a logical place to spend an overnight; it is 7.5 miles from the southern end and 9.4 miles from the northern trailhead.

The southern portion of the traverse has some wet portions and some rugged sections of trail, with some of the steepest and most difficult miles just south of South Kinsman. There are restricted views in the southern half, with more as you traverse the higher peaks. Kinsman Pond is a unique lake, gorgeously situated beneath North Kinsman, that also has a great campsite and shelter. North of North Kinsman are the Cannon Balls and the steep section of trail from Coppermine Col north to the summit of Cannon Mountain, where an observation tower provides good views.

Kinsman Pond sits just below North Kinsman Mountain. The shelter and campsite there make for a great place to camp while doing a Kinsman Ridge traverse.

Trails used: Kinsman Ridge Trail, Rim Trail

Route: This hike goes to/from Kinsman Notch at the southern end to the parking area near the Cannon Mountain Tramway at the northern end. Traveling in either direction, the route follows the Kinsman Ridge Trail the entire way, with a very short loop to the observation tower on Cannon Mountain.

Distance: 16.9 miles point to point

Elevation gain: 6,600 feet

4,000-footers: Cannon Mountain, North Kinsman, South Kinsman

Trailheads:

Southern trailhead: From I-93, take exit 32 and turn right onto NH 112 West. Follow NH 112 West for 6.5 miles to the parking area on the left for the Beaver Brook Trailhead at the top of Kinsman Notch. The trailhead for the Kinsman Ridge Trail is across the road on the north side of NH 112. **GPS:** N44 02.40' / W71 47.46'

Northern trailhead: From I-93, take exit 34B toward the Cannon Mountain Tramway. Turn left onto Tramway Drive; then take the first left into the main parking area. In a few hundred feet, you will see a dirt road on the left. You can park in the main lot; the dirt road leads to an open area and the trailhead is at the southeast corner of the open area. *From I-91 (from the south),* take exit 16 and head east on VT 25 South toward Bradford. In 0.5 mile turn left onto US 5 North. Turn right onto Newbury Crossing road in 7.7 miles. After 0.5 mile cross the Connecticut River and turn left onto NH 10. In 2.3 miles turn right onto NH 116 East; follow this winding road for 10.2 miles until the junction with NH 112. Turn right, and in 0.9 mile turn left onto NH 116 North. Take NH 116 North for 8.5 then turn right onto Wells Road and in 2.0 miles turn right onto NH 18 South and after 2.1 miles get onto I-93 South. Take exit 34B and turn right onto Tramway Drive. In a few hundred feet, you will see a dirt road on the left. You can park in the main lot; the dirt road leads to an open area and the trailhead is at the southeast corner of the open area. **GPS:** N44 10.17' / W71 41.25'

2 Franconia Ridge Traverse (point-to-point and loop options)

Description: Franconia Ridge is one of the most iconic ridgelines in New England. With steep sides falling away to Franconia Notch to the west and the Pemigewasset Wilderness to the east, the views are spectacular, and you may feel like you are flying high above the valleys below. The climb up the Flume Slide Trail is one of the most challenging hikes in the White Mountains.

This traverse can be done as a point-to-point with a car drop or a longer loop by returning along the flat Pemi Trail in the notch. You can do this as a single day hike or make it an overnight by hiking the 0.3 mile down off the ridge to the Liberty Spring Tentsite or reserving a spot at the Greenleaf Hut on the shoulder of Mount Lafayette.

Trails used: Whitehouse Trail, Flume Slide Trail, Franconia Ridge Trail, Greenleaf Trail, Old Bridle Path, Pemi Trail

Route: Take the Whitehouse Trail 0.6 mile to the Franconia Notch Recreation Path and head left to the Liberty Spring Trail a few hundred yards up on the right. Take the Liberty Spring Trail for 0.6 mile (1.4 from trailhead) then head up to the steep Flume Slide Trail, reaching the top at 4.7 miles. Turn left to the summit of Mount Flume at 4.8 miles and continue north along the ridge on the Franconia Ridge Trail. You pass over Mount Liberty at 6.0 miles. You climb above tree line near Little Haystack Mountain at 8.1 miles where the Falling Waters Trail comes in from the west. Continue north on the Franconia Ridge Trail over Mount Lincoln at 8.8 miles and finally to Mount Lafayette at 9.8 miles, where you then head down the western shoulder of Mount Lafayette on the Greenleaf Trail. From the Greenleaf Hut take the Old Bridle Path down to the main parking area at 13.7 miles.

To make this a loop, cross under the highway to the Lonesome Lake Trailhead, then follow the mostly flat Pemi Trail south to the Whitehouse Trail and back to the trailhead.

Distance: 13.7 miles point to point; 17.2-mile loop

Elevation gain: 5,800 feet

4,000-footers: Mount Flume, Mount Liberty, Mount Lincoln, Mount Lafayette

White blazes signify that this section of Franconia Ridge is part of the Appalachian Trail.

Trailheads:

Southern Trailhead: From I-93 (from the south), take exit 34A and merge onto US 3 North. The road to the parking lot for the Liberty Spring Trail will be on the right in 0.9 mile, past the main entrance to the Flume Gorge. *From I-93 (from the north),* take exit 33 and turn left onto US 3 North. The road to the parking lot for the Liberty Spring Trail will be on the right in 2.8 miles, past the main entrance to the Flume Gorge. The Whitehouse Trailhead is located at the south end of the parking area. **GPS:** N44 06.05' / W71 40.90'

Northern Trailhead: From I-93 (from the south), take the "Trailhead Parking" exit in Franconia Notch. This exit is two exits past exit 34A and one exit past the exit signed for "The Basin." *From I-93 (from the north),* take exit 34A and get back on I-93 North/US 3 North. In 3.1 miles take the "Trailhead Parking" exit. This is one exit past the exit for "The Basin." **GPS:** N44 08.52' / W71 40.88'

3 Galehead-Garfield Loop

Description: A fairly short road walk allows for a nice loop up over Mount Gale-head and Mount Garfield. On this loop you get to visit the Galehead Hut and summit Mount Garfield, one of the most aesthetically pleasing summits in the White Mountains. The Gale River and Garfield Trails provide access and egress from the ridge and are both fairly straightforward hikes with only short steep sections. That is counterbalanced by the fact that the route from Galehead Hut to Mount Garfield traverses some extremely rugged terrain capped by a super-steep climb to the summit of Mount Garfield.

Few summits in the White Mountains have as stunning a view as the one from the top of Mount Garfield.

Trails used: Gale River Trail, Garfield Ridge Trail, Frost Trail, Garfield Trail, Gale River Loop Road

Route: Begin by heading up the Gale River Trail 4.1 miles to the Garfield Ridge Trail. Head east on the Garfield Ridge Trail for 0.6 miles to the Galehead Hut and go out and back on the Frost Trail (1.0 mile round trip) to the summit of Galehead Mountain. Then get back on the Garfield Ridge Trail, heading west for 2.9 miles to the summit of Mount Garfield at 8.6 miles, passing the Garfield Trail on your right 0.25 mile before the summit.

Head back down from the summit to the junction with the Garfield Trail and follow it down at a consistent moderate grade for just under 5.0 miles back down to Gale River Loop Road. At the road, turn right and walk over a small hill for 1.7 miles to get back to the Gale River Trailhead for a total of 15.6 miles.

Distance: 15.6-mile loop

Elevation gain: 4,400 feet

4,000-footers: Galehead Mountain, Mount Garfield

Trailhead: *From I-93 (from the south),* take exit 35 and continue onto US 3 North. Follow this for 5.1 miles and turn right onto Gale River Trail (just past Gale River Loop Road). In 1.3 miles turn right at the junction; the parking lot will be on the left in about 0.25 mile. *From I-93 (from the north),* take exit 36 and turn left onto NH 141 East toward US 3 North. In 0.8 mile join US 3 North for 4.2 miles; turn right onto Gale River Trail (just past Gale River Loop Road). In 1.3 miles turn right at the junction; the parking lot will be on the left in about 0.25 mile. *From the junction of US 302 and US 3 in Twin Mountain/Carroll,* head south on US 3 for 5.2 miles. Turn right onto Gale River Trail. In 1.3 miles turn right at the junction; the parking lot will be on the left in about 0.25 mile. **GPS:** N44 13.97' / W71 36.63'

4 Galehead and the Twins (point-to-point)

Description: This hike is best done when water levels are fairly low, as the North Twin Trail requires multiple river crossings. Along the way you get to stop by the Galehead Hut and ascend a steep section of trail to the summit of South Twin, which rewards you with 360-degree views from the eighth-tallest mountain in the state, bagging three 4,000-footers along the way.

Trails used: Gale River Trail, Garfield Ridge Trail, Frost Trail, Twinway, North Twin Spur, North Twin Trail

Route: Follow the Gale River Trail up to the Garfield Ridge Trail at 4.1 miles and then follow that east for 0.6 mile to the Galehead Hut. Take the Frost Trail out and back (1.0 mile round trip) from the hut to the summit of Galehead Mountain and then from the hut climb the Twinway up to the summit of South Twin for a total of 6.5 miles.

Follow the North Twin Spur north along the ridge to North Twin Mountain at 7.9 miles, where ledges off to the west of the summit provide good views. Descend on the North Twin Trail, crossing the Little River multiple times reaching the parking area at 12.2 miles.

Distance: 12.2 miles point to point

Elevation gain: 4,200 feet

4,000-footers: Galehead Mountain, South Twin Mountain, North Twin Mountain

Trailheads:

Starting trailhead: *From I-93 (from the south),* take exit 35 and continue onto US 3 North. Follow this for 5.1 miles and turn right onto Gale River Trail (just past Gale River Loop Road). In 1.3 miles turn right at the junction; the parking lot will be on the left in about 0.25 mile. *From I-93 (from the north),* take exit 36 and turn left onto NH 141 East toward US 3 North. In 0.8 mile join US 3 North for 4.2 miles; turn right onto Gale River Trail (just past Gale River Loop Road). In 1.3 miles turn right at the junction; the parking lot will be on the left in about 0.25 mile. *From the junction of US 302 and US 3 in Twin Mountain/Carroll,* head south on US 3 for 5.2 miles. Turn right onto Gale River Trail. In 1.3 miles turn right at the junction; the parking lot will be on the left in about 0.25 mile. **GPS:** N44 13.97' / W71 36.63'

Ending trailhead: *From I-93 (from the south),* take exit 35 and continue onto US 3 North. Follow US 3 North for 7.8 miles. Turn right onto Haystack Road; the trailhead is at the end of the road in 2.5 miles. *From I-93 (from the north),* take exit 36 and turn left onto NH 141 East toward US 3 North. In 0.8 mile, join US 3 North for 7 miles. Turn right onto Haystack Road; the trailhead is at the end of the road in 2.5 miles. *From the junction of US 302 and US 3 in Twin Mountain/Carroll,* head south on US 3 for 2.5 miles. Turn left onto Haystack Road; the trailhead is at the end of the road in 2.5 miles. **GPS:** N44 14.28' / W71 32.85'

The journey up the Twinway from Galehead Hut is steep, but the view is worth it.

5 Tripyramids Loop

Description: A loop over the Tripyramids is a hike you won't soon forget, mostly due to the challenge—and rewards—of climbing the North Slide. The steep rockslide up North Tripyramid starts out as narrow, steep slabs and widens to an impressive boulder-strewn swath with extensive views, climbing 1,000 vertical feet in just 0.5 mile.

Descending the South Slide off South Tripyramid is only slightly less steep and affords great views along the way. On the way up to the slides, you get to pass some nice cascades as you transition from the developed Waterville Valley to the rugged terrain of the Sandwich Range Wilderness. Truly one of the most classic and challenging hikes in the White Mountains, this memorable hike should only be attempted in good, dry weather.

The slide up North Tripyramid is steep and exciting, and the views get better the higher you climb.

Trails used: Livermore Trail, Mount Tripyramid Trail

Route: Follow the Livermore Trail out of Waterville Valley for 2.6 miles until the Mount Tripyramid Trail comes in on the right. Continue following the Livermore Trail for another mile along a logging road, turning right on the Mount Tripyramid Trail at 3.6 miles. Soon you hit the base of the North Slide, which is narrowest and steepest near the bottom. Take your time, using trees as handholds as you work your way up the slope, following rock cairns along the way.

You leave the slide just below the summit of North Tripyramid, which is reached at 4.8 miles. Follow the trail around the ridge, over Middle Tripyramid, then over South Tripyramid back down the only slightly less steep South Slide, taking in the views to the west. At the trail junction with the Livermore Trail at 8.5 miles, turn left onto the Livermore Trail back down to the parking area for a total of 11.1 miles.

Distance: 11.1-mile loop

Elevation gain: 3,200 feet

4,000-footers: North Tripyramid, Middle Tripyramid

Trailhead: *From I-93* take exit 28 and turn (right from the south, left from the north) onto NH 49 East. Keep straight and follow this for 10.2 miles. Turn left onto Tripoli Road and continue for 1.2 miles, then veer left to continue on Tripoli Road for another 0.6 miles. Turn right onto West Branch Road, then almost immediately turn left into the Livermore Trailhead parking. *Note*: Much of Tripoli Road is closed in the winter so you will need to continue past Tripoli Road on NH 49 through the village of Waterville Valley (11.6 miles from I-93 exit), then turn right onto West Branch Road and in 0.7 mile turn right into the Livermore Trailhead parking. **GPS:** N43 57.96' / W71 30.84'

6 Pierce and Eisenhower (out-and-back)

Description: The Crawford Path between Mount Eisenhower and Mount Pierce is an extremely nice portion of trail as it rolls through sections of alpine and subalpine vegetation with numerous long-range views, including the stunningly open summit of Mount Eisenhower. This hike involves heading over to Mount Eisenhower and then returning to the trailhead via the Crawford Path. (**Option:** This route can be made into a loop by heading down Edmands Path from Mount Eisenhower and road-walking back down Mount Clinton Road to the Crawford Connector.)

The broad summit of Mount Eisenhower stretches to the south, with the summit of Mount Pierce visible farther along the ridge.

Trails used: Crawford Connector, Crawford Path, Webster Cliff Trail, Mount Eisenhower Loop

Route: Take the Crawford Connector to the Crawford Path, reaching the Webster Cliff Trail in 3.1 miles. Turn right onto the Webster Cliff Trail, summiting Mount Pierce in 0.1 mile. Turn around and head back north to the junction; continue straight ahead on the Crawford Path and follow it northward along the ridge to the junction of the Mount Eisenhower Loop in 1.2 miles. Turn left (north) onto the loop and follow it for 0.4 mile to the summit of Mount Eisenhower, 4.9 miles from the trailhead. Turn around and take the Crawford Path to the Crawford Connector to return to the trailhead parking area for a total distance of 9.6 miles.

Distance: 9.6 miles out and back

Elevation gain: 3,700 feet

4,000-footers: Mount Pierce, Mount Eisenhower

Trailhead: *From the junction of US 302 and US 3 in Twin Mountain/Carroll,* follow US 302 East for 8.2 miles. Turn left onto Mount Clinton Road just before a big curve in the road and the AMC Highland Center. The parking lot is on the left in 0.1 mile. *From the junction of US 302 and NH 16 in Glen,* follow US 302 West for 20.8 miles. Turn right onto Mount Clinton Road, which is just past the entrance to the AMC Highland Center. The parking lot is on the left in 0.1 mile. **GPS:** N44 13.42' / W71 24.68'

7 Mount Monroe to Mount Jackson (point-to-point)

Description: Basically half a Presi Traverse, this hike takes you over the four 4,000-foot peaks of the southern Presidentials. Even though this is a point-to-point hike, you can take the AMC Hiker Shuttle from the AMC Highland Center to the Ammonoosuc Ravine Trailhead and walk back to your car. By going from north to south, you also have the advantage of starting from a higher trailhead, with a total net loss of 600 vertical feet.

The traverse along the ridge is stunning, with Mount Monroe and Mount Eisenhower high above timberline, showcasing stunning views in all directions. You start dipping below the shrubbery on the way to Mount Pierce but still have multiple viewpoints along the way, with the summit of Mount Jackson an aesthetic finish to the traverse. Along the way you pass the Lakes of the Clouds and Mizpah Spring Huts.

Trails used: Ammonoosuc Ravine Trail, Crawford Path, Mount Monroe Loop, Mount Eisenhower Loop, Webster Cliff Trail, Webster-Jackson Trail

Route: Head up the Amonoosuc Ravine Trail reaching the Lakes of the Clouds Hut in 3.1 miles. Take the Crawford Path south to the Monroe Loop. Head over Mount Monroe, reaching the summit at 3.5 miles, then continue along the loop, rejoining the Crawford Path in 0.4 miles. Continue south on the Crawford Path for another 1.4 miles, then take the Eisenhower Loop up to the summit of Mount Eisenhower at 5.7 miles.

Continue over the summit another 0.4 miles to the Crawford Path, turn right and continue heading south. At the junction with the Webster Cliff Trail, head left/straight on the Webster Cliff Trail to the summit of Mount Pierce at 7.4 miles, then continue down the ridge along the Webster Cliff Trail all the way to Mount Jackson at 9.9 miles. At the summit of Mount Jackson, turn right (east) and take the Webster-Jackson Trail down to the parking area just south of Saco Lake, near the AMC Highland Center for a total of 12.5 miles.

Distance: 12.5 miles point to point

Elevation gain: 4,650 feet

4,000-footers: Mount Monroe, Mount Eisenhower, Mount Pierce, Mount Jackson

Trailheads:

Starting trailhead: *From the junction of US 302 and US 3 in Twin Mountain/Carroll,* follow US 302 East for 4.4 miles. Turn left onto Base Station Road; you'll see a sign for the cog railway. The parking lot for the Ammonoosuc Ravine Trail is on the right in 5.6 miles. *From the junction of US 302 and NH 16 in Glen,* follow US 302 West for 24.6 miles. Turn right onto Base Station Road; you'll see a sign for the cog railway. The parking lot for the Ammonoosuc Ravine Trail is on the right in 5.6 miles. **GPS:** N44 16.03' / W71 21.68'

Hikers enjoy easy walking on the Crawford Path.

Ending trailhead: *From the junction of US 302 and US 3 in Twin Mountain/Carroll,* follow US 302 East for 8.7 miles. Parking is on the right just past Saco Lake and right before the sign for Crawford Notch State Park. The trailhead is across the road. *From the junction of US 302 and NH 16 in Glen,* follow US 302 West for 20.3 miles. Parking is on the left just after you pop out of the notch at the top of the hill. If you pass Saco Lake on the right, you have gone too far. The trailhead is across from the parking area. **GPS:** N44 12.90' / W71 24.50'

8 Kilkenny Ridge Traverse (point-to-point)

Description: This traverse takes you through the most northern and most remote regions in the White Mountains. Along the way you will pass over Mount Cabot and Mount Waumbek along with numerous other interesting sub-4,000-foot peaks, such as the Horn and Mount Starr King, as well as one of the best clifftop views at Rogers Ledge. If you do this hike in late summer / early fall, you may even see a moose.

If you want to break this hike up into multiple days, you can stay at the Rogers Ledge Tentsite, Unknown Pond Tentsite, or the Fire Warden's Cabin atop Mount Cabot. The entire route is part of the Cohos Trail, a long-distance trail that stretches from the Canadian border to Crawford Notch through the entire length of Coos County.

You are much more likely to find solitude along this route than almost any other hike in this book, especially through the northern section. This traverse can be done in either direction but is described from north to south.

The view from Rogers Ledge over the Kilkenny to the Presidential Range is a real highlight of a Kilkenny traverse.

Trails used: Kilkenny Ridge Trail, Horn Spur, Starr King Trail

Route: From the trailhead at the South Pond Recreation Area, head south on the Kilkenny Ridge Trail; in 4.1 miles you get to the incredible views from Rogers Ledge. Although there is no water here, it's a great place to enjoy lunch—the vista extends past the nearby peak of Mount Cabot to the northern Presidentials farther south. You can also camp at the Rogers Ledge Tentsite 0.5 mile farther, but it's worth hiking back up to the ledge for sunset.

Continue south on the Kilkenny Ridge Trail past Unknown Pond to the Horn at 8.8 miles, a cool rock promontory accessed by a 0.3-mile spur trail and well worth the visit. Continue southward, reaching the summit of Mount Cabot at 10.5 miles, then a number of smaller peaks, eventually reaching Mount Waumbek at 21.2 miles. Continue south on the Kilkenny Ridge Trail over Mount Starr King, where a standing chimney is the only thing left of the former building on the summit at 22.2 miles. Head down to the parking area on the Starr King Trail for a total of 24.8 miles.

Distance: 24.8 miles point to point

Elevation gain: 8,550 feet

4,000-footers: Mount Cabot, Mount Waumbek

Trailheads:

Northern trailhead: *From the western intersection of US 2 and NH 16 in Gorham*, head north on NH 16 for 5.0 miles, then turn left onto NH 110 and go 14.7 miles, then turn left onto South Pond Road. Follow this to the end parking area in 2 miles. *From the western junction of US 2 and US 3 in Lancaster*, head north on US 3 for 9 miles then turn right onto NH 110 East. Go 10.2 miles, then turn right onto South Pond Road. Follow this to the end parking area in 2 miles. **Note:** This is a day use recreation area in a remote location and car break-ins have been reported here, so don't leave anything visible or valuable in your car. **GPS:** N44 35.82' / W71 22.08'

Southern trailhead: *From I-93*, take exit 42. Turn (left if coming from the north, right if coming from the south) onto US 302 West and follow this for 1.5 miles to the junction with NH 116. Head east on NH 116 for 10.5 miles. In the town of Whitefield, NH 116 joins US 3 North for 500 feet. After making a right turn off US 3 back onto NH 116, head east for 8.8 miles. In the town of Jefferson, turn right onto US 2 East and in 0.6 mile turn left onto Starr King Road. Follow this road (which can be bumpy/rutted and veers left from Cottage Road) for 0.2 mile to the trailhead parking. *From the junction of US 2 and NH 16 in Gorham (western junction)*, follow US 2 West for 16.2 miles. Turn right onto Starr King Road and follow this road (which can be bumpy/rutted and veers left from Cottage Road) for 0.2 mile to the trailhead parking. **GPS:** N44 25.12' / W71 28.03'

About the Author

Eli Burakian is a photographer and author based out of Brownsville, Vermont. He is author, photographer, or contributor to fifteen books, including his self-published landscape coffee table book, *Moosilauke—Portrait of a Mountain*. He is an avid hiker and ultrarunner and has through-hiked numerous long- and middle-distance trails. He has attempted to break the Long Trail unsupported speed record (FKT; fastest known time) multiple times and is working on a book and podcast series about mountain and trail speed records.

Eli works full-time at Dartmouth College, his alma mater, as the college photographer. More of his work can be seen on his website: eliburakian.com.